THE RAF'S ARMOURERS

One of the main reasons for writing this book was to capture some of the wonderful stories that Armourers would relate whenever they got together over a pint or three. We were well aware that many of the people with the greatest tales to tell were getting older, and when they were no longer around those stories would disappear. Sadly, since we finished writing the book but before it was published, one of our major contributors, Mike Steel, passed away. We would like to dedicate this book to Mike, and all of the other Armourers who are no longer with us.

THE RAF'S ARMOURERS

Safely Making Aircraft Dangerous Since the First World War

TONY LAMSDALE
AND
PHIL APPLEBY

THE RAF'S ARMOURERS
Safely Making Aircraft Dangerous Since the First World War

First published in Great Britain in 2023 by
Air World
An imprint of
Pen & Sword Books Ltd
Yorkshire – Philadelphia

Copyright © Tony Lamsdale and Phil Appleby, 2023

ISBN 978 1 39901 033 7

The right of Tony Lamsdale and Phil Appleby to be identified as Authors of this work has been asserted by them in accordance with the Copyright, Designs and Patents Act 1988.

A CIP catalogue record for this book is available from the British Library.

All rights reserved. No part of this book may be reproduced or transmitted in any form or by any means, electronic or mechanical including photocopying, recording or by any information storage and retrieval system, without permission from the Publisher in writing.

Typeset by SJmagic DESIGN SERVICES, India.

Printed and bound in the UK by CPI Group (UK) Ltd.

Pen & Sword Books Limited incorporates the imprints of After the Battle, Atlas, Archaeology, Aviation, Discovery, Family History, Fiction, History, Maritime, Military, Military Classics, Politics, Select, Transport, True Crime, Air World, Frontline Publishing, Leo Cooper, Remember When, Seaforth Publishing, The Praetorian Press, Wharncliffe Local History, Wharncliffe Transport, Wharncliffe True Crime and White Owl.

For a complete list of Pen & Sword titles please contact

PEN & SWORD BOOKS LIMITED
George House, Units 12 & 13, Beevor Street, Off Pontefract Road,
Barnsley, South Yorkshire, S71 1HN, England
E-mail: enquiries@pen-and-sword.co.uk
Website: www.pen-and-sword.co.uk

or
PEN AND SWORD BOOKS
1950 Lawrence Rd, Havertown, PA 19083, USA
E-mail: uspen-and-sword@casematepublishers.com
Website: www.penandswordbooks.com

Contents

Preface		vi
Three Cheers for the Man on the Ground		ix
A Tour of the Camp		xi
Chapter 1	The History of the RAF Armourers	1
Chapter 2	Starting Out as an RAF Armourer	16
Chapter 3	The Bomb Dump	50
Chapter 4	Squadron Life	68
Chapter 5	EOD	107
Chapter 6	Bay Work	134
Chapter 7	Small Arms	151
Chapter 8	Detachments	161
Chapter 9	Conflicts and Terrorism	186
Chapter 10	Pull Up a Sandbag	223
Chapter 11	Life as an Ex-Armourer	245
Chapter 12	Ade Thorne's Falklands Diary	256
How to Talk Like an Armourer: A Glossary of Trade Terms		284
Index		312

Preface

Writing a book has been a life-long ambition and what better place to start than one about your own family. The motivation to write this book is partly driven by the knowledge that the experiences of those family members is lost when they leave us on that final flight. The 1366, RAF Armourers RAFA branch does a wonderful job of keeping us all in touch but, sadly, some of the more frequent notices are about departed brethren. This book is an attempt to capture just some of our history and give you a taste of what it was like to be an Armourer in the RAF.

The collection of stories and details covers some, but by no means all, of a trade that has been around since the beginning of time (well, at least since we started falling out with each other and having fights). The creation of the RFC, and subsequently the RAF, was an opportunity for Armourers to flex their muscles at a new challenge, and the years have led to much blood, sweat and tears given in the cause of defending the realm. An equal if not greater amount of beer has been consumed to replace those fluids – hydration is everything!

This is not a definitive anthology of everything an Armourer has ever done in the history of the RFC or RAF. To try and capture over 100 years of history is an impossible task; there are no longer any eyewitnesses to the First World War, and those who served during the Second World War are also somewhat scarce. Not every aircraft gets a mention, and I am sure there are many jobs and postings that haven't made it between these covers. There are always niche jobs or one-off, never to be repeated experiences; and sometimes the fog of war or beer is just too thick to penetrate.

I could not have undertaken this task without my great friend Phil. I vividly recall the chat where I persuaded him that we could work together to write this book; I am sure he will forgive me one day. Along the way we have met some wonderful people and been privileged to have them share their stories with us. The most important thing for Phil and I was to recount the story just as it was explained to us.

PREFACE

Writing this book has been, on the whole, a lot of fun. There have been moments when the enormity of the task weighed heavy, but this was massively offset by meeting all the Armourers who have contributed. It really was a constant round of 'pull up a sandbag'!

On days when inspiration was scarce, I found myself wandering to a local café, Grays in Bedlington, where I could sit with a pot of tea and the occasional fried breakfast, purely for energy of course. The girls, Frances, Susan, Carina and Nicole, certainly know how to keep a chap well fed and ready to work!

This book is meant to be enjoyed, and if you served as an Armourer, we hope it brings back memories. If you served in any other trade or service, never mind, and if you never have served then trust me when I say it is fun and challenging in ways beyond imagination.

There are so many people to thank for their help and support; those who have contributed appear between these covers and their stories are the lifeblood of the trade. Just to hear them has been a privilege, so thank you for sharing. Mark 'Beany' Bean deserves a massive thanks for contributing some of the photos and answering our many questions to clarify some details. His razor-sharp knowledge has helped clear the fog of time that has replaced that of war and beer. Dick Lindsay stepped in with some fantastic photos from back in the day; his selection of photos from the 1940s and 1950s shows plumbers in their natural habitat and that things haven't changed much over the decades.

Finally, the biggest thank you is to my wife, Lesleyanne. She is one who swore before she met me that she would never marry an Armourer. At the time of writing, we are approaching thirty-three years married, and she has almost stopped swearing! Thank you, my darling.

Tony

When Tony asked me if I'd be interested in working with him on a book about the RAF Armourers, my immediate thought was, 'What's an RAF Armourer'? Nearly two years on I'm still not entirely sure, but I do know that the people who inhabit the Armourers community are a fantastic bunch. I have always been made to feel like I'm a part of the family, even though I've never touched a gun or flown in anything more exciting than a passenger plane to Majorca.

My role has been asking lots of questions, and writing up many of the stories that our contributors have told us. I did also write the chapter on the history of the Armourers, which involved lots of fascinating research. It's amazing what you can find on Wikipedia these days. Sadly, we weren't able to talk to any Armourers who had served in the Second World War, but we did speak to people who had joined up in the 1950s, so we were able to gather a wide historical perspective on the Armourer's role.

I very much hope that I can remain a part of the Armourers family long after my active involvement, in the form of working on this book, has ceased. On the one occasion when I did get to meet people we'd talked to online, everyone was extremely welcoming, and I did my best to keep pace with the beer consumption. The fact that we all caught Covid-19 afterwards did little to spoil the good memories. In years to come I look forward to attending further events and becoming personally acquainted with one or two of the airbases that I've learnt so much about.

My thanks go to all those who have contributed to the book, and of course my wife Tomoko, who has supported me throughout the writing process.

Phil

Three Cheers for the Man on the Ground

By Eric Sykes[1]

Wherever you walk, you will hear people talk,
Of the men who go up in the air.
Of the daredevil way they go into the fray,
Facing death without turning a hair.

They'll raise a big cheer (and buy lots of beer)
For the Pilot who's come home on leave.
But they don't give a jigger, for the Flight Mech., or Rigger,
With nothing but 'props' on his sleeve.

They just say, 'Nice day' – and then turn away,
With never a mention of praise…
For the poor bloody Erk, who does all the work,
And then orders his own beer – and pays!

They've never been told of the hours in the cold
That he spends, sealing Germany's fate.
How he works on a kite, 'till all hours of the night,
And then turns up next morning at eight.

He gets no rake-off, for working 'til take-off,
Or helping the aircrew prepare.
But whenever there's trouble, it's 'Quick at the double!'
The man on the ground must be there.
Each flying crew can confirm it as true –
That they know what this man's *really* worth.
They know that he's part of the Air Force's heart,
Even though he stays close to the Earth.

THE RAF'S ARMOURERS

He doesn't want glory,
But please tell his story.
Spread tuppence of *his* fame around.
One of only a few – so give him his due: *'THREE CHEERS FOR THE MAN ON THE GROUND!'*

---

1. Note that this poem was not written by *the* Eric Sykes, who went on to become one of the UK's favourite comedians, and who, in 1942, was serving in the RAF as a wireless operator. It was written by a totally unconnected Eric Sykes who, in 1942, was serving in the RAF as a mechanic.

A Tour of the Camp

This book is about RAF Armourers, past and present. In putting the book together, we talked to lots of members of the trade from across the years; among many others, we interviewed someone who joined up for his National Service in the early 1950s, and we also chatted with an Armourer who is still serving. Over the years the trade has changed hugely, but everyone we spoke to had stories to tell of their time as an Armourer, stories we've tried to capture in the chapters that follow.

But let's begin in the early 1990s, when Tony was serving. Imagine that you've never experienced the world of the RAF Armourers before. What was it like at the airbase? What are the Armourers like? And what did they do? Let Tony give you a quick tour of the camp, as it was then …

As you drive through the main gate you'll be stopped and asked for ID by a gate guard or sentry. They'll be carrying a personal weapon (either an SA80 or an SLP). The weapon will have been serviced and issued by the Station Armoury, and at the end of the shift the weapon will be handed back to the armoury and stored on the racks, ready for its next day (or night) on duty.

After your ID has been verified and you drive into the camp, you pass the Aircraft Assisted Escape System (AAES) bay, AKA the seat bay. This is where the ejection seats come for servicing and maintenance. Outside the seat bay you may well see some trolleys used for transporting the seats from the jet to the bay and back again. These trolleys or trailers will have been serviced by the AGSE (Armament Ground Support Equipment) team. They look after all the equipment used by the Armourers on that station, including trolleys, trailers, Wendy Loaders, jacks, hoists, lifting equipment, and possibly even the Spartan or Scimitars used by the Airfield Explosive Ordnance Disposal (AEOD) team.

Drive further on and you will pass the AEOD team building. Their job is to render safe any bombs, rockets, missiles or other dangerous ordnance launched at the station, to allow business as usual; it might be dealing with an IED (improvised explosive device) or an unexploded bomb (UXB).

THE RAF'S ARMOURERS

At the moment they probably won't be in. They may be working on their main job in one of the other armament sections, coming together during exercises or training days to practise their craft. Whatever the issue, the team will deploy and deal with the problem before it becomes an issue, probably by blowing it up!

Somewhere on camp you will pass the Armament HQ. This may be annexed to another building, or it may be separate. Typically, it's well hidden because they don't like being disturbed when there are big discussions to be had. Here the senior Armourers on camp will sit and debate gnarly issues such as staffing, training, regulations, H&S, and why there are no biscuits left in the tea bar … 'Who is on teas and keys this week, and why didn't they top up the hobnobs?'

Nearby is the role equipment bay. Its job is to maintain all the devices which fix the rockets and bombs to the aircraft: carriers, ejector release units (ERUs), pylons, crutching units, and all manner of trickery to keep things firmly attached to aircraft until the time comes for the two to part. There might be a gun bay too. It services and maintains the various machine guns or cannon fitted to the front-line aircraft, including the mini gun, M60, 27mm Mauser or 30mm Aden gun.

You drive past the station range without even noticing it – a high-walled edifice with a small door to let you in or out, and a red flag fluttering in the breeze to let you know that a cohort of nervous RAF personnel are having their annual trip to the range to re-qualify for their green card. The guns will have been serviced and issued by the Armourers, and the bullets will have been dragged from storage and faithfully counted before asking the rock ape (a representative from the RAF Regiment) in charge of the range that day for a signature. Most likely the range will be looked after by a grizzly civilian who every now and again makes an appearance in the armoury tea bar to get a brew and complain bitterly about the job, weather, rock apes, lack of work, too much work and the general state of the country.

You will now be leaving the main complex of buildings and starting to head out onto the airfield side. Keep an eye on the lights controlling access to taxiways, and after carefully avoiding taxiing aircraft you'll eventually find yourself on the ring road, or perry track.

In the distance looms the high fence and solid concrete buildings of the Explosive Storage Area (ESA), or 'bomb dump'. This is where everything dangerous is stored: bombs, rockets, missiles, ammunition, grenades, plastic explosive, detonators, fuzes, and Armourers. All the buildings are made of reinforced concrete with solid steel doors. They are surrounded by blast walls or revetments, and there is always a good distance between

A TOUR OF THE CAMP

each building to prevent sympathetic detonation should the worst happen. The electrical supplies are sheathed and bonded, with archaic-looking switches on the outside to turn on the lights. Lightning protection wraps the building with copper strips, all running to earth. Dotted around are static tanks, big reservoirs of water readily available to douse fires or dunk newly arrived or leaving Armourers. Everything is counted here: bullets, bombs, fuzes, cartridges, rockets. You name it and it's counted. All the numbers have to add up. Too many, not a problem, pop the spares aside for a rainy day. Too few, not a problem, it would appear to be raining, now where did I put those …?

Bombs are built here, tail units fitted, fuzes removed from their tins and inserted in fuze pockets, cables connected (Lead Electrical Fuze Arming (LEFA)) are selected, just the right length to meet the connection on the aircraft when the time comes. Rocket packs for the ejection seats, grenades for the rock apes, flares for Air Traffic Control so they can communicate with aircraft when someone runs out of money for the meter … Boxes are painted and certified Free From Explosive (FFE), then returned to be filled again. Drums of ammunition are filled, ready to be fitted to the aircraft to feed the hungry guns, belts of 30mm rounds are made using links and the linking tool. All are carefully prepared and boxed, then lovingly delivered to the squadron.

Within the ESA or very close, you may well find a bay dedicated to building or servicing missiles, rockets or torpedoes – stored in deep, dark, concrete buildings with good ventilation and no light so as not to disturb them. They are brought from slumber, unboxed, unwrapped and built; wings are attached, guidance systems connected, rocket pack or motor and warhead all joined together by complex electrical wiring and held together with just the right amount of torque on the bolts and screws.

While admiring the view you pass entrances to the HAS (hardened aircraft shelter) sites or dispersals. This is the sharp end. Turn up at one of these and you will find front-line squadrons equipped with the latest and greatest aircraft – through time, Spitfire, Hurricane, Lancaster, Shackleton, Nimrod, Harrier, Jaguar, Hunter, Lightning, Phantom, Hawk, Tornado and Typhoon. All are names indelibly printed in the history of the RAF and our nation. The squadron Armourer works alongside the other trades to care for their aircraft like children: fitting and removing the bombs, guns, carriers, ERUs and ejection seats; making the aircraft safe for the other trades to do their work; safely making it dangerous for the aircrew to take it for a spin. This is where is all comes together, the reason for all the other buildings, jobs, equipment and personnel – providing aircraft capable of attack or defence, search, rescue, drop-off or pick-up, all in the defence of our realm. Ready to serve at a moment's notice. It's all in a day's work for an Armourer.

Oh, and one other thing to mention. Every section will have a bar equally ready to deploy at a moment's notice, because even Armourers need a few hours off now and again!

Chapter 1

The History of the RAF Armourers

Early Days

Armourers, defined in the Oxford Dictionary as makers, suppliers, or repairers of weapons or armour, have been around for a very long time. Chances are that when two groups of cavemen got into a bit of a spat, someone in each group would have been running around gathering sharp stones and wooden stakes, while a dexterous cavewoman tied them together to make ancient knives and spears.

Throughout history, Armourers have played a significant role in military conflicts, ensuring that the troops who were fighting the battles were suitably equipped for their job. In medieval times, the Armourer's main responsibility was supplying suits of armour, primarily to knights and noblemen. As such, the medieval Armourer was a highly skilled craftsman with expert knowledge of working with various materials – not just metal, but also leather and wood. Each suit of armour was custom fitted, so the Armourer's skills extended to detailed measuring of clients. Accuracy was crucial. If a suit of armour turned out to be too tight for a corpulent knight, the withholding of payment might be the least of the Armourer's worries.

In more recent times, the Armourer's role has centred on weapons: providing, testing, repairing and maintaining them. Armies and navies have Armourers, police have Armourers, even movie studios have Armourers, although one would hope that on a film set the weapons provided would be for show rather than utility.

RAF Armourers are a breed apart. As the Forces War Records state: 'Within the British Royal Air Force (RAF), Armourers are considered the most specialised of any trade', and the founder of the RAF, Lord Trenchard, held the Armourers in great esteem, saying: 'The Armourer – without him there is no need for an air force.' Armourers even have their own patron saint, Saint Barbara, who is traditionally invoked against thunder and lightning, and all accidents involving explosives.

THE RAF'S ARMOURERS

The very nature of the Armourer's work means that much is being done behind the scenes. In the sections that follow, wherever armaments are mentioned, think of the Armourers. Always first in and last out, they're the ones preparing the bombs and weaponry and ensuring that they're fitted correctly to the aircraft. They're the ones fitting and removing ejection seats. They're the ones attempting to make safe any bombs, rockets, missiles and other ordnance launched at an RAF station. They're the ones preparing guns and ammunition for testing on the ranges. They're the ones ensuring that aircraft are safe and ready for crucial missions. And at the end of the day, they're the ones returning all the equipment and munitions back to safe storage. In short, they're an integral part of everything that goes on at an RAF base.

The first mention of Armourers in relation to the air force can be traced back to 13 April 1912, the date on which King George V signed a royal warrant establishing the Royal Flying Corps. The RFC was established in recognition of the potential of aircraft to fulfil a perceived need for reconnaissance and surveillance of military sites. The original list of RFC ranks included Air Mechanic (1st, 2nd and 3rd class), and 'Armourer' was listed in each of these classes, alongside trades such as blacksmith, coppersmith, aircraft rigger and sailmaker.

Ironically, in 1910, two years before the formation of the RFC, the Chief of the Imperial General Staff, Sir William Nicholson, had described the concept of military aviation as 'a useless and expensive fad'. One of the UK's earliest army pilots, Bertram Dickson, provided a far more perceptive assessment: 'In the case of a European war, both sides would be equipped with large corps of aeroplanes, each trying to obtain information from the other, and to hide its own movements. The efforts which each would exert would lead to the inevitable result of a war in the air, for the supremacy of the air, by armed aeroplanes against each other. This fight for the supremacy of the air in future wars will be of the first and greatest importance.'

One can imagine that in the first two years of its existence, the RFC had little need of its Armourers. There were few planes in those early days (at the end of 1912, the RFC had twelve manned balloons and thirty-six planes), and pilot safety was a more pressing concern than arming aircraft. However, on 28 July 1914, everything changed. The First World War began.

First World War

In the early days of the war, the RFC's role was primarily one of photographic reconnaissance, in order to support the British Army on the ground. The planes themselves were not armed, and there are even stories of rival aircrews on reconnaissance missions smiling and waving at each other as they passed by in the sky. But any such camaraderie was short-lived.

RFC pilots and their accompanying observers began to carry their own weapons. One pilot, Lieutenant Eric Conran, dropped hand grenades from his cockpit over enemy troops. Although they caused little physical damage, the noise of the grenades allegedly resulted in cavalry horses stampeding, which might well have caused considerably more chaos than the grenades themselves. Another celebrated airman, Captain Louis Strange, destroyed two German trucks by dropping home-made petrol bombs on them.

But soon the bombs became more sophisticated. In March 1915, Captain Strange flew a bombing raid on a troop train at a railway station, during which he released four 25lb Cooper bombs that were fitted on wing racks and released by pulling a cable in the cockpit. There were substantial casualties. In a synchronised mission, another pilot, George Carmichael, dropped a 100lb bomb that destroyed part of the railway track next to the station. Later in the year a New Zealand-born pilot, Will Rhodes Moorhouse, flew a solo raid in which he dropped a 112lb bomb on the same station, causing significant damage and disruption. He was seriously wounded during the mission and died from his injuries shortly after returning to his base; he was posthumously awarded the Victoria Cross for his bravery.

Bombing was seen by the senior officers in the RFC, and indeed the other forces, as a key factor in the conflict, and over the course of the war the production of bombs increased dramatically. In July 1914, the total supply of aerial bombs was twenty-six 20-pounders; as the end of the war approached, more than 26,000 bombs were being manufactured every week. The variety of bombs was also eye-catching. In addition to the well-known 25lb Cooper bombs, there were bombs weighing in at over 500lb. Bomb types included phosphorous bombs, designed to shower burning phosphorous over targets such as airships, and sweeper bombs, which included metal bars that were scattered on impact, in the hope of imposing maximum damage on machinery and buildings.

The arms available for aerial combat similarly evolved during the course of the war. At first pilots and their observers carried hand-held firearms, such as pistols and single shot rifles, but these were far from effective. During one aerial battle, with both planes having exhausted their ammunition, the British pilot flew close to his adversary while his observer threw his revolver towards the German plane's propeller, attempting to bring the plane down. The attempt was unsuccessful.

It was a French plane, piloted by Louis Quenault, that carried the first machine gun into battle in October 1914. However, earlier experiments with machine guns and aircraft had taken place in Britain before the war. In 1913, the London Aero Show featured an experimental fighting biplane, developed by the engineering company Vickers, which included an integrated machine gun. A fully developed version of this plane, the FB.5, was drafted into action in February 1915. However, the FB.5 was a 'pusher' aircraft, with the engine and propeller at the back of the plane. It was slow, and less manoeuvrable than aircraft with front-mounted engines and propellers, the 'tractor' configuration. It soon became apparent that the future lay in tractor-configured planes, so the new challenge was to enable the pilot to use a front-mounted machine gun.

Attempts to address this requirement included mounting the machine gun at an angle where it could fire past the propeller, but this made aiming the gun very difficult. Clearly the optimal approach was to fire the gun straight ahead. The problem was the propeller. It seemed that firing the gun through the propeller itself was likely to be suicidal, because of the damage it might cause, so one early solution was to mount the gun on the top wing; however, this made changing the magazine somewhat hazardous. A French innovation was to fit the propeller blades with deflectors, so bullets that hit the blades would be deflected rather than penetrating them. But it was the Germans who were the first to successfully synchronize the timing of the shots from the machine gun so that they passed cleanly between the propeller blades. This was incorporated into the Fokker aircraft, and for a while this gave the Germans a distinct advantage in the aerial battle. Equality was restored when the Vickers company managed to replicate the synchronization achieved by the Fokkers.

A less well-known element of First World War aerial combat was the ammunition itself. In the early days, machine guns tended to jam because the ammunition was not of sufficiently high quality. In 1917 the British introduced 'Green Label' (later superseded by 'Red Label') ammunition specifically for synchronised guns, and this was a great success. At the same time, different types of bullets were being developed, involving the use of explosive and incendiary materials. These were particularly useful for shooting down balloons and airships.

Pilots in the First World War were viewed as folk heroes, albeit short-lived ones in most cases; on average, a pilot could expect to live for a mere three weeks from the time of joining the airborne battle, and in 'bloody April' in 1917, life expectancy for a pilot dropped to a matter of hours.

In contrast to the perceived glamour of the pilot, there are few records of RFC Armourers during the First World War, although we can be sure they were feverishly working away in the background, building, testing and fitting bombs, and setting up machine guns on fighter planes, most of which were destined to be shot down within a matter of hours or days.

THE HISTORY OF THE RAF ARMOURERS

Cartoon of an aircraft dropping bombs over the side. (Mark Bean)

One thing that *is* known about early RFC Armourers is the vehicle that was used to transport ammunition and bombs across the Channel for No. 5 Squadron in late 1914. Bizarrely, it was a bright red van emblazoned with gold lettering proclaiming the merits of HP sauce. It turned out that its eye-catching colour had its benefits – on more than one occasion, a disorientated Allied pilot was able to locate his base as a result of spotting the scarlet ammunition van.

The early Armourers would also have been involved in helping to set up anti-aircraft shell fire, although this was notoriously unsuccessful as a means of shooting down enemy aircraft. Happily, the Germans were no better, and many more Allied pilots died as a result of mechanical failures than succumbed to anti-aircraft fire. That said, there were several incidents when RFC planes were shot down by French gunmen, a situation that led to one well-known RFC observer, Dermot Allen, politely enquiring of his French colleagues: 'Do you mind telling your men not to fire on us. It puts us off.'

As the conflicts intensified, and both the number of aircraft and the variety and complexity of armaments increased rapidly, the Armourer's job became ever more complex and challenging. And important. Towards the end of the war, with strategic bombing missions far more frequent and the skies over the battlefields filled with aircraft strafing the enemy troops, the contribution of the Armourers was crucial.

For the final few months of the war, they were no longer RFC Armourers. On 1 April 1918, the structure of the British air force changed. The RFC and the Royal Naval Air Service, which had been formed as an offshoot of the RFC in July 1914, were combined in the new Royal Air Force (RAF).

Between the Wars

At the end of the First World War, the RAF was the most powerful air force in the world, with over 20,000 planes and almost 300,000 personnel. However, within eighteen months the number of personnel had dropped to just 20,000. Let's face it, no one could have anticipated that within twenty years the world would be back at war.

Between the wars, the main task of the RAF was the policing of the British Empire from the air, although RAF forces did also see action in Iraq, helping to quell tribal unrest, and Afghanistan, where civil war broke out in 1928 – a strange mirroring of RAF missions that took place almost a century later.

So, what of the weapons themselves? In the case of bombs, throughout the 1920s the emphasis was on standardisation, with General Purpose (GP) bombs of various sizes – 50, 120, 250 and 500lb – forming the backbone of the supply. These bombs were rarely used in action, the only exception being a few raids in Iraq in 1923. But in the mid-1930s the approach began to change, as fears of a second European war started to emerge. A new type of incendiary bomb was developed, entering production in 1937 – although bizarrely these bombs were not actually tested until early 1939, when over 650,000 had been produced. As a result of the tests, a fundamental flaw was discovered that resulted in numerous modifications having to be made. Testing of anti-submarine bombs also took place in the mid-1930s, and again numerous modifications were made following the tests. There was some experimentation with larger bombs, up to 1,000lb, but the consensus was that it was better for bombers to carry more, smaller bombs.

The armaments fitted on the aircraft themselves were similarly stagnant during the early inter-war years, with the Vickers and Lewis guns used towards the end of the First World War continuing to be the standard well into the 1930s. It was only in 1937 that things began to change, when a US-manufactured machine gun, the Browning, which had a higher firing rate than the Vickers and Lewis, was fitted to many RAF aircraft.

There was also a significant change of strategic direction in 1937. For most of the inter-war years, the overwhelming doctrine was that bombers were unstoppable, and that the only legitimate way of achieving air superiority was to do more damage through bombing than your enemy.

Following the formation of RAF Fighter Command in 1936, its leader Hugh Dowding argued against this doctrine, and in 1937 the minister in charge of defence co-ordination, Sir Thomas Inskip, decided in favour of Dowding with the words: 'The role of our air force is not an early knock-out blow, but rather to prevent the Germans from knocking us out.'

Nevertheless, it is clear that there was little coherent strategy throughout this inter-war period. Lack of funding was the main factor, but attitudes in the RAF were a major contributor too. Officers with responsibility for armaments were not required to have a technical background or an in-depth knowledge of the weapons they were working with, and the emphasis was still very much on flying. This always took precedence over ground duties.

Consequently, on 1 September 1939, when the Second World War began, the RAF was far from ideally prepared, in terms of both its aircraft and its armaments.

Second World War

The Battle of Britain, which prompted Winston Churchill's famous quote, 'Never in the field of human conflict was so much owed by so many to so few', has rightly become one of the most celebrated military conflicts in modern history. However, the Battle of Britain began many months after the start of the Second World War. The first significant action for the RAF, towards the end of 1939, was to send aircraft to help the French military. Small bombing raids were carried out, and propaganda leaflets were dropped. These early months of the war became known as 'the Phoney War'; prior to 10 May 1940, when Germany launched its invasion of France and the Low Countries, there was no large-scale military action.

In 1939 the German Luftwaffe was vastly superior to the RAF in terms of both the number of aircraft and their weaponry, and there had been some expectation that the Germans would start bombing the UK immediately after the war began. The Phoney War undoubtedly helped the UK, in that it was able to manufacture fighter planes and bombers and improve the armaments on these planes.

The Battle of Britain started in July 1940. Initially, German bomber raids focused on naval targets, such as shipping convoys and ports. This focus then shifted to attempts to disable the RAF, with attacks on airfields and aircraft factories. The original hope of Adolf Hitler had been that Britain would agree to an armistice, or even to surrender, but it soon became clear that prime minister Winston Churchill had no such thoughts. As far as Churchill was concerned, this was a battle that had to be fought and won.

THE RAF'S ARMOURERS

The two main RAF fighter aircraft were the Hawker Hurricane and the Supermarine Spitfire. Both were armed with eight Browning machine guns, which gave them greater firepower than their main foe, the German Messerschmitt Bf 109, which had only four guns. However, the machine guns on the Hurricane and Spitfire, 0.30 calibre, were less powerful than those of the Messerschmitt, and on occasion enemy bombers were able to limp home to Germany despite extensive hits. Nevertheless, as a result of the manoeuvrability and speed of the aircraft, the intense efforts of the ground crew, and the skill and determination of the RAF pilots, the Hurricanes and Spitfires succeeded in seeing off the enemy and triumphing in the Battle of Britain.

So, what of the RAF Armourers during this critical phase of the war? Happily, the Imperial War Museum has a written record provided by a senior Armourer, Chief Technician Ronald Pountain BEM, who worked on Spitfires with No. 64 Squadron at RAF Kenley during the Battle of Britain. His record contains detailed descriptions of what the Armourers would do in order to ensure that the planes were ready for battle.

The Armourer would begin by harmonising the aircraft's guns. This process ensured that all of the bullets fired from the aircraft's eight machine guns would converge at a single point.

The gunsight itself was highly sophisticated, and involved images displayed on a reflector screen. The range of attack had to be set by the pilot on the gunsight, and the value of this range varied for different enemy aircraft, based on their wingspan. Different-coloured dots were painted onto the span adjuster, for different types of aircraft. Depending on the plane that the Spitfire was targeting, the pilot would set the appropriate coloured dot and launch the attack.

The Spitfires were armed with ammunition belts that comprised a series of different cartridges. These included solid bullet cartridges, armour-piercing cartridges, and 'De Wilde' cartridges that included incendiary material designed to set target aircraft on fire. The combination of cartridges helped to inflict the maximum level of damage. The Armourers had to ensure that each cartridge in a belt was positioned very precisely. If a cartridge was even a fraction of an inch out of place, the gun might not work.

The Armourers worked incredibly long days during the Battle of Britain. They had to be up well in advance of the pilots to ensure that the planes were ready for action as soon as they were needed. And when the aircraft returned, the Armourers would immediately be back in action, checking for damage and removing unused ammunition, prior to rearming the planes in preparation for their next mission.

THE HISTORY OF THE RAF ARMOURERS

In September 1940, the German bombers were redirected to non-military targets. This signified the end of the Battle of Britain and the start of the Blitz, when London and other UK cities became the main focus for the German bomber raids. During the Blitz, Spitfires and Hurricanes continued to battle against the German bombers, but they were joined by a new specialist night fighter, the Bristol Beaufighter. Again, the RAF demonstrated its resilience and strength, and in May 1941 the Germans redeployed their bombers to Eastern Europe.

RAF Fighter Command continued to target the Luftwaffe over the next few years, with operations centring over continental Europe rather than the UK, and from 1943 onwards there were also extensive operations in the Far East. However, as the war progressed the activities of the RAF Armourers focused on bombs rather than artillery shells, with Bomber Command playing the lead role.

At the start of the war, RAF Bomber Command was not in a good place. Bombs were in short supply and predominantly of the GP (General Purpose) type developed during the inter-war period. Maximum bomb loads for the existing planes, such as Battle, Blenheim and Hampden, were between 1,000 and 4,000lb, with most bombs being 250 or 500lb. Furthermore, the facilities for navigation and accuracy were woefully inadequate.

Remarkably, by 1943 everything had changed. New planes, in the form of the Halifax and Lancaster bombers, were now flying most of the key missions. They were faster and could carry significantly more bombs than their predecessors – a mixed load of up to 14,000lb of high-explosive and incendiary bombs. Just as significantly, they were equipped with navigation aids that gave them far more accuracy.

The bombs themselves were also much more effective. Instead of the 250 and 500lb GP bombs, which had a detonation failure rate of 10–15 per cent, new Medium Capacity (MC) and High Capacity (HC) bombs were being manufactured, with weights of up to 12,000lb for a single bomb. These bombs were far more destructive, and far more reliable. Then there were the much-improved incendiary bombs, primarily made from phosphorous, which were designed to ignite destructive fires when they hit their targets. The catastrophic firestorms in Hamburg and Dresden were the consequence of these devices.

Led through most of the conflict by Air Chief Marshal Arthur 'Bomber' Harris, RAF Bomber Command dropped an astonishing total of 955,044 tons of bombs during the Second World War, and on the Dresden mission alone over 750 Lancaster bombers were involved.

Armourers played a significant role in the success of Bomber Command and, like their colleagues on the fighter aircraft, their working

THE RAF'S ARMOURERS

days were long, particularly during the busiest years of 1943 to 1945. The aircraft would generally take off between 8 and 9 in the evening, so the Armourers would often be working from early afternoon preparing the bomb loads. A Lancaster bomber had sixteen bomb stations, and these had to be loaded in the right order to keep the aircraft stable when the bombs were dropped. Bombs could be nose-fuzed or tail-fuzed; this determined how they would explode. A typical Lancaster bomb load might include one 4,000lb MC bomb, 640 4lb incendiary bombs, and 16 30lb incendiary bombs.

Some squadrons, particularly those with Mosquitos, were Pathfinder units. Pathfinders would fly ahead of the main bombing force, marking targets through the use of flares. This enabled the main bombers to hit the targets with greater accuracy. For Pathfinders, the Armourers had the responsibility for loading the flares.

When the Lancasters returned from their mission in the middle of the night, the Armourers would check to ensure that all of the bombs had been released successfully. On the odd occasion when a bomb had failed to release, the loading process would be reversed and the bomb would be returned to the bomb dump. Finally, around 9 a.m., the Armourers would be finished and could get a few hours of sleep before starting the bomb-loading process all over again.

For the RAF Armourers, one of the biggest dangers towards the end of the Second World War wasn't German attacks; rather, it was the unreliability of the RAF's own bombs. One of the worst incidents occurred at RAF Spilsby in Lincolnshire, on 11 April 1944. Shortly before 8 p.m., there was a huge explosion at the airfield's bomb dump. It was found that a 1,000lb bomb, one which was due to be used in bombing operations that evening, had exploded. Ten armourers who were working at the bomb dump were killed, and many others were injured. The explosion was so intense that no remains were found of three of those who died.

Similar disasters occurred at East Kirby airfield, where four Armourers died and six Lancaster bombers were damaged such that they were declared 'beyond repair', at RAF Graveley, where seven Armourers died, and at RAF Waterbeach, where nine ground crew were killed when a large bomb that was being loaded onto a Lancaster fell and exploded.

When such incidents occurred, not only were there immediate casualties, but other bombs that were in close proximity to the one that exploded had to be made safe. It can't have been much fun being sent over to the site of an explosion to check the remaining weapons.

THE HISTORY OF THE RAF ARMOURERS

12000lb Tall Boy and the 22000lb Grand Slam. Known as "earthquake" bombs, they were used during the latter years of the war with devastating effect. (Mark Bean)

Armourer completing checks before loading. (Dick Lindsay)

THE RAF'S ARMOURERS

Above left: Hoisting 1000lb HE bomb off the stack at Linton on Ouse. (Dick Lindsay)

Above right: 1000lb HE bomb on the trolley Linton On Ouse. (Dick Lindsay)

Hoisting a 2000lb SAP bomb off the stack at Linton On Ouse. (Dick Lindsay)

THE HISTORY OF THE RAF ARMOURERS

2000lb SAP bomb ready to go. (Dick Lindsay)

The infamous "Bouncing bomb" designed by Barnes-Wallis for operation Chastise. The raid to breach the three dams in the Rhur Valley was carried out by 617 Sqn led by Wing Commander Guy Gibson. The model in this picture is displayed outside Wing Commander Gibson's old office at RAF Scampton. (Mark Bean)

THE RAF'S ARMOURERS

In May 1945, the war in Europe ended. A significant factor towards the end of the conflict was Allied bombing of German cities, with many thousands of German civilians killed. While there was justifiable controversy over the number of civilians who died, the RAF and its Armourers undoubtedly fulfilled their roles successfully in helping to implement the Allied strategy.

Post-War and Recent Times

Immediately after the end of the Second World War, spending on the armed forces inevitably dropped significantly. Within a year of the war ending, the number of RAF personnel dropped from 963,000 to 150,000. But from the late 1940s, tensions began to build with the Soviet Union – this was the period known as the Cold War – and the RAF numbers started to increase. By 1956, RAF personnel numbered 257,000, which included 6,000 women in the Women's Royal Air Force (WRAF). The Cold War continued for more than thirty years, although the number of RAF personnel fluctuated. When tensions rose, the UK government would increase defence spending and employ more military personnel; when tensions dropped, numbers would decrease. But throughout this period, the armed forces were seen as being crucial during the standoff between East and West.

It takes a war to instigate technological development at pace. Radar, jet engines, new aircraft design and conventional weapons were all a legacy of the Second World War, and the Cold War served to keep the momentum going. For the Armourers this meant learning to work with nuclear weapons, fondly known as 'buckets of sunshine'. These were the ultimate deterrent to a full-scale war. Safety has always been a key aspect of the armament trade and never had this been more true. Ejection seats also came under the care of the Armourers and remain so to this day. New aircraft, new missions, new weapons and systems; all required new training and new ways of working, something everyone who has ever served understands and adapts to.

In terms of location, West Germany became the focal point for NATO in the post-war years, because of its geographical position. There were several RAF bases in West Germany, and many Armourers served time there. In every sense, it was at the heart of the Cold War. But there were RAF bases all over the world, from Singapore in the Far East to Belize in Central America. Many of the stories in this book paint a picture of the locations where the Armourers served.

THE HISTORY OF THE RAF ARMOURERS

Happily, nuclear weapons have never been used. But for many Armourers there were active conflicts, most notably the Falklands War in 1982, Bosnia in the 1990s, and the ongoing unrest in the Middle East.

But perhaps the most challenging time of all for the British armed forces came in the early 1990s. In 1989 the Berlin Wall came down, leading to a unified Germany, and in 1991, following the break-up of the Soviet Union, the Cold War finally ended. During the 1990s, government spending on the military was slashed. RAF bases in the UK and around the world were shut down, and the number of personnel was significantly reduced. This was achieved largely through redundancies, contracts not being extended, and minimal recruitment. Even for those who stayed on, life would never be quite the same again. The defence cuts meant that there were fewer training options, many people were asked to change their job roles, and the opportunities for travel to sites in Europe and the Far East were significantly reduced. At the same time, there were others who applied for voluntary redundancy and were refused – another bone of contention.

But despite everything that has happened, throughout the conflicts and the cuts, the RAF Armourers have retained their zest for life and their sense of humour. They have continued to uphold the Armourers' traditions, and provide the kind of service to the RAF that so impressed Lord Trenchard all those years ago. They've worked hard, but also played hard – after all, when you know you've done a good job, surely you deserve a few beers? The stories in this book help to give a flavour of life as an RAF Armourer over the years – its ups and downs, its characters, its conflicts and its rewards.

Chapter 2

Starting Out as an RAF Armourer

In the process of gathering information for this book, one phrase kept coming up: 'Once an Armourer, always an Armourer'. Although the preferred term for the trade at the time of writing this book was 'Weapon Technician', everyone we spoke to referred to themselves as Armourers, so that's the term we're going to use. Throughout our interviews, the strong bonds and the camaraderie shone through. So, what is it that makes someone become an RAF Armourer? Is it a case of being born to be an Armourer? Are there little children all over the world who, throughout their formative years, dream of spending their lives loading weapons onto war planes?

The reality is that Armourers come from many different backgrounds and join the trade for many different reasons. Often, people know that they want to join the RAF, but they don't know exactly what trades are available. And there were others who didn't intend to join the RAF at all, but who were persuaded by an RAF recruitment officer that a job in the air force might be more to their liking than an army or navy role.

Some have been given an insight into possible military careers through organisations such as the Air Cadets, or as a result of family connections. Some start out doing other jobs, but circumstances point them in the direction of the armed forces. And some are taken along to their local CIOs (Careers Information Offices for the armed forces) by desperate parents, in the hope of finding some kind of reputable job for their bored teenagers. At the CIO each potential applicant is given a glossy brochure to take away. These brochures paint a wonderful picture of life in the RAF, a life full of excitement and opportunity. The hope is that, bolstered by this sunny prospect, young recruits will come back, full of enthusiasm.

So why an Armourer, rather than a pilot, or a mechanic, or an engineer? This decision will be based on a number of things: school and college qualifications, the results of doing a series of tests that identify the specific strengths of applicants, and of course people's personal preferences.

Sometimes decisions are based more on what roles are available, or which trades are desperate for new recruits. Another factor might be who

STARTING OUT AS AN RAF ARMOURER

happens to be working in the CIO on a particular day. If the person sitting behind the desk is an Armourer, why wouldn't they sell their trade in preference to others?

The Armourers we spoke to while writing this book fall into many of the categories described above. So let's introduce you to our contributors, and find out what prompted them to join the trade. You'll read much more about these characters in the chapters that follow.

The oldest Armourer we spoke to was **Bill Lanfear**, who signed up in January 1954. Bill joined the RAF as a National Service conscript. National Service started in 1949, and for the next twelve years all healthy young men between the ages of 17 and 21 were required to serve in the armed forces for a minimum of eighteen months, and remain on the reserve list for four years. Bill served as an RAF Armourer for two years.

Brian Polson was born in 1937, so many of his formative childhood experiences took place during the Second World War. Unsurprisingly, and in line with many of his contemporaries, he enjoyed playing with toy guns; it's not difficult to imagine who 'the enemy' was. The armed forces always seemed a likely career direction. Brian had originally planned to join the Royal Navy; several family members had served in the navy, so it seemed the obvious place to go. But somehow the RAF was more appealing. So, on 10 December 1954, at the age of 17, he approached his local RAF recruiting office and signed up.

For **Bill Morton**, joining the RAF had been a dream since his early teens, even though his parents weren't keen. So in September 1960, at the age of 17, he headed off on his own to the local RAF recruitment centre. He took an exam and clearly did well, because he was offered a choice of any ground-based job. He looked around, saw a Javelin loaded with Firestreak missiles, and thought, 'That's the job for me.' His mother, now resigned to Bill's military ambitions, signed the requisite forms, and he was ready to start his new life.

Mike Steel is an example of an Armourer who came to the trade via the army, which he joined in the early 1960s. Over the next few years, he was promoted through the ranks, ending up as a corporal. His main role was that of an instructor, teaching new recruits how to fire guns, among other things. Mike left after six years but couldn't get a job on civvy street. Now aged 27, he didn't want to rejoin the army, so applied to the RAF instead. Having enjoyed the world of weapons during his time as an instructor, he didn't take much persuading to become an Armourer.

For **Martyn Mander**, links with the RAF were part of his ancestry. In fact, for Martyn, they went back beyond the RAF – his grandfather had joined the Royal Flying Corps prior to the First World War, as an air

17

mechanic. Martyn's father applied to join up in 1938, when the winds of war were starting to blow once again, but was rejected on the grounds that he was too small; instead, he did his bit for the war effort by working in an ammunitions factory. Martyn joined the Air Cadets as a youngster, and although he passed his 11+ exam and got a place in grammar school, his desire was always to join the RAF. He left school before sixth form and in 1973 he signed up at his nearest recruitment office, with strong support from his family. After passing all the aptitude tests, he looked at the trade options that were available and decided that becoming an Armourer sounded like a fun direction to take.

Martin 'Taff' Turner was 16 in 1977, when his dad took him to the local RAF CIO. He hadn't planned to join the armed forces, but at the time there weren't many jobs available in Newport, where his family lived. He recalls being greatly impressed by the glossy brochures, which made life in the RAF sound fantastic. Clearly buoyed by the prospect, he did well enough in the tests to be offered several different job roles, one of which was Armourer.

Ade Thorne was born and brought up in Amesbury next to RAF Boscombe Down, which is best known as the base for the testing of new military aircraft and its equipment. So as a child, his dad would take him up to the end of the runway, aircraft spotting. Unsurprisingly, the excitement of watching fast jets flashing overhead made him decide to join the RAF in 1978, at the age of 17. So why an Armourer? The fact that he was working in a fireworks factory prior to signing up may have been a factor!

The majority of new recruits are men, but some intrepid young women decide that their future also lies in the military. **Jane Erskine** joined up in 1985. Her father had served in the army during the Second World War, and Jane remembers being transfixed by the stories he told her about his wartime experiences. She had tried to get a job as a civilian engineer, but was rejected because her potential employer didn't want a woman. So she decided to try the armed forces. Originally she'd planned to join the navy, but there was a six-year waiting list. What's more, she discovered that women weren't allowed to go to sea. Who would want to join a navy but be confined to shore? (Note that this restriction was removed in 1990.) So she joined the RAF instead. She had planned to be a sooty or a rigger, but there were no openings. However, she was offered a weapons mechanic course as an alternative. She had absolutely no idea what that involved, but after talking it over with the recruitment officer, Derek, who happened to be an Armourer himself, she signed up and headed off to Swinderby. Five years later Jane met Derek during an event at Coltishall. He recognised her, and mentioned that he'd been the recruiting officer who signed her up.

STARTING OUT AS AN RAF ARMOURER

His next words reflected something that Jane had to get used to during her years as an Armourer: 'I didn't think you'd make it. You were so little.' Jane did make it, and had a long and successful career.

Jon Eaton joined up in May 1980, after chatting with an old schoolfriend who was a Flight-Line Mechanic at RAF Swinderby, and who was loving life in the forces. At the time Jon's long-term plan was to work in agriculture, and after leaving agricultural college he was working on a farm. But for various reasons he wasn't enjoying the job he'd been given, and after talking things over with his grandfather Jon decided to join the RAF as an Armourer. His contract was for three years, after which he planned to leave and return to agriculture. Instead, he ended up serving in the RAF for twenty-six years.

From an early age **Garron Clark-Darby** had a fascination with military vehicles and used to spend hours in the local library poring over the Jane's guide to fighting vehicles, so obviously the only career for him was an army driver. That was until the Troubles in Northern Ireland were on the TV every night, at which point he started to have second thoughts, watching the Land Rovers getting petrol bombed. Nevertheless, he was genuinely on his way to an appointment at the Army Recruitment Office in Bedford when he noticed that the RAF Recruitment Office was just upstairs in the same building. For some inexplicable reason, he went in there instead. He was sent to RAF Stafford for a three-day selection process and as a result was offered a craft apprenticeship. They wanted him to do avionics, but his second love of firearms made him ask about being an Armourer instead, and luckily they agreed. A few months later, aged just 15½, he turned up at Halton to start a new life.

Brendan Lucey joined up in December 1983. His dad had served in the RAF in the 1950s so, like many others, the armed forces seed had been sown early in Brendan's life. He'd made an enquiry about the RAF when he was still at school, but thought little more about it and after leaving school he was working in a garage, while doing a car mechanics course at college. Then one day, out of the blue, he got a letter from the RAF asking if he was still interested. So he went down to the recruitment centre in Ilford for an interview and some tests. However, it was a year later when he finally signed up. His intention had been to join as a mechanic, working on vehicles, but he was told that he'd failed the mechs test and would he be interested in an Armourer role instead. The reality was probably that there were no openings for mechanics at the time.

In **Tony**'s case, he was working as a grave digger in Taunton when he decided to join up. Initially he wasn't sure which service to apply for, although the navy was a non-starter because he couldn't swim. Again there was family history, in that his uncle had served in the Second World War as an Air Gunner and Wireless Operator on Short Sunderlands, but it was long conversations in the pub about aircraft with his best mate, who at the time was in the Fleet Air Arm, that really got Tony hooked and pointed him in the direction of the RAF.

The ages of the recruits can vary significantly. Some are just 16, straight out of school. Some, such as Tony, have already been working and are over 20 when they sign up for the first time. There are others, such as Mike Steel, who have re-joined the armed forces, perhaps switching from the army to the RAF. There are also different entry levels: apprentice, mechanic and DE (Direct Entrant). DEs are generally a little older, often with experience of civilian work, and are on a fast-track route to earlier promotion. This doesn't always go down well with other recent recruits, and occasionally there was bitter rivalry.

Podge Middleton joined as a DE in 1975, even though he was only 17 at the time. He had started sixth form at school, but after a year he decided that he didn't want to continue with his academic education. He'd been a member of the Air Cadets, and a friend of his who'd also been an Air Cadet had recently joined the RAF as an Armourer. So Podge thought he'd give it a go too. In his words, 'Who wouldn't want to blow things up?'

Sometimes the parents have no idea that their child is about to join up – perhaps because joining up wasn't even being considered by the young person themself! In the case of **Derek Binnie**, as a 17-year-old he was working as a trainee Architectural Technician in Edinburgh's West End. He remembers looking out of his office window one sunny day and thinking, 'I really need to get a job with a bit more excitement.' So the following week, during his lunch hour, he walked into the RAF Careers Office and asked for information on what was available. When his qualifications were disclosed, like Podge he was offered a direct entry to become either an Aircraft Electrical or an Aircraft Weapons Technician. When it was disclosed that the electrical option involved a year's training, whereas weapons training was nine months, it was an easy choice. Plus the fact he couldn't even wire a plug at the time. So he joined up, and when he got home he remembers his mum, dad and brother sitting eating tea and watching *Crossroads* on TV, at which point he announced, 'Oh, I joined the RAF today, I leave in February.' Completely out of the blue, none of it planned, and they were all totally shocked. He went on to have twenty-nine great years of service.

Bob Worthington-Harris was born and brought up in Northern Ireland. In 1982, when the Falklands War broke out, he was an 11-year-old schoolboy. Seeing what was going on in the South Atlantic had a big effect on him, and he decided that he wanted to join the army. His dad wasn't happy about

STARTING OUT AS AN RAF ARMOURER

this, and told Bob that if he was going to join the armed forces he should choose one that offered trades. So, when he was 16½ Bob excitedly applied to join the RAF – and was rejected on the grounds that he was too young. Undaunted, he reapplied shortly after his 18th birthday. It was only later that he discovered that he was only the forty-seventh person from Northern Ireland to have been accepted to join the RAF in five years. It seems that getting security clearance, while the Troubles were still ongoing, was a major stumbling block.

Having set his heart on an RAF career seven years previously, Bob was a bit taken aback when he arrived at Swinderby for initial training and overheard another new recruit commenting that his main reason for joining was because he hated his mum and dad and wanted to get away from them!

Towards the end of his RAF career, Bob found himself on the other side of the fence, working as a recruiting officer in Sheffield. He was able to provide us with an interesting perspective on the decision-making process for recruiting future Armourers. Everything has to be done by the book, so that there is no potential for legal challenges, and a series of cross-checks takes place, checks of which the excited new recruits are generally completely unaware.

One hard and fast rule involves health issues. There are a number of health issues that are complete no-nos when it comes to joining the RAF. On one occasion in Sheffield, a young lad climbed the stairs to the recruitment office and walked in gasping for breath. Bob immediately asked him if he had asthma, to which the reply was yes. End of interview. If you have asthma, you can't join up, even if you're in very good physical shape otherwise – that was the case with a young female applicant who had successfully run the London Marathon, despite her asthma. She still couldn't join the RAF.

Sometimes the medical issues are more complex. A colleague of Bob's told him of a teenage applicant whose medical records stated that he was asthmatic and was using an inhaler. The young man said that he wasn't. The reality was that it was his father who was using the inhaler, but had managed to get a prescription made out in his son's name so that he wouldn't have to pay for it. This posed a dilemma for the family: have the son's application rejected based on his medical record, or admit that they had been defrauding the NHS. Bob never did find out what actually happened.

Having a criminal record was another prohibitor. Minor offences might be overlooked, but lengthy jail sentences definitely wouldn't. Bob recalls a young woman who seemed like an excellent candidate, until he asked her whether she had a criminal record. After a moment's hesitation she said 'Yes'. Next question: Have you served more than two and a half years in prison? Again, the answer was 'Yes'. It turned out that the young woman's boyfriend at the time had murdered someone, and she had participated in the killing and been convicted of manslaughter. It goes without saying that she didn't get the job.

Mike Steel's failure to find a job after leaving the army ties in with another common theme: that joining the armed forces is nothing like a regular job. It is a career, a vocation, a lifestyle choice and, for some, a calling.

The RAF starts taking control of potential new recruits even before they join. Details are sent out on when to attend a medical, where and when the various tests will be taken, and the interview date. In the past, after your interview and medical test you were told whether or not you had been accepted into the RAF. Nowadays, all potential new recruits are given the opportunity to go for a taster week, which provides them with the chance to became acquainted with the kind of work they'd be doing. The taster week also includes the physical tests. Only after completing the taster week do applicants find out whether or not they have been selected – assuming they haven't decided that the military life is not for them after all.

Those who are lucky enough to pass selection are given a date and location to attest; this is where each new recruit attends a careers office and, in the presence of an officer, swears an oath of allegiance to the ruling monarch. Tony attested on 20 July 1987, at Exeter careers office.

After signing the necessary papers, the new recruits are sent off for their initial or basic training. Prior to 1964, training of new recruits took place at a number of different stations including RAF Halton, in Buckinghamshire, and RAF Padgate, in Cheshire. From 1964 to 1993, the training moved to RAF Swinderby, in Lincolnshire, before returning to RAF Halton in recent years. Basic training is the first real test of character and an opportunity to find out whether both parties (recruit and RAF) are suited to a long and happy relationship together. The duration of basic training has changed over the years. In the early days and times of crisis, it may only have lasted a few weeks; from the 1970s to the late 1990s it was six weeks; now, it is ten weeks.

Tony describes his experience of attesting and being sent for training:

> I travelled to Exeter on the train from Taunton. You were allowed to take someone along, so my Mum came. I remember that I was wearing a suit and there were a few of us attesting on the same day. I am sure we arrived for about 11 a.m. and were all called into a room. I don't really have a clear memory, more a sense that at some point we were all invited to stand and collectively swear the oath. There would have been some

STARTING OUT AS AN RAF ARMOURER

handshaking and congratulations; there may even have been tea and biscuits. I don't recall. I do remember feeling a great sense of pride and a little bit of, 'Oh God, what have I got myself into?'

We were each given a rail warrant and instructions for the next step. I was instructed to arrive at Swinderby the next day. The warrant could be exchanged for a train ticket from wherever you lived to your destination.

So that was that. Mum and I travelled home, and I got all my gear together. The kit list was impressive; you had to take an iron, coat hangers, shoe polish and brushes, braces (black) to support one's trousers, labels, marker pens, dusters and goodness knows what else. I had bought two rucksacks, one large and one smaller one, and just about managed to get everything crammed in. We had a meal, and the next day I got a taxi to the train station, said goodbye to Mum, and that was it. The date was 21st July, which happened to be her birthday. Happy birthday Mum!

Day one of initial training is a rude awakening for many, particularly those who have never lived away from home. In the days when initial training took place at Swinderby, day one and beyond might go something like this, as described by Tony:

> You'd be collected from Newark station by DI staff, put on a bus and driven to Swinderby. You got off the bus, grabbed your bags, and got marched to the welcome hangar. You were given a haircut even though you were told to (and did) turn up with short hair. The station barber did it and charged you a couple of quid for a butcher's job.
>
> From there you were marched to the stores to get your kit. By this time you were fully loaded and taken to your block. You were in a multi-person room – in my case eighteen people – and were allocated a bed space with a bedside locker, wardrobe and top locker. This was now home – an 8 x 8 bed space.
>
> Everything was structured: meals at set times, scheduled lessons and drills, skill at arms, history of the RAF, rank structure, the padre, PE, how to protect yourself, firefighting, first aid, etc. There was regular room cleaning and allocated areas, and inspections. And there was shouting. Lots of shouting.

THE RAF'S ARMOURERS

It's at this point that new recruits discover that life in the armed forces isn't quite the same as the picture painted in the glossy brochure, and that they need to adjust to being yelled at on a regular basis. In the 1970s and 1980s, the emphasis in initial training was very much one of character building: 'They would try to break you down, and then build you back up again.' Some people would decide that the rigours of life in the armed forces wasn't for them and would drop out. But those who remained came out stronger. As one Armourer said: 'If you can't hack it in training, how can you be expected to deal with the situations that occur in the real world? Situations that might involve danger and death.'

The experiences of Brian Polson give a feel for how things were in the mid-1950s. When Brian joined up, he was sent off to Cardington to be kitted up and sign the oath of allegiance forms. Three days later he headed off to West Kirby on Merseyside, for eight weeks of square bashing. There he met many interesting characters, including the infamous Irishman Corporal Parkinson ('My name's Parkinson, and I'm a bastard') and another corporal named Jim Watson, who was doing his National Service. It turned out that Jim was a member of the Jack Parnell band, one of the best-known jazz bands at the time; no one was excused National Service, even if they were the equivalent of a contemporary boy band member. Brian's time at West Kirby included some unexpected non-military activities including caddying at Hoylake Golf Course, perhaps better known as Royal Liverpool, one of the venues for the British Open.

Brian's training then moved on to St Athan in Wales. At the time St Athan was the main physical training centre for the RAF, and Brian was invited to help out at the Royal Tournament in 1955. His role would have been organisational rather than competitive, and would no doubt have involved lengthy stints in the cookhouse, but unfortunately he injured his right knee during training and had to drop out. Instead, he was posted to RAF Gaydon in Warwickshire, the first UK site for the V bombers. Gaydon was his base for the next four years.

A fundamental part of service life is the ability to look after yourself and your kit. When you have mastered this, you are no longer a liability who needs to be taken care of.

In the past, an early introduction to looking after yourself was the bed pack. On joining and arriving at the training camp, recruits were kindly issued with bedding for the use of: pillows, two; blankets, four; sheets, two; counterpane, one; and mattress protector, one. The kindness was mitigated slightly when you realised that you had to arrange this bedding every day in a very specific order ready for inspection:

STARTING OUT AS AN RAF ARMOURER

Mattress protector fitted tightly to mattress.

Blanket, grey (with three narrow stripes) over the mattress with stripes running down the bed; blanket must be fitted tightly over the bed so that a coin can be bounced off it; include hospital corners.

Remaining three blankets and two sheets folded neatly to form a rectangular pack alternating blanket, sheet, blanket, sheet, blanket.

This pack is then neatly wrapped by the counterpane ensuring that the full 'sandwich' effect is visible.

Finally, the pack is neatly topped by the two pillows.

Failure to display the bedding to the correct standard would result in bedding being thrown by the inspecting NCO. Where it was thrown depended on the mood of the NCO. If you were lucky it was distributed around the room. If you were less lucky it involved a trip outside to recover said items. The sheer stress of the morning arranging of the bed pack prior to inspection often resulted in recruits choosing to leave their bed pack intact while they slept on the floor.

These days are different, of course. Since the 2000s bed packs have been consigned to the great blanket store in the sky. Recruits now have duvets, which are doubtless more comfortable and snuggly. Another change is the accommodation. Rooms now have carpets, of all things. Gone are the days of using the mop and bucket to clean and the 'bumper' to polish the floor to within an inch of its life; the hoover is now the weapon of choice. One

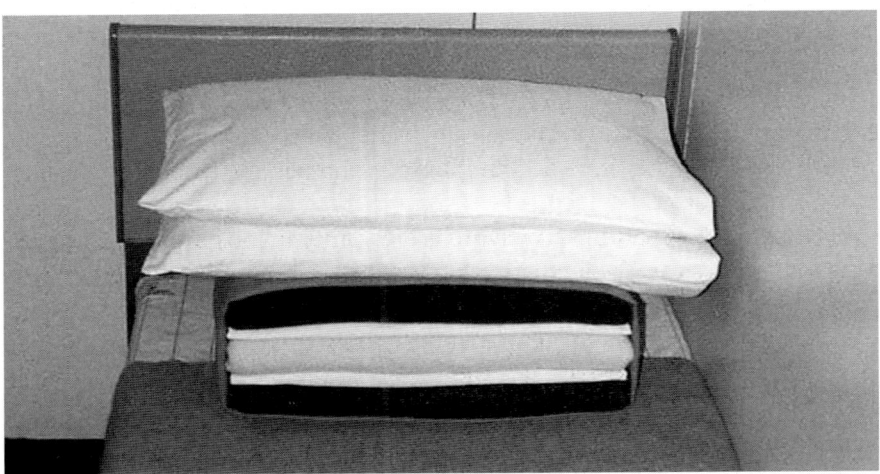

Bed pack. (Mark Bean)

thing that hasn't changed is the need for things to be kept clean and tidy, so while the methods are different, the stress of 'bull nights' still exist, and that horrible moment in the morning where all are stood to attention at the end of their bed while the snec inspects bedspace and kit still very much exists.

A combination of beds and ablutions (used in military circles to refer to the building or room containing washing facilities and toilets) was crucial to the operation of one of the best-executed practical jokes Garron Clark-Darby ever experienced.

> The ablutions were positioned centrally on each floor, with two barrack rooms leading off, forming a 'T' shape. Every apprentice had an identical iron bed, identical brown blankets and identical white bedding, so it was all totally interchangeable. One lad was a particularly heavy sleeper, so one night his roommates carried him, still sleeping, in his bed and left him in the ablutions, then replaced his bed with an identical one, bedding and all, from the room opposite, even with the sheets pulled down as if somebody had just got out.
>
> As people started to go for showers in the morning he duly awoke and ran back into the room hurling insults on those who he alleged had moved his bed. He was met with blank/confused stares from his roommates who swore he had just got out of his bed which was so clearly still right there. He then insisted his 'friends' accompany him to the ablutions so he could show them where his bed was – but of course it wasn't, as unbeknown to him while this was all going on the other bed was removed from the ablutions and used to replace the one that had been taken from the room opposite. Everybody then just walked away, shaking their heads and muttering that he had finally 'lost it'. I can't remember who he was, but I wonder to this day if anybody ever told him what really happened.

Having a birthday during training could be a dangerous time for a new recruit. You would inevitably be bought lots of booze and had to be prepared to be the butt of the practical joke. Bob Worthington-Harris remembers an incident from his training days at Swinderby:

> There was a young lad in our room, and it was his birthday. We were parallel to the WRAF block, so we'd got to know them a bit, and told them to come to the window at 6 o'clock. We stripped off the birthday boy, strapped him to a bed, and raised

STARTING OUT AS AN RAF ARMOURER

it up to the window, where the WRAFs had a good view of what was going on.

Next thing a WRAF corporal came storming over and demanded to know what was going on. Someone replied, 'Nothing, Mum.' She was not amused, and retorted: 'I'm not your f***ing mother!' When she realised what was going on, and that it was his birthday, she asked us to let him down. And that was it.

This was a classic example of how practical jokes during training would be dealt with. The officers knew that this was a time when people were under a lot of pressure and needed to let off steam occasionally. No serious damage had been done, so there was no need for repercussions.

It's not just other new recruits who are the victims of practical jokes during training, as Podge Middleton recalls:

In the summer of '76, the hottest summer in living memory, I was doing DE training at Halton. Because it was so hot we had lessons outside, starting at 6 in the morning and finishing at 2. We had a couple of sheds allocated to the Armourers, and we took our tables and chairs outside. There was a row of trees which gave some shade, so we sat under the trees having our lessons.

We had an instructor at Halford that we nicknamed 'Bike Chain', because he had a length of lifting chain with a chunky piece of metal attached to it. If ever he thought one of us had nodded off in the heat, he'd swing the chain and whack the table with the metal, to wake up whoever had fallen asleep.

One day we managed to get hold of this chain, and Araldited it into a loop. The next time Bike Chain lifted his chain and tried to swing it against the desk, he almost wrenched his arm off.

Of course, for people like Mike Steel, who had done it all before in the army, training was a bit of a doddle. In Mike's words, 'I thought they should have given me a red coat. I thought I'd gone to Butlins.' He would continually be singled out by his instructors as an example of how things should be done – hardly surprising when he'd been an instructor himself. Mike remembers a field training exercise, when small teams of recruits were sent on an exercise that involved map reading and observation:

All the teams were going to the left, and I said to my team, 'We're going to the right.' Some members of my team weren't happy and pointed out that all the other teams were going left. I said: 'That's their f***ing problem. We'll meet them halfway round.' For me, doing map-reading and field craft was a natural thing.

After a short while the other members of the team realised that we were going the right way and all the other teams were going the wrong way, so they were happy after that.

I made a note of all the things they wanted – the ground, where we set up, ambushes, firing points, the enemy – all that type of thing. Came back to do my report, then went in the hut. I didn't salute the senior officer when I walked in. In the army you don't salute in the field. You get the officers killed if you do that. Of course I got a bollocking for not saluting. But they did seem to be impressed with the report.

The staff who supervise the initial training often develop a sense for which of the young Armourers have what it takes to survive and flourish, even when things don't seem to be going well. Jon Eaton was one of those who experienced this first-hand.

Jon's initial training was at Swinderby, but for a short period he moved over to North Luffenham, doing fieldcraft training. Jon describes what happened there:

A group of us were walking around Luffenham, and I thought I wouldn't mind putting some night lines out in Luffenham Water, maybe catch some trout. So I snuck out at night, put some lines out, and went to bed. At that time I could survive on an hour's sleep, so in the early morning I snuck out again and started to pull in the line. At that point I heard voices approaching. I was on the wall of the reservoir, with nowhere to go, so I got into the water, thinking I'd just keep my head above water and dip down if anyone came along.

No one did, so I got out and went back to the camp. It had been raining the day before, so I had all this wet kit which I had to put on. Two days later I came down with a really bad cold. I felt terrible, but I knew I had to push through.

Late that afternoon, we had our first session in the gas chamber, which is a brick-based room. You have a respirator on, and you do these drills that are supposed to help you survive in a biological or chemical attack. It's called NBC training, nuclear, biological and chemical, and involves the use of CS gas. At the end of the session they make you take your mask off, and you have to say your service number. The first thing you do when you take your mask off is to breathe in. And immediately the gas is in your nose, throat, eyes etc. Because of my cold, it affected me really badly, and when I came out of the chamber I felt awful. I just couldn't get it out of my sinuses, and couldn't breathe properly. I ended up having a really bad night's sleep.

I got up the next morning and was really struggling. Reveille was at 5.30 a.m., and you needed to clean the room, get your uniform ready, make your bed pack. A corporal came in, and he was bawling at me. All my stuff goes out the window, and he rips all my stuff out of my locker. I was on a real low, and I just thought, 'There's no way I'm going to get through this. I just can't function.'

Everyone else went for breakfast, but I didn't want to eat. So I thought, 'There's only one thing you can do.' So I took myself down to the sergeants' and corporals' office at the end of the block, and knocked on the door. A sergeant answered the door.

'What do you want Eaton?'

'I'm chucking the hat in. I can't get through this. The training yesterday did me in. I've got this cold …'

'So what do you want to do?'

'I'm going to phone my parents and get them to come and fetch me.'

'OK. I'll get all the paperwork ready. You phone your parents.'

So I phoned my dad, and asked him to come and fetch me. Dad asked why, and I told him I couldn't get through it – that I had to rethink everything.

I put the phone down, and the sergeant said, 'I'll just go through your records, and get all the paperwork done. So get off back to your room and get the rest of your stuff ready. Then carry on. You have to carry on until your parents come.'

It was now between 6.30 and 7 o'clock. I'm thinking it'll be two and a half hours until my dad can get things sorted and be here. So I'm thinking: 'Morning tea break. That'll be me gone.'

It gets to morning tea break, and there's no sign of him. Gets to lunch, still nothing. My parents ran a pub, and I know he's going to be working now, so I reckon he'll come when it's not busy, maybe between 2.30 and 6 o'clock.

It reaches 5 o'clock, and there's still no sign of him. I couldn't ring my dad directly, so I went back to the office and asked if they'd heard anything from him, if anything had happened to him. So I said I'd try to ring him, and the sergeant said: 'You're not ringing him. Get back to your bed. Get into bed and get yourself dosed up. You ain't going anywhere.' He gave me a bottle of paracetamol, told me to take two now, and two more when I woke up in the middle of night.

It turned out that what he'd done, straight after I left the office in the morning, was to ring my dad up and tell him not to come.

A few weeks later, at the leaving parade, the sergeant came over to my dad, and they were chatting away. This is what he said to my dad: 'I'll tell you now. You get lads coming into the office, they say they want to leave, and I can't get them out of the door quick enough. But you have other lads, like your lad, who come in because they've had a s*** day. You just need to get them through it, because you know they'll be fine after that.'

That sergeant clearly knew what he was doing, based on Jon's long and fulfilling career.

From the perspective of the new recruits, being part of the armed forces gives you a sense of belonging. From the moment you attest, you feel that you are wanted, and that you have a purpose; for many, this is the first time they have experienced that sense. Many of those who join in their mid to late teens have barely worked out who they are. Even those who join later in life have their perceptions challenged and re-formed.

Of course, what the brochures don't tell you is that the military want you on their terms. Individuality is all very well, and there is room to be your own person in the military, but primarily you are part of something bigger. You are recruited for your potential, not who you are when you join. Training is the process of turning you into who the RAF want you to be, and anyone who resists soon comes to question why they joined. You are challenged in ways you never thought you could survive, both physically and mentally. Everyone comes to a point in their training where they question their choice and think about leaving; this is the rite of passage, and the RAF only wants you if you face that question and choose to stay. That point is the lowest, but from then on it is about building you up. You start to appreciate the environment and the process and, more importantly, the people around you: the training staff (it's very difficult to appreciate them at the time, but most appreciate them after the event) and more importantly your fellow recruits – your muckers, oppos, mates.

STARTING OUT AS AN RAF ARMOURER

The first big lesson to learn is that you are no longer in control of your own life. Choices are taken away: when to go to bed, when to get up, what to wear, when to eat, when to work, when to relax – these are no longer your decisions to make. The only choice you have is whether to comply. As you progress through training you become more confident, you learn to rely on and trust in your mates, to support each other, to barter skills and just get the job done. You develop resilience, the ability to shrug and get on with it. You learn when to question and when to obey without thinking, and above all you learn about who you are.

An aspect that everyone associates with the military is uniform. You all dress the same and therefore have a common bond from the start. During square bashing (marching up and down a lot) the uniform is used as part of the break-down and build-up process. To start with you all wear overalls, or 'denims' as they are known. Originally the denims were blue, but by the 1970s green was being issued. The wearing of denims singles you out as the newbies. Course attendees who have been in training longer would progress to wearing the more standard uniform of light blue shirt and tie, blue trousers, blue jumper and shoes, and all topped off with the beret. Each flight is distinguished by the colour of the disc behind the RAF cap band and the shoulder flashes. Those in denims wear a coloured cravat. As you progress through your square bashing you get to change from denims to working blue, and finally there's the passing out parade when you have the chance to wear your full number 1 or dress uniform.

The passing out parade is a moment of great pride and achievement. You have survived your basic training and, while still not qualified in your chosen trade, you have met some massive challenges and overcome them. You have earned the right to wear your number 1 uniform on parade in front of your invited family and friends and show them just how far you have come. This is a special moment in your career and will live long in the memory; there may even be the odd tear shed. One thing is guaranteed – you will never stand straighter or march more sharply; you will throw your whole being into this parade, your heels will be hammered into the tarmac, your responses to the shouted commands will be lightning quick and in perfect time with the rest of your flight. Your chest will burst with pride and you will feel on top of the world.

The passing out parade marks the end of basic training and the starting of the next phase, which is trade training. You have learnt how to be an airman or airwoman (actually the phrase these days is 'aviator') and now need to learn how to be an Armourer. This involves packing up your kit, saying goodbye to the friends you have made during basic training, and heading off to your trade training camp. Trade training has varied in duration depending on whether you were recruited as a mechanic, apprentice or direct entrant. The most common route to join in the 1950s was apprentice, because while the training was tough and lasted at least eighteen months, you qualified as a time-served apprentice, which was recognised in civvy street. During the 1970s, 1980s and 1990s, most people joined as mechanics, did six months of initial trade training, then went off to experience the 'real' RAF for a few years before returning to do further trade training and become a Technician. Since the early 2000s, new Armourers spend up to fourteen months learning their trade. On leaving training they continue their studies at their new camp and eventually gain a Level 3 NVQ, a modern apprenticeship. Trade training has taken place at numerous camps over the years, including RAF Halton and RAF Cosford. Armourer trade training has been taking place RAF Cosford for the last forty years or so, which means generations of Armourers have fond memories of the camp. In its early days as a training camp Fulton Block became notorious, so notorious in fact that it now has its own memorial.

By the time you reach trade training you are all in working blues, unless you're in the workshop, in which case you put on your denims. Shoulder flashes and coloured discs behind the RAF cap band are still used, but this time to distinguish between trades. The Armourer wears yellow shoulder tabs and has a yellow disc. The moment you graduate from training and can remove the shoulder tabs and backing disc is one to savour. Those who return to training for their fitters course have to wear a coloured shoulder flash under their rank badge and put a disc behind their cap badge.

Most people expect the military to be consistent in their dress and have an expectation that uniform means, well, 'uniform', in that everyone should be dressed the same. However, the chances of anyone turning up for work dressed exactly the same as their oppos diminishes greatly after you leave training. Uniform continuously evolves, not always for the best, but one effect of this is a certain randomness to what people wear. Typically, your working blue uniform would be blue shirt, blue trousers and jumper, black socks, black footwear and a hat adorned with the RAF badge – much the same as during the later stages of initial training. Over time, kit being issued changed such that the variety of uniform being worn was almost limitless:

- Blue shirt – choice of light blue long or short sleeve (in the summer unless worn under the jumper or jacket) and tie (no tie required in the summer or if working with machinery), or dark blue working shirt.
- Trousers – summer or winter weight.
- Jumper – round or V-neck depending on when you joined and what stores had in stock. May be replaced with the Thunderbirds jacket.
- Black socks – long in winter or short in summer.

STARTING OUT AS AN RAF ARMOURER

Fulton Block sign. (Mark Bean)

- Black footwear – shoes or boots. Boots could be DMS (Direct Moulded Sole) pattern, steel toe safety, high leg, flying boots (not issued but could be available if you knew the right person!)
- Hat – beret, chip hat or even the peaked cap (number 1 dress).

For training courses that involved RAF, army and navy personnel, there was often a marked contrast in the attire worn by the trainees. Invariably the army and navy representatives would turn out in immaculately matching uniforms. For the RAF trainees, 'uniform' could be, and generally was, interpreted in many different ways – while still conforming to the list above.

Oddly enough, while many things have changed over the decades, the blue uniform of the RAF hasn't changed much. Minor changes such as style of raincoat, round-neck to V-neck and back to round-neck jumpers, and the introduction and subsequent demise of the 'Thunderbirds' jackets are ones that spring immediately to mind. The latter item really was a Marmite choice. During the 1980s and 1990s you tended to see snecs and warrant officers sporting this natty little number while the more junior ranks avoided it like the plague. When being demobbed, you are required to hand in all items of kit issued, and the Thunderbirds jacket was consistently placed back on the counter at stores.

THE RAF'S ARMOURERS

The biggest change in uniform was a realisation in the 1970s and 1980s that the RAF was actually part of the military, and that the issue of green or camouflage uniform might be sensible. Anyone in RAF Germany (the front line in those days) was issued combat trousers and jackets and, if they were lucky, a green shirt. Initially known as OGs (olive greens), RAF personnel in the UK would gradually receive combat gear as it became available. It was not uncommon to see people turn up for their annual GDT with the RAF Regiment in varying levels of combat gear, from fully 'cabbaged' up down to the more urbane combat jacket and trousers with shoes and puttees. At the time of writing this book a new uniform has just been announced with pictures being released in the press. The general consensus so far seems to be not favourable, at least among those of us who are no longer serving.

Ade Thorne recalls a bomb disposal course that was attended by all three services. The RAF trainees, and their officers, made a pledge at the start of the course never to wear the same outfits as each other, to the extent that if two people turned up for breakfast wearing the same clothes, they would draw lots to decide who would go back upstairs and get changed. Needless to say, this didn't go down too well with the army and navy – which of course was the whole objective of the exercise!

Another example of the variety in uniform is remembered by Tony:

> In the early '90s I went to RAF St Athan to do my HGV training. The powers that be decided that Armourers should have an HGV driving licence so they could transport their own bombs rather than use MT drivers. There were eighteen of us on the course, all Armourers. We arrived on the Sunday night and had to parade outside the mess at 8 a.m. on the Monday morning, at which point the station staff would come and take us to the training area. We were all there at the appointed time, and lined up when ordered to by the staff. The sergeant looked us over and you could see he wasn't happy. Not one of us was dressed the same. Some had jumper and trousers, some wore coats, some of us had Gore-Tex kit, some were wearing the beret, and one lad had his No. 1 hat on. A few of us were wearing boots and the others wore shoes. It was quite funny.
>
> This snec started shouting at us for not being properly dressed, but it was pointed out that there were no orders about uniform in the joining instructions other than normal working blue. Now because we all had different jobs at different stations, we all had different working blue. The snec tried to achieve unity by ordering those of us wearing coats to take

them off. It was raining quite hard so I felt obliged to point out that if we all got colds it would cost the RAF a lot of money in abandoned training. I did it nicely, and it worked. You could see his shoulders drop and he muttered something about Armourers – I'm sure it was a compliment. He then said to follow the signs for the MT training area but don't go as a group; split up into small groups so no one knew we were together on a course. By rights, because St Athan was in part a training camp, we should have all marched over together in columns looking very smart and military. The snec quickly realised that this was not going to happen.

The lessons learned in training stay with you forever; the details may become blurred, faces may be fuzzy, but your experiences – the feelings and the sense of achievement – are with you for life, along with the ability to recite your service number on command in any circumstance.

All through training and beyond you are becoming the person the RAF needs you to be. You are starting to achieve your potential and you never stop throughout your career. (Well, some do, but for different reasons.) Training does incur losses. Those who choose to leave have made the right choice for them at the time; to stay would likely end in unhappiness, which suits no one. The more difficult situation is those who have to leave through injury. This seems harsh, but then the military life is not easy. Injury can hit at any point and end a promising career.

Conversely, a minor injury can help a trainee to demonstrate their resilience. Jane Erskine broke her wrist during 'hacking and bashing', the workshop phase of the mechanics and fitters training. But she continued on the course as an observer, then did an extra two weeks after her plaster cast was removed, and duly passed. At the same time, she earned the respect of her colleagues and instructors.

On a lighter note, training was also a time when friendships would be formed in the NAAFI bar, as large amounts of beer were consumed. For some teenagers, this might be their very first experience of drinking. Podge Middleton recalls a 16-year-old trainee who was generously provided with copious amounts of Pernod and orange juice by his colleagues – needless to say, he didn't see out the evening.

But sometimes alcohol was exactly what was needed. When Ade Thorne was doing his hacking and bashing, things weren't going well. The instructor, a well-known character called Dick Bates, told the trainees that there would be 'No tea tonight', and that they had to come back for extra training. The disconsolate trainees arrived back to find fourteen portions of fish and chips

THE RAF'S ARMOURERS

and a crate of beer awaiting them, courtesy of Dick. Suitably invigorated, and with morale restored, they knuckled down and everyone passed.

During training, there would often be an inspection of the training camp in the form of an AOC's parade. This was when the senior officer in charge of the RAF group would come to inspect the new recruits, and everything on the camp would have to be at its shining best.

Podge Middleton's experience of an AOC's parade was a little unusual. He had just moved to Halton from Swinderby, to complete his trade training. While he was at Halton he celebrated his 18th birthday. Unfortunately, this was the night before the AOC inspection. However, that didn't stop Podge and his mates from consuming large quantities of drink at the NAAFI bar, including some of the infamous NAAFI-labelled whisky ('horrible stuff, like rocket fuel'). Podge had to be carried back to his eight-man room, considerably the worse for wear. This is what happened next, in Podge's words …

> At some point during the night, I had to go and throw up. I headed for the doors of the barrack block, but misjudged the doors and ran into the corner of the wall. Knocked myself unconscious. Flat out. The guys had to call the medics.
>
> I remember waking up, being carried downstairs on a stretcher, then passed out. I woke up again in the Med Centre, and a guy was asking me how many fingers I could see, and could I count back from 100 in sevens. Someone said: 'He's an Armourer. He couldn't count upwards in sevens.'
>
> Eventually I came round properly, and there was a guy in the bed next to me who'd taken a real good beating – he'd been giving unwanted advice to his mates, who'd taken offence.
>
> Next morning, as part of the inspection, the AOC was due to visit the Med Centre. So before this happened OC Med came round and said: 'A C Middleton, so what happened to you?'
>
> 'It was my 18th birthday. I got pissed and ran into a wall.'
>
> 'No you didn't, A C Middleton. You slipped on the polished floor, didn't you?'
>
> 'Yes sir.'
>
> Then he moved on to the lad next door. 'And you had a run-in with some of the locals, didn't you?'
>
> 'Yes, sir.'

For the next two weeks Podge had to walk around with a bandage on his head, and had to wear his number 1 hat, because it was the only one that would fit over the bandage.

STARTING OUT AS AN RAF ARMOURER

Trade training covers so many individual subjects, and all come together at the end to give you the background knowledge you need to be an Armourer. The approach to trade training has changed over the years. Whereas in the past all the training involved working directly with weapons and equipment, in more recent times some of the training has involved using virtual reality and, increasingly and in line with modern practices, there are plans to provide more online learning going forward. This is not something that many instructors welcome; how can you learn practical skills without actually doing the hands-on work? However, while the learning processes may be evolving, the subjects themselves have remained much the same.

The subjects are divided into phases, and the length of each phase is determined by the amount of material there is to learn. Some of the simpler phases might be just a few days and others span a few weeks or longer. You cover how APs work, all the forms relevant to the work you may be involved in for the various job roles, and the correct way to complete them. Paperwork is everything, especially in the armament trade. It is an audit trail for accounting, but more importantly, safety. The forms provide a written declaration of all manner of details, including who did a job, who with, and when. That's how they know who to blame if it goes wrong!

You are also introduced to the fundamental principles of RAF maintenance. Aircraft and equipment servicing is a big subject, so worthy of a proper explanation. The RAF applies a preventative maintenance policy, which means every item of kit will have a finite life assigned to it. During the life of the equipment, detailed schedules of maintenance are specified together with specific instructions on how to carry out the maintenance. There are various levels of servicing. First-line servicing on an aircraft is all about preparation for use or after use and is carried out by the line section or squadron. Second-line servicing is more in depth and is carried out in a bay or by a team. It may require the item of equipment to be removed from the aircraft. Third-line servicing requires significant checks and involves the aircraft being placed in a hangar so that detailed inspections can be carried out. Fourth-line involves the aircraft being stripped down to its component parts. The aircraft or item of equipment may well be sent to a specialist site, and the work may be carried out by the manufacturer rather than RAF personnel. This is a very general description. Specific aircraft and equipment will have very clearly defined definitions and requirements; the idea is to prevent very expensive equipment dropping out of the sky.

You will be introduced to flight servicing, which is a key aspect of working on aircraft. The term is a catch-all phrase for carrying out routine, pre- and post-flight checks. The work is completed by the lineys and includes things such as inspections for damage, refuelling, pressures, fluid level checks, arming, rearming and de-arming. There are a number of types of service: before flight (BF), after flight (AF), turn round (TR) and operational turn round (OTR). The first two are self-explanatory. A TR service is carried out when an aircraft has returned from a flight or sortie and is going on another flight or sortie immediately. There are strict protocols and servicing instructions to be followed and much paperwork to complete. An OTR service relaxes the rules a little based on the fact that OTRs take place during real operations, so things will be a little fraught. For example, an Armourer's TR on a Herc carrying chaff and flare would require the aircraft to be shut down and powered off prior to fitting more flares. An OTR may well be done with engines turning and power on, because this means less time on the ground in a potentially dangerous area.

Basic Engineering, or 'hacking and bashing' as it was affectionately known, was anything other than basic. Mechs, fitters, DEs and appos all started their respective courses with this subject. It was a mix of theory and practical and, depending on your course, could last from four weeks to several months. For mechs and fitters, the first week was classroom orientated and went into great detail about types of metal, corrosion, standards such as drawing and thread sizes, the measuring units used in engineering, how to measure a variety of surfaces and shapes, how to calculate area, mass and volume, the principles of workshop safety, and the various tools (hand and powered) in use.

The practical element involved working metal by hand to a standard specified in a drawing. You are given a length of mild steel, roughly 4ft long (the newer recruits are lucky as theirs is roughly 10cm), and it's vaguely circular in profile. Your first task is to turn it into a rectangular block with all six sides filed flat and square to each other. Once you've completed this, all by hand, you use an engineer's square and Engineer Blue, a type of pigmented paste, to find the lumps. You then use files to chase the lumps around, then you start drilling holes into it – a blind hole and one that passes right through. The blind hole is tapped to accept the threaded rod you have to make from scratch. Once this is complete you start work on the duralumin plate – cutting two pieces that have to be riveted together and then joined to the steel block. You form angles and curves on the corners of the plate and, if you are a fitter, DE or appo, you then take it with you to the next gruelling phase, which is electrics.

Your task is then to learn all about the rules of electricity (Ohm's Law etc.), all the components in circuits, how to read a circuit diagram, wiring, looming and soldering. With your head full to bursting you then have to deploy this knowledge to create a working circuit of wires and plugs that is fitted to your metal block and plate. ('Here's one I made earlier' springs to mind.)

STARTING OUT AS AN RAF ARMOURER

Once you've done this for practice in the workshop, you are then expected to do it all again in the exercise known as the final test job (FTJ). The FTJ must be submitted within the prescribed time and meet the engineering criteria (standard of work and built to tolerance using the prescribed methods and tools). To say it is difficult for most is an understatement. It is hard to find the words to describe the potential pain and torment suffered during this little phase. Even the hardened engineers, those who perhaps served an apprenticeship before joining the RAF, cannot fail to become emotionally attached to their work. The care that is lavished on it is beyond comprehension, even to the point of wrapping it in oilcloth for the night to make sure it gets plenty of comfortable rest. Without passing the FTJ, there is no progression to the rest of the course, so the atmosphere in the workshop is electric to say the least. To see Armourers hunched over their benches filing, measuring, drilling, riveting and tapping, is a sight to behold. Every now and again the block or plate will be raised to the light and the square offered gently to the edge. The smallest imperfection will mean that light is visible along the surface between the square and the metal. This will cause a groan, and the Armourer will note the place of the imperfection, bend to their bench and secure the metal in the vice (using the vice clamps they made to protect the hand-finished surfaces). There will be a few gently applied strokes of the file and, depending on how lucky, frustrated or desperate the individual is, one for luck. The block will be released from the vice and offered once more to the light for inspection with the square. A silent prayer will be offered to all that is great and good and ... Lo! There is still light. So back again for more gentle filing until that blessed and hallowed moment when there is no light. A friend, and perhaps even the instructor, will be consulted to check the diagnosis. Confirmation or denial of light determines sanity. Light means getting back to it. Darkness is relief, and onto the next phase.

Armourers are tough, rugged, dependable and doughty, and all these attributes are forged in this workshop. These skills are valuable, and although deploying them in anger may seem a lifetime away, when you are working in a bay gauging a vital component, checking the wiring connection on a pylon, screwing the fuze into a pocket in a 1,000-pounder, or loading a belt of 30mm ammo, your mind can drift back to that workshop. You remember the light streaming through the windows at the top of the room, the smell of metal filings, the oil cloth, and Armourers sweating over their FTJ, and you offer thanks that it is all behind you!

Other subjects covered include guns, which focuses on aircraft guns like the 27mm Mauser cannon and the 30mm Aden gun. Bombs, Components and Pyrotechnics (bombs and comps) gives a fascinating insight into all the parts of a bomb and how to make it ready for use. Aircraft Assisted Escape Systems (the ejection seat phase) is fascinating and covers some really vital equipment that can save lives. Small arms covers all the in-service personal weapons of the time. Back in the day you would have learned all about

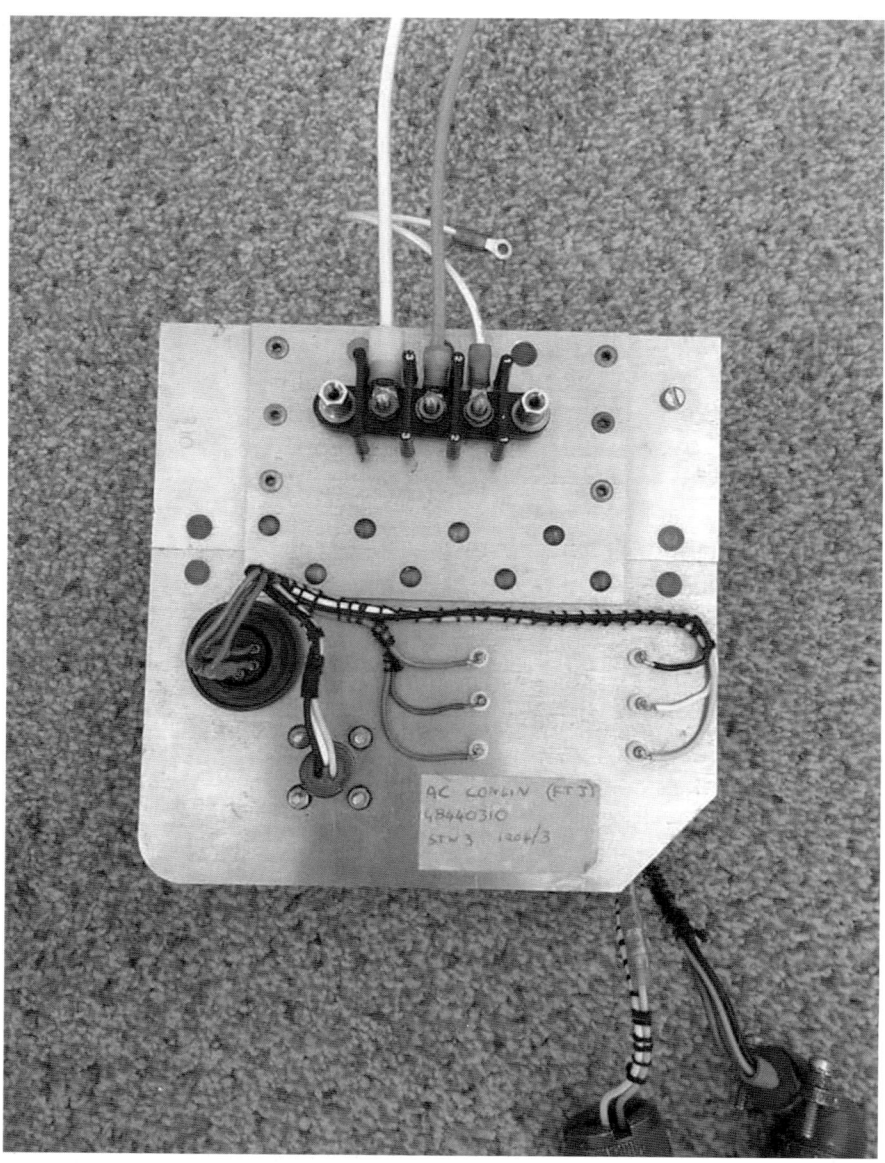

Armourers FTJ. (Mark Bean)

STARTING OUT AS AN RAF ARMOURER

the .303 Short Magazine Lee Enfield (SMLE) or the 7.62 Self-Loading Rifle (SLR); modern times sees the L85 A1 (SA80) and its variants on the syllabus. Firm and long-standing favourites include the Shotgun, Signal Pistol, GPMG and Browning 9mm Self-Loading Pistol (SLP). A less effective weapon, the 9mm Sub-machine Gun (SMG), was removed from service in the 1990s. At the time it was issued to WRAFs, SNCOs and officers but was notoriously inaccurate; barn doors within 100m were safe, as were the enemy.

Guided Missiles, Release Equipment, Ground Support Equipment, Basic Engineering and Engineering Science all come together to form the core knowledge required to be an Armourer. During training you start to understand that you are part of something bigger; individual knowledge is important, but you also learn that you are part of a team and just as reliant on the person next to you as they are reliant on you. What cannot be taught is experience, but that said, the instructors are drawn from serving and ex-Armourers so between them they own pretty much every T-shirt there is. Every phase is accompanied by 'pull-up-a-sandbag' moments where the instructor reminisces about past postings and old friends. They have even been known to become dewy eyed, at which point the students recognise the opportunity to exploit the situation and prompt further reminiscence, smoke breaks or an early stack.

There is a strong emphasis on hands-on or practical elements throughout the training, and wherever possible trainees get the opportunity to actually touch and play with whatever is being discussed. The classrooms often open out onto areas in the hangar dedicated to the equipment. For example, during the guns phase there are a number of benches set up, all with 30mm Aden guns sat on them. At various points there is the opportunity to go out and play around with the gun. Of course, they are deactivated training aids, but they have all the components and functions of the live-firing model. It is all very well to discuss the removal of the two massive springs in the cradle, but nothing beats walking up to the gun on the bench, placing your palm on the locking nut on the back of the spring, and trying to compress and remove it. To be an Armourer it is useful to have a gorilla-like grip and the ability to be ambidextrous and double jointed. The continuous hands-on practice builds confidence and, in many ways, replicates doing the job for real as far as possible. The lessons learned during the early phases are repeated throughout subsequent phases; workshop practice, tools and techniques are all embedded and start to become second nature.

One of the key skills found in pretty much every aspect of Armourers' work is lock wiring. Lock wiring is a method of securing a moveable component to something solid. Vibration during flight can be severe, and even locking nuts and other vital securing devices are tightened to tolerance using torque wrenches. Certain components are so critical that just making sure they don't come loose is necessary. Locking wire is 22 SWG chromium nickel, corrosion resistant and fully softened. The component to be locked has a hole drilled through it to accept the wire. The wire is then passed through the hole, then the two ends are twisted together, starting at the hole using between six and twelve twists (at 180°) and working towards the securing point. The wire must be kept taut and then finished by passing one end through the securing hole then twisting the two wires together to form a tail. For neatness, the tail is trimmed then turned over to tuck away the ends. This all sounds complicated, but it's easier done than written about, and by the time you leave training, how to lock wire professionally is embedded into you so the first time you are faced with the task in your job, it comes naturally. Then you find out all about lock wiring pliers!

The final phase is known as the Airfield phase. It is the culmination of all the modules, and everyone looked forward to it. For those who trained at Cosford it meant marching across to the airfield side of the camp every day and was as much like being at a proper camp as could be achieved during training. You turn up to work every morning and put on overalls, then gather in the crew room to await the instructor. Aircraft handling, starting procedures, start-ups, see-offs and see-ins, and marshalling are all on the syllabus. At Cosford the planes in the museum were used for some of the static training like loading weapons and guns. Cosford also had serviceable Jet Provost aircraft, and these were used for 'live' training. It is important at this stage to give trainees the most realistic experience possible. This is vital for the mechanics or DEs as they have never been out in the 'real' air force but it's also important for those on their fitters course as some will not have had aircraft experience. Their next posting could be to a squadron or line, so hands-on experience makes all the difference. Tony remembers the airfield phase from his mechs course in 1988:

> To make it over to the airfield was just amazing. You were treated like a real person and were away from the admin and bullshit. You made yourself cups of tea or coffee in the crew room and chatted with the instructors on a more casual basis. They had a tea bar so you could buy snacks and stuff just like being on a squadron. I remember the first time we did marshalling (the art of manoeuvring an aircraft around an airfield by communicating with the crew by hand signals). We learnt the theory quickly in the tea bar. The instructor showed us the hand signals and we all had a practice, then it was off

outside. We gathered on a pan just outside the hangar and the instructor brought out a push bike. One of us got on the bike and they were now the aircraft. Then we each took turns at marshalling. Hold your arms up above your head to signal you are ready and wait for the aircrew to signal they are ready by flashing the taxi lamp. A cruel crew would keep you waiting with your arms above your head for ages, like some sort of demented hostage. Once they are ready you wave them on by bending your arms at the elbow and waving; the faster you wave the quicker the aircraft goes, and vice versa. To get them to turn, keep the appropriate arm still pointing in the direction of the turn and keep waving with the other arm. You need to stay in sight of the captain at all times so position is key. If you have to start moving around you risk tripping or falling over because generally you will be moving backwards. Marshalling an aircraft is a fantastic experience. Even the Jet Provost is a lot of fun, but practice is the key.

Using a bicycle to practise marshalling aircraft is clearly quite ridiculous, so these days students have the opportunity to practise it using a computer. Essentially you practise your marshalling skills using VR, which is obviously much more effective and modern.

During training you are asked to put in your options. You can list up to three camps in the UK in order of preference. During the late 1970s and early 1980s this was reckoned to be a bit of a pointless exercise because the drafters were known to post you wherever they wanted. These people, whom you probably never met, were credited with superhuman powers such as the ability to look into your head and then do the opposite of what you were thinking.

Tony remembers putting in his choices while on his mechs course at Cosford:

> I'm sure we put our options in during the hacking and bashing phase, which was the first four weeks of the course. I remember there being a map of the UK on a wall in one of the tea break areas. It had all the camps listed and we spent hours poring over this, looking for the prime camps. Our thinking was mainly influenced by what aircraft a camp had. The majority wanted fast jets; they were cool, bristling with weapons and the sharp end – exactly why we joined. Places like Cottesmore, Leuchars, Coltishall and Finningley all had fast jet squadrons,

and many hosted squadrons that were known for their exploits during World War Two.

A few of the lads went for camps close to home, but I could never see the point in that. I had joined to travel. I made my three choices, which were Leuchars, Lossiemouth and Kinloss, in that order. For a boy who grew up in Somerset and had never been further north than Birmingham, that was a definite statement.

The final day of trade training was huge. The idea was that everyone sat the final exams, packed up their kit and cleared camp ready to travel by 4 p.m. The pressure was massive and failing the exams could cause major problems for everyone.

Training was defined by a regular series of tests. Each phase had tick tests throughout, normally multiple-choice questions, also referred to as 'vote for Joe's'. Of course, when in doubt the answer is 'C' was always the advice. Competition could be fierce, and no one wanted to be at the bottom of the table. The end of a phase was marked with an end-of-phase test. There were four progress tests, which tested recruits on all the preceding phases, and then the final test: more multiple-choice questions. Candidates had to get enough marks in each section of the test to get an overall pass. A failure in one section would require a resit of that section.

The exam was sat in the morning, and everyone then spent the rest of the day running around 'camp clearing'. This process and the corresponding 'arriving' consisted of being given a blue card with all the key sections on camp listed. People had to go to each section in turn to get a signature to acknowledge their arrival or leaving. Clearing would involve handing back any items of kit that had been loaned to recruits which were specific to that camp. At Cosford, on arrival everyone was issued with a library of books or Air Publications (also known as Pubs or APs).

Tony has these memories of APs at Cosford:

> When we arrived at Cosford we were marched around the camp on the first day and taken to all the relevant sections, one being the Station Library. We filed in, and there on the counter were eleven neat piles of APs which we signed for and then piled into our blue canvas holdall. They weighed a ton, and I honestly don't remember looking at them once during my mechs course. I put them in my overhead locker that lunchtime and didn't take them out until we cleared Cosford six months later.

STARTING OUT AS AN RAF ARMOURER

At some point during that final day people would check in at the Armourers' hangar to make sure everything was OK, and that no one was requested to see the training officer; this would signify that an airman needed to resit a part of the exam. Around mid-afternoon the course gathered in the presence of the training officer to be given their results and also their postings. At that point there was a scramble to get back to the block, gather all one's kit, and leave the camp that had been home for six months. Everyone said goodbye, and set off on their next big adventure, their first real posting.

There is a lot of symbolism in the act of sending off the newly qualified personnel, on their own, to their first postings. It's like proud parents recognising that they have done all they can, that their youngsters are as ready as they will ever be to thrive in their service lives. Each of the new airmen knows that they have been trusted to 'get on with it'.

Tony recalls his final day at Cosford, and heading off for his first posting:

> It was incredible. Six months all came down to this one afternoon. I don't remember if anyone on the course had trouble with their results. I think someone did, but you were all so caught up in the day it's a blur. I remember we were all in the room and the officer called out our names, gave us our scores (no particular order) and gave us our posting.
>
> I got through with good scores, which pleased me, and was posted to Kinloss. There were another three heading to Scotland, so that made life a bit easier. Simon Hunt, Dinger Bell and another whom I can't remember got Lossiemouth, and Simon had a car. We couldn't all fit in the car with our kit, so two of us said we would travel by train with enough gear for a few days, and Simon would take everything else with him. Lossie is fairly close to Kinloss, so he could drop my gear off once we were settled.
>
> Dinger and I got the train from Cosford to Brum then travelled up via Aberdeen. We missed the last train from Aberdeen, which was a bit of a disaster because neither of us had much money. We left Aberdeen station and decided to ask a friendly-looking porter at the Aberdeen Station Hotel for suggestions for somewhere cheap to stay. He instantly saw we were military and said that we could dump our kit with him then come back after midnight. He would find somewhere for us to kip until the first train in the morning. Result!
>
> We decided to go for a wander. I drew my last £20 out of a cashpoint, and we went to a pub. It was a half-decent looking

place down near the docks. As we walked in the whole place went silent. I am now thinking, 'Oh s**t', but there's no going back so I walked up to the bar with everyone staring at us. I had a quick look along the bar and then in my finest West Country accent said: 'Two pints of 80 shilling please mate.' The barman nodded and started pulling the beer. He used long glasses which had the 80-shilling logo on, if I remember right.

This massive bloke came up to us and said something like, 'You're not from round here are you?', to which I nodded and then said we were on our way up north to Lossie and Kinloss. He smiled and said it was great to see us.

The other occupants of the pub had all just come in off a rig and were spending the evening in convivial company to celebrate their return to dry land. We never put our hands in our pockets all night and eventually tumbled back to the hotel about 1 a.m. The porter let us in and showed us to a corner of a conference room where all our kit was. He said, 'There's a party going on at the moment with booze and food all laid out, so if you want anything just mingle and help yourselves.' We ventured out to see everything in full swing.

My memory is a bit fogged, but I seem to recall lots of very well-dressed people in various states of sobriety mingling and having a good time, so Dinger and I joined in. At some point the porter came and fetched us, saying that the train would be leaving in about thirty minutes, so we gathered our kit and said our goodbyes. I had a feeling I was going to like Scotland.

Tony's posting was to one of his favoured choices. This wasn't always the case. Ade Thorne, who had joined up as a mech, spent six months doing basic training at RAF Halton, during which he learnt all of the skills required to be an RAF Armourer. Having completed the final course, he was looking forward to putting all of his new skills into action – and was promptly sent off to 5131 Squadron, which was solely responsible for bomb disposal, which involved only a tiny part of his acquired skill set. A couple of years later he spent another six months doing his fitters course. His reward? Being sent straight back to 5131.

For a young person who has never really spent time away from home, the first posting could be quite challenging. After completing his mechs course, Brendan Lucey was posted to 27 Squadron at RAF Marham. In many ways it was a dream posting, but the accommodation wasn't great, with basic single-man rooms. And at first Brendan felt a bit lost; he didn't

STARTING OUT AS AN RAF ARMOURER

know anyone and spent much of his first weekend in his room, reading a book and listening to music on a radio and cassette player. On the Monday he and two other new joiners were sent to put up barbed wire around the HAS site. It was a lovely September day, with a clear blue sky. As he worked, Brendan noticed a roar, just over the horizon. It turned out to be two Lightnings doing a low pass over the runway. As they approached the HAS, they did a 90° flip-up and soared off into the distance. It was a wonderful sight, and helped to provide him with validation that he had made the right decision.

Your first posting as an Armourer is special. You are a real Armourer, albeit with a lot to learn. You are brimming with confidence and itching to get on with the job and prove that you can do it. Your first aim is to become an SAC. You leave training with shiny new LAC badges, but they mark you out as a newbie – they need to go as soon as possible. To achieve the dizzy heights of SAC all you needed to do is complete your Trade Ability Tests (TATS). The tasks are based around the job you are doing in your posting as well as your general armament knowledge. You are assessed by a snec, and given help and support to prepare for the test. Once you have passed your TATS you are promoted to SAC and can now wear the three-propellor rank badge. This is the badge worn by the backbone of the RAF; we all know it's the SACs who do the work!

Note that, less than a week before we finished working on this book, the RAF announced that the names of the ranks were changing. The LAC became an Air Specialist 2 (AS2), the SAC became an AS1, and the JT, which you'll hear more about later, became AS1(T). For the purposes of the book, we'll stick with LAC, SAC and JT. There's every chance that by the time you read this, the names of the ranks will have changed again.

Training is a constant theme throughout your time as an Armourer. When you arrive at your posting you will have been trained on all the aspects of your job that are specific to your location; even Ade Thorne had learnt the basics of bomb disposal before arriving at 5131 Squadron! A busy flying station with lots of Armourers is likely to have its own training team, known as the training cell. It will be staffed by snecs, who have experience and the authority to sign people off as being competent. They will have completed courses on how to train or instruct and have training plans for all the various jobs that the Armourers will need to be qualified for. Local training is carried out either on the job or by attending the training cell for as long as is needed to learn the ropes. The training normally concludes with the trainee performing the task and being observed by a member of the training cell. If the task is completed properly, they will be signed off and their engineering record updated accordingly.

THE RAF'S ARMOURERS

Many tasks, such as loading weapons, require regular checks to be carried out to ensure that standards are maintained, so the training cell is kept busy all year round recertifying all the Armourers. A typical fast jet squadron will have its regular shifts, and a shift will have a number of people who make up the teams. A team will be a group of people who carry out specific tasks on an aircraft to ready it for operations, for example fuelling, arming and snagging, and routine fluid, pressure and damage checks. The teams may all be Armourers, or they may be made up of different aircraft trades – composite teams. It is efficient (in some circumstances) to have the different trades (Armourers, sooties, riggers and fairies) working together as they can cover all the basic jobs on an aircraft. Another method used for efficiency is cross training, so Armourers may be trained to refuel an aircraft, which is typically the job of a sooty. During the Cold War (and probably before), and in critical operational situations (i.e. war!), the most important thing is to get the aircraft in the air to carry out its job, so they would make up load teams of many different trades, not always aircraft trained. There would be an Armourer in charge of the rest of the team, usually another two or three people brought in from other sections like catering or admin. Of course there is always an exception and in the case of Tornados load teams were always taken from aircraft trades.

A squadron may have a training cell made up of different trades, so a newly posted arrival will spend time learning about the aircraft and how the squadron works. The key aspect of being in the RAF is that you can go anywhere at any time and, with the correct support, be productive in your role quickly. Part of your basic and trade training helps you develop the ability to go somewhere new and fit in quickly and easily. You learn to make friends and orientate yourself within a few hours. Tony recalls:

> Change was constant in the mob and that's why I joined. You never knew what the day may bring. I went away a lot in my time, and often to places I had never been before with people I had never met. You quickly learn to be open and get to know folks; I am happy to start chatting to people I don't know. Whenever I travel anywhere, even to this day, I unpack quickly as soon as I get to my room. I get everything sorted and then go for a wander to find out what's around me. The location of the food and the bar are the first two on the list. I think as an Armourer this was even more important because the job involves working with very dangerous things, so knowing who you are working with was all about survival.

STARTING OUT AS AN RAF ARMOURER

The trade training you receive sets you up to be an Armourer anywhere within the RAF. You carry with you knowledge that can be applied anywhere. It also helps you to learn the process of learning, which sounds strange but means that, when faced with something new, it is already natural to start learning all about the new environment. You instinctively soak up new things and also know the questions to ask. The idea of being able to post anyone anywhere gives almost limitless possibilities in terms of manpower. This ability to adapt is critical because war is fluid, and you need people who can get on with the job in spite of things, and not sit there in a fug moaning that nobody told them about the new tool and they don't know what to do. The only thing that matters is whether you can do the job. If you can, then great. If you need some help to master it, there is always someone prepared to help, provided you step up and are prepared to graft.

Some jobs are really specialised so need specialist training before you reach your new posting. For example, a posting to Small Arms guarantees you a trip back to RAF Cosford to do the Small Arms course and gain the Small Arms Q. While small arms training is covered in the trade training, it doesn't go into the depth required for someone who is going to be servicing small arms as their main job. Another example is becoming part of a Station EOD team. Up until April 2020 this would have guaranteed you a trip to at least RAF Wittering, home to 5131 Bomb Disposal Squadron; in April 2020 they were disbanded.

During your time in the RAF you receive some of the best training, and when you leave, you do so with qualifications and experience. Oh, and a big pile of training course notes. The following picture shows just some of the notes collected by Tony through his career.

Training notes. (Tony Lamsdale)

Chapter 3

The Bomb Dump

At some point in an Armourer's career, there is a good chance that they will work in an Explosive Storage Area, or ESA. 'Bomb dumps', or just plain 'dumps', are the more common names for this area of a camp dedicated to all things that go bang.

The size of the area is determined by the needs of the camp. A busy flying station that hosts several squadrons will need a bigger bomb dump to store all the weapons and explosives required to carry out its operational role. A dump may just be one building surrounded by a fence, and cover less than an acre of ground, or it may be much, much bigger. Some dumps act as distribution points or central stores and service many other camps or establishments, so may cover hundreds of acres. In recent years, the number of bomb dumps has started to dwindle, and the remaining dumps tend to be smaller. Instead, ready use armament storage (RUAS) is increasingly used, with smaller storage areas in existing buildings found on HAS sites and/or around the camp, distanced from built-up areas. This reflects improvements in weapon safety; in the past, no one would have wanted the airfield's armaments to be anywhere near them!

Typically, the bomb dump is situated well away from anything else, often across the airfield a considerable distance away from the main camp, hangars and general habitation. The reason for this should be self-explanatory; should anything untoward happen you don't want to blow up the NAAFI – there'd be nowhere to go for a beer!

All bomb dumps have the following features in common: they are secure; typically, they have a perimeter fence; and they have alarms up the ying-yang (a colloquial term meaning 'lots').

Access is strictly controlled and monitored, usually through the main building that forms part of the perimeter of the dump site. There will always be someone on duty to control access using a tally system. Anyone entering the dump has to hand over their ID card and get a tally tag. When they exit the dump, they swap the tally for their ID. This is an easy way of seeing who is on the site should the brown stuff hit the motorised rotating

THE BOMB DUMP

cooling system. If vehicle access is required, the driver and passenger get their tags and the vehicle reg is noted down. On entering the dump, you are also required to leave any flammable materials or electrical devices at the control point; the reason for this should not need additional explanation!

The highly responsible and demanding job of controlling access is usually given to one of the junior ranks. The LACs, SACs or JTs who form the backbone of the RAF are deemed trustworthy, capable of counting people in and out, and opening and locking gates.

Tony remembers:

> My first posting from training was to the bomb dump at Kinloss. It was right over the other side of the airfield, so well out of the way. It actually backed on to the beach. It was a cracking spot.
>
> They had a duty called 'teas and keys'. From memory, it lasted a week and was always done by one of the junior ranks (LAC, SAC or JT). There was always a duty NCO as well. Their role was more titular!
>
> You had to collect the wagon (we had a long wheel-base Land Rover) from the Armourers' hangar, along with the keys for the dump. This was about a two-mile cycle from where I lived. You then drove to the mess to get those who needed a lift (all the singlies) before driving over to the dump, stopping off at MT to sign for the wagon's daily inspection and fill it with fuel. Once at the dump you opened up the main office area, switching off all the alarms, and got the first round of brews ready for everyone. Once the screaming hordes had had their first brew, they would start to drift off to whatever jobs they had to do. That would be when you went to the picket post and started tagging people into the dump and issuing building keys. All the keys to the various buildings were kept in another safe. Whoever needed keys would have to sign the key register. You also controlled the tool kits for basic jobs so would have to sign those out as well. You'd then have to clear up the tea bar and get it ready for tea break: clean the cups, wash the sides, top up the urn, check the tea bar stock, hoover the carpet, and sweep the floor. In the meantime, you'd be answering the phone and monitoring the comings and goings.
>
> At some point you would do a mail run and any gash jobs that needed doing. This might be dropping off one of the snecs, picking up some spares, or whatever. We also had a

ready use building which stored flares for the aircraft. It was a brick building on the end of the main dispersal and could hold enough flares to replace those used on an aircraft without having to drive all the way over to the dump. You did a stock check and loaded up any empties to take back for refilling.

You had to get back in time for tea break to make all the whingers their brew. The banter was relentless, but if you were getting it that week it was someone else's turn the following week. It never bothered me because I knew it was all done in fun, and we had a laugh.

The rest of the day was rinse repeat. At knock-off time you had to do a building check which involved driving the landy round the site as fast as you could, checking that every building and store was locked and the electrics were turned off. You then did a key, tool and person check to make sure everyone and everything was accounted for, and then locked up. You returned the keys, went to the mess, returned the landy to the hangar, and cycled home for a kip prior to popping out for a social beer or three.

The dump will always have an access gate and well-defined roads within to allow access to the buildings, magazines and stacks. The buildings are made of reinforced concrete with steel doors, full lightning protection, and a bonded wiring system with control and cut-off switches on the outside. Fire suppression systems might also be fitted. Some have large blast walls surrounding them, which may even be covered in soil and turf, with only one side or face showing (the one with the doors, for obvious reasons). They have a security system with trembler switches and contact breakers fitted, and they all have flipping big padlocks.

Each building has a purpose, and the dump is laid out in such a way as to maximise safety and minimise movement and handling of whatever is stored there. Generally speaking, explosives are quite safe until people start mucking around with them, so limiting the opportunities is always a good strategy. The majority of buildings are used for storage of explosives; these are typically called magazines. At the time of licensing, it is determined exactly what can be stored and in what quantity. This figure is known as the net explosive quantity, or NEQ. Not all magazines are buildings. Some are stacks outside; for example, bombs can be stacked outside a building. A 1,000lb bomb is quite safe to be stored outside. The explosive is secure within a steel case, the fuze pockets are plugged up so no water or moisture can penetrate, and they have a lovely coating of weatherproof

THE BOMB DUMP

paint. By storing them in a stack outside, they are more easily accessible and easier to handle.

Licensing is taken care of at command level initially; inspectors will visit the site, study maps of the local area and factor in the operational requirements of a station. Once these factors have been determined, licences are issued. Whoever is in charge of the bomb dump, usually a snec, will work together with OC Arm to regularly review the licences against operational needs and request any changes or updates as required. Some stations may need more than one dump, and there may be smaller storage facilities placed around the station to make life easier. Ready use stores are common in guardrooms; traditionally the ammo needed by the guards would be stored and accounted for by the use of stack cards. Every time ammo was issued or returned the stack card would be filled in to record the transaction. Nowadays many units use electronic stock control, although where electronic stock control measures are not available the good old 957 card is still used in its paper form.

Another thing to avoid is mixing certain types of explosives. This could be for compatibility reasons or security. Top tip: Never store your detonators with your plastic explosive (PE); should anyone break in they have all they need to ruin someone's day. The licence also determines what can be done in the building, how many people are allowed in it at any one time, what tools and equipment can be used, and whether anything is barred from use. For example, radios are not used in a bomb dump because of the emissions (and we don't mean $CO2$); similarly, mobile phones are banned. Any communications systems must be an integral part of the dump infrastructure and known to be safe; for example, there may be telephone points around the site well away from storage buildings.

An easy way to spot an Armourer is their propensity to earth themselves constantly to discharge any static electricity. In any building that is licensed to store explosives, there will be earthing points near the entrance for this very purpose. A trained Armourer will instinctively spot and move towards an earthing point to make contact.

Some buildings are licensed to prepare or maintain the various explosives stored. Everything in the RAF needs to be looked after and will have a maintenance schedule, and explosives are no different. Everything needs to be checked to make sure it is 'serviceable', a ubiquitous term in the RAF to declare an item fit for purpose and readiness. Unserviceable is the opposite, and the common phrase is U/S. Note the forward slash to distinguish between 'unserviceable' and 'US' – this is done to avoid a diplomatic incident.

A typical task would be prepping bombs for fitting to an aircraft. The required number of bombs (no more, no less) would be collected from the stack. The Armourers would use a loader and load them onto an S-type trolley. The bombs would be secured in place using cradles and straps. The trolley would be towed to the weapon prep shed. Once in the shed, the bombs would be checked, fuzed, and each would have a tail unit fitted.

1,000lb High Explosive (HE) bombs waiting for their turn. (Mark Bean)

1,000lb with 117 tail unit on American loader. (Mark Bean)

THE BOMB DUMP

Any wiring to connect the tail unit to the aircraft needs to be prepared in accordance with the requirements for the mission. The tail unit is there to stabilise the bomb in flight. The type 114 tail unit is cone-shaped with fins at the end. The type 117 tail unit has blades that pop out and retard the descent of the bomb. Paveway is now the bomb of choice and has been in service for a number of years. It has evolved and there are a number of different variants that we would love to describe in great detail, however we don't want to give away secrets so let's just say that when they hit the target, they blow it up.

The paperwork and admin associated with this job is enormous, so in the interests of entertainment we have spared you a full description. Suffice to say that every job in the RAF is fully documented in an Air Publication (AP). Sometimes the detail goes to a level that many would prefer not to know about. For example, a well-preserved copy of AP 3242B, Volume 5, Chapter 3, page 36, Amendment List 1 (AL 1) listed the emergency procedures for eating, urinating and defecating, including a summary of the general principles. It contained both written instructions and photos – most helpful. Everything needs an audit trail, so forms must be filled out in full, with multiple signatures to say it is going to happen, it is happening, it has happened, and that sometime ago nothing went wrong.

1,000lb practice bomb with Paveway II fitted, Tucson. (Mark Bean)

THE RAF'S ARMOURERS

Left: Transporting a 1,000-pounder with Paveway II nose around the dump in Dhahran. (Mark Bean)

Below: Locking the nose on the Paveway IV. (Mark Bean)

In addition to magazines, prep sheds and explosive maintenance, you'll find an empty box store or compound. All explosives and ammunition come in containers, tins, boxes or crates that can be reused. Once the container is empty it is taken to the store, ready to return for refilling. Remember the days when you could return bottles for reuse (beer, milk and pop)? Sometimes you even got money for returning them. Well, the same

THE BOMB DUMP

principle applies, apart from getting money back. A good job on a Friday is to head over to the empty box store with a tin of brown or green paint, a brush, some lockwire, snips, and the station seal. Your first task is to open all the boxes and check that they are empty apart from the reusable packing material. A liberal amount of paint is applied to the outside of the box to obliterate any markings or indications of what the box may have held. Once the paint is dry you fill in a linen slip (form RAF F6485), which you put in the box. This declares that the box is free from explosives (FFE), so that the person opening it at the other end knows what to expect. If explosives or a round are found, they know who to come after for telling lies. The box lid is shut, and a seal is placed over the lid onto one of the sides to show if the box has been opened; shellac was used to secure it in place. The final step is to lockwire the lid shut and place a brass seal on the end of the lockwire. The brass seal is unique to the station, so is an easy way of identifying the origins and seeing if the box has been tampered with.

If you think this is a lot of hassle for an empty box, consider some of the alternatives. For example, an empty box, still with its original markings, falls from a lorry onto the public highway. The police are called and see the markings, and believe that the box contains explosive. So they close the road to all traffic and call out the bomb disposal team. Three hours later the bomb disposal team ascertain that the box is empty. Meanwhile, the M25 has become a bit gridlocked.

The process for dealing with fired brass or empty cartridge cases is similar. Ammunition usually comprises a bullet (the round or projectile), a cartridge case filled with explosive material, and some form of primary ignition usually initiated by being struck. After the round has been fired, you are left with the empty cartridge case. Brass is an expensive commodity, so wherever possible the cases are collected and returned as scrap. This is easy on a small arms range or if the aircraft collects the empty cases in a tank; it's not so convenient on a battlefield or if the cases are ejected from the aircraft during firing. Once the cases are returned, the brass can be melted down and reused. It is vital that the cases are empty because applying heat to explosives can cause ructions, so a stray complete round could kill someone. As the brass is collected, it is inspected by the Armourers to make sure all the cases are empty. For small arms cases, the brass will be returned in sandbags that have to be certified FFE.

Many bomb dumps have their own means of fighting fires. All buildings have suitable fire extinguishers on hand, possibly fitted with sprinklers. But let's face it, if something big goes bang, a 5kg water gas extinguisher isn't going to cut it. Hydrants and static water tanks (SWT) are a common feature. If the station has a good water supply, you may find hydrants, but if

THE RAF'S ARMOURERS

not, static water tanks are used. An SWT is a concrete-lined pool or reservoir holding thousands of gallons of water. Remember that due to dumps being isolated, it may take the fire service some time to get to the problem, so having the means to contain an incident is vital. The size of the bomb dump would determine how many tanks there are and where they are sited. Each tank may have a pump next to it, or the dump may have a trailer pump that can be towed anywhere on site.

Occasionally an alternative use is found for the water tanks. Shortly after being promoted to sergeant, Derek Binnie was posted to the Brüggen bomb dump. That summer, his team was given the job of emptying all the water tanks on the site. Being enterprising types, they promptly refilled one of the tanks and converted it into a swimming pool.

Static tanks are also used when celebrating an event such as a newbie being posted in, promotions and also leaving. The ritual is known as tanking and involves the individual being thrown in the tank.

Fire training is a regular feature of service life, and drills are run all the time. While running from a burning building full of explosives was always the preferred option, the big question is how far would you have to run to be safe? Doing maths while sprinting is not easy, therefore training people

Pool preparation. (Derek Binnie)

THE BOMB DUMP

A proper tanking. (Mark Bean)

how to respond to a situation is a lifesaver. Everyone who joins the military is shown how to operate extinguishers and gets to practise what they've been shown. Armourers practise using proper hoses, pumps and other equipment, including breathing apparatus (BA). A BA set allows you to operate in areas of smoke or toxic fumes, and possibly even enter a building to tackle the source of the fire.

Tony remembers:

> At Kinloss we had loads of static tanks around the site; from memory we had three BA sets. This was because we had torpedoes on the site, and they gave off quite nasty gases even without being on fire.
>
> We had regular drills, and if the siren went off you rushed to your post. We always had a Land Rover at the dump, and its job in a fire was to go and get the trailer pump and tow it to the fire. You had hoses to deploy, one of which you dropped into the static tank to suck up the water, and more lengths to spray the water on the fire. The pump was powered by a diesel engine.

THE RAF'S ARMOURERS

One day the siren went off (it was a drill), and me and another lad had the Land Rover so we set off for the pump. I was the driver, so I backed up the Rover and the other lad hooked on the pump. Normally roads in the dump have strict speed limits and a one-way system. You could ignore those during a fire alarm and have a bit of fun.

We only took a couple of minutes to get to the building which was 'on fire'. I parked up and the other lad jumped out to unhitch the pump. I started getting out the hoses while he got the starting handle for the pump. He went to the tank and dropped an end of hose, but forgot that he hadn't connected it to the pump, so it all went in. No drama – I got another piece of hose. Then he couldn't start the pump. It was a bugger sometimes. He was swinging the handle with no luck, so I said I'd have a go. He stomped off and still had the handle, which he dropped in the tank by mistake. No drama – we had another handle. I got the pump going and we coupled up the other hoses so we were ready to start pumping. I grabbed the business end, and he turned the water on only to find that the hose wasn't properly connected, and he got soaked. Not our finest hour.

Bomb dumps can be very busy places to work, and flying stations place frequent demands for loads to be prepped and delivered. The station bomb dump handles all the explosives so is responsible for issuing, among other things, ejection seat carts, fire bottle carts, small arms ammunition, pyrotechnics for life-preserving equipment, release unit carts, missiles, torpedoes ... and the list goes on. There can be a high turnover of stock, so regular checks on quantities are vital. Every stack of explosives has a stack card or its electronic equivalent, and all transactions are recorded. Whoever is tasked with getting out the equipment logs what is being issued and by whom, and the total is reduced accordingly. In this way, it is easy to keep a track of all the dangerous kit – well, you would hope so.

The main accounting ledger is known as a Kalamazoo, which is a wonderful word in its own right. It conjures images of far-off places, tropical climates and sandy beaches, and sounds as if it harks back to the days of Empire and pith helmets. The reality is just as interesting and goes back to 1664 when Sir Samuel Morland, private secretary to Oliver Cromwell, was appointed Master of Mechanics to King Charles II. Sir Samuel invented a calculating machine that was capable of addition, subtraction, division and multiplication. He also invented a pocket version. We now need to fast

THE BOMB DUMP

forward to 1904, when his direct descendant, Oliver Morland, head of the English printing firm of Morland & Impey Ltd, heard of and bought the rights to a loose-leaf binder system invented in Kalamazoo, Michigan. Its principal selling point was a flexible thong (now we know what attracted the Armourers) that facilitates the easy insertion and removal of pages. The RAF Kalamazoo is used to store all the stock details of explosives. It is a hardcover binder and the metal mechanism for inserting and removing records is robust, a key selling point given that Armourers use it on a daily basis. The details of the explosives (serial number, date of manufacture, lot number, expiry date etc.) are printed on an A5 record sheet with holes down each side. When the bomb dump receives the stock, its associated record is stored in the Kalamazoo. The firm, now called Kalamazoo and based in Australia since 1919, is still in operation today. In recent years the RAF has embraced new technology and some stations are moving to more digital records; it makes you wonder how much longer the Kalamazoo has in service.

Let's say you have a big stack of small arms ammunition. On a pallet there are thirty boxes of 5.56mm Ball ammunition. Each box (an H83 for the anoraks out there) holds 900 rounds. 30 x 900 = 27,000 rounds of ammo. An unnamed SAC has been tasked with getting out 60 rounds of ammo. They drive to the store and open the building. It's raining, so they turn on the lights (switch located on outside as per regulations) and make their way through the gloom to the correct stack of ammunition. By the way, alongside that stack of 27,000 rounds there are other stacks of exactly the same ammo in the same boxes; they are just different lot numbers. Like most things in life, ammunition has a use-by or best-before date; we will leave it there. By some miracle, said SAC navigates their way to the correct

Kalamazoo. (Tony Lamsdale)

stack. They open the box, get out 60 rounds, reseal the box and fill out the stack card entry, all in the gloomy darkness of the building. They head back to the picket post and issue requested ammunition to the person who needs it. Later that day, the person returns any unused ammo. Said SAC repeats the ritual in reverse, returning the unused ammo to the stack and annotating the stack card. Do this multiple times a day over a week and longer, and mistakes can happen. The saying 'better to be up than down' has relevance. Rounds found spare over the required amount can be 'banked' for that rainy day when you expect to find 70,201 but can only find 70,200. It can happen. Now small arms ammunition is not a good thing to misplace, but try to explain a missing 1,000lb bomb. Armourers have a massive responsibility to look after and account for the kit in their charge. Mistakes are rare, such is the professionalism and counting ability of the trade.

Increased use of satellite technology during the Cold War led to care having to be taken when moving certain items around the bomb dump. The RAF would be tracking the Soviet satellites and issuing daily briefings on when to expect satellites in orbit. When a satellite was orbiting over your bomb dump, weapons movement was restricted. The timings would be pinned on the noticeboard, a little bit like a bus timetable, and an announcement would be made on the bomb dump Tannoy at the start and end of the restriction. If you were in the dump, you found a building and stayed inside until the satellite was clear, and then you went back to work.

If the dump is big enough, you can challenge your motoring skills by seeing how quickly you can complete the building check at the end of the day. Or how about some off-road driving up and down the traverses or revetments around the building? A traverse or revetment is a steep, often grassy, bank with a sharp apex.

Martin Turner, whose first posting after training was Lossiemouth, remembers an early experience of driving weapons across the airfield. Although he was just 17 and didn't have an official driving licence, he knew how to handle a vehicle and was allowed to drive the Land Rover that was assigned to the bomb dump.

On this occasion, an urgent call came through requesting several Hunter gun packs for the Hunter line on the other side of the airfield. Martin was quick to volunteer for the job:

> I was well chuffed, getting to drive the Land Rover, and towing all these gun packs. It was a long drive around the peri-track, and it took me ages. I wanted to make sure I kept to the speed limit, and didn't do anything that would draw attention. Eventually I got all the way over to the Hunter squadron –

THE BOMB DUMP

Number 2 Tactical Weapons Unit it was – and dropped off all the gun packs, feeling very pleased with myself.

So then I drove back. When I got back, one of the corporals says to me, 'Did you take barrels with you?'

'Yeah, I did. Why?'

'Are you sure? Because they just phoned up and said there were no barrels.'

I was so sure I'd taken them over. I went back to the building where I'd picked up the gun packs, to see if the barrels were there – they weren't. The corporal said, 'Drive back over there and see what's going on.'

So I started driving over, and immediately saw a barrel on the peri-track. Then another. Then another.

Now if you know what a Hunter gun pack trolley looks like, it has a cradle for the gun packs, and on the side there are little racks to take four barrels. It turned out that the barrels had bounced out of the racks while I was driving over.

Luckily I found all the barrels, and because it was early in the morning and most of the camp was still asleep, I pretty much got away with it. I just took the barrels back and said, 'It's all right. Here they are.' I couldn't bring myself to tell them that they'd been scattered all over the peri-track.

Podge Middleton recalls an incident when he was driving a Land Rover from the bomb dump at Honington. He was working on Buccaneers at the time, and every day an S-type trolley loaded with practice bombs would be delivered to the flight line. At night, with the bomb dump closed, it would be taken to a secure area where it would be locked up.

On this particular day, Podge was driving back from the bomb dump, towing the trolley with its practice bombs. Suddenly, shortly after he crossed the threshold, the gear stick of the Land Rover snapped off and he ground to a halt. He was stranded, with his load of bombs, in an area where incoming aircraft would be coming in to land. He had no radio, so apart from standing up and waving the broken gear stick, hoping that someone would notice, he was helpless. Fortunately for Podge, he'd broken down quite close to the 'caravan', a small air traffic control tower on the back of a truck close to the runway that is used to check on aircraft coming in and taking off. The caravan operator spotted that Podge was a man in distress, and he and the stricken Land Rover were quickly moved out of danger.

Stations and squadrons are not permanent. They come and go based on need. It is not uncommon for a once thriving camp to dwindle and become a shadow of its former self. The end of both world wars saw a rapid decline in the numbers of serving personnel and associated stations, and there were similar reductions at the end of the Cold War. Sometimes though, a station declines because its primary role changes.

For example, during the early years of the Cold War, RAF Marham in Norfolk was a thriving hubbub of activity, hosting all manner of RAF and USAF aircraft. However, by 1981 a lot of the operational capability had been moved to RAF bases in Germany, which were closer to the front line. This, coupled with the fact that the RAF was no longer the primary nuclear strike force (this role had been handed to the navy some decades before), meant that Marham was quiet. So quiet that, when he arrived, a young JT Martyn Mander thought a neutron bomb had gone off. All the buildings were intact, but the place was empty. He had just returned from RAF Gütersloh in Germany, which, by comparison, was absolutely heaving.

As a result of the airfield's diminished status, the outer bomb dump at Marham had been effectively closed down. One of Martyn's jobs was to help get it up and running again:

> The outer bomb dump was all revetments, with rows of gravel in between. I remember us opening the gate, for the very first time in years. There was a little gatehouse with an Elsan toilet, which was all rusty. It had probably been taken over years before, perhaps by a Valiant guy.
>
> The HASs were already being built around the dump, ready for the Tornados, although we didn't actually have any yet. Bombs were being brought in from Chilmark, and they had to be escorted by someone with a sub-machine gun on their lap – and that was us lot. So we all went down to Chilmark in a Sherpa, carrying our guns. Then 2MT from Stafford arrived [the Military Transport people] with a convoy of big articulated lorries. The lorries were loaded up with bombs – loads and loads of them – and each of us was allocated to escort an individual lorry. We did the trip to Chilmark several times, until the bomb dump was fully stocked once more – all with 1,000-pounders.
>
> On one occasion we were told that we had to use 'the war route'. The war route – and bearing in mind that these artics were fully loaded up with 1,000-pounders – went straight through the middle of Slough along the A4. Maybe someone thought it didn't matter if Slough got blown up.

THE BOMB DUMP

Some bomb dumps can be a haven for local wildlife. The dump at Kinloss was one such place, as Tony recalls:

> There was a corner of the dump which, during nesting season, you dare not go. The Arctic terns would come in and lay their eggs. During that time they became very territorial, so if you needed to get to a building in that area you had to wear a hard hat and a big parka, and take a pickaxe handle to defend yourself. The birds would dive-bomb you and get really aggressive. The best you could expect was to get covered in droppings, but if you were unlucky you could get a nasty peck. To be fair, it wasn't as bad as the NAAFI bop, but it was still a bit hairy.

Birds weren't just responsible for pecks and droppings; sometimes, something more unexpected turned up. Ade Thorne recalls a human bone being found in the bomb dump at Kinloss. Initially the expectation was that it would turn out to be an old bone, possibly belonging to someone who had been caught up in a known accident with explosives during the war. However, forensic examination revealed that the bone was that of a recently deceased young woman. Immediately, the bomb dump was cordoned off, and military investigators and civilian police conducted a thorough search, but no other bones were found. After further forensic work, it was confirmed that the bone came from a young woman who had fallen overboard from a boat in the Western Isles. It was thought that her body had been attacked by sea birds, one of which had flown over to Kinloss and deposited one of her bones in the bomb dump.

Depending on the aircraft operating from your station, you might find yourself prepping 1,000-pounders, missiles such as the Sidewinder, or rounds of ammunition for the guns. This would involve getting the required amount of ammo from the store, taking it to the prep shed, and fitting it into the links to make up belts of ammo to feed the guns. To make up a belt of ammo you lay out the links and then place the rounds into the links one at a time. They need to be pushed into place and positioned correctly so that the gun doesn't jam, so the Armourers use a linking tool to seat everything properly. The tool presses the round into the link and seats it in the correct position for it to be fed into the gun. Once prepped, the belts of ammo can be transported in a box to the aircraft or loaded into ammo tanks that can then be fitted into the aircraft at the line.

27mm HE linked rounds (Mark Bean)

THE BOMB DUMP

One of the key roles of the Nimrod was search and rescue (SAR), and there would be an aircraft on standby 24/7. If deployed, the SAR aircraft would patrol the area using its state-of-the-art navigation equipment to look for the vessel in trouble. This might be a ship in trouble, another aircraft, or even an oil rig. When the Piper Alpha oil rig caught fire in 1988, Nimrods were on the scene to co-ordinate the rescue operation.

Marker flares were a key piece of equipment used in SAR. On a Nimrod, the flares were fired out of the rear of the aircraft using a bit of kit called the rotary launcher and used to mark a specific location in the sea. The flares would emit flame and/or smoke, and could be used by other aircraft or vessels to navigate to that point. The flares would be launched at the same speed rearwards as the aircraft was travelling forwards, so would drop on the exact spot needed. To achieve this the flares were fitted into a holder that had seven explosive cartridges fitted to it. Each cartridge was a different size, so when initiated would give off a measured amount of power. Using electronics on board the aircraft, the airspeed would determine which combination of the seven cartridges would be fired to enable the flare to be launched rearwards at the correct speed. One of the daily jobs at the Kinloss dump was to prep enough flares for the daily operations ('ops' for short) or to cover the weekend. The cartridges, flares and holders would be taken to the prep shed and laid out on the prep table. The holders would have the cartridges inserted using the precision seating tool. Once the holders were ready you inserted the flares; they fitted tightly, so were held in place nicely. You put all the flares in a box and then put a sheet of paper in the box that recorded the serial number of all the holders, cartridges fitted, and flare types. This was used by the lineys when they loaded the flares into the holder on the aircraft.

Bomb dumps aren't glamorous, and often the work can be repetitive, but there is also a lot of variety and the opportunity to have some fun. Keeping the site tidy can equate to a nice afternoon strolling around in the sunshine picking up litter, checking firebreaks, and making sure all the extinguishers are in the correct place. You're not going to win any medals, but it is a great way of topping up the tan and getting away from the office. Of course, the same jobs need to be done in both winter and summer, so it isn't always costa-da-bomb-dump.

During operations they become frenetic hives of activity, a veritable production line of munitions to be readied. The technology has changed massively since the early 1900s, but any Armourer from those days would soon catch on and be able to be a productive part of the team. Safety has always been top of the list, followed by getting on with the job when it needs to be done. When the dust settles and the bomb trolleys are being towed out to the pan, it's time to get a brew on and dust off the Uckers board before you do it all again.

Chapter 4

Squadron Life

For many Armourers, the ultimate career goal is to work on aircraft. A posting to a squadron or aircraft line represents the opportunity to put into practice much of what is learned through training. Airfields are exciting, noisy and visceral places; your senses are assaulted by sights, smells and noises that stir the blood. If you have ever walked across the pan to your holiday aircraft, you will know the feeling. The ground power unit (GPU) will be running somewhere nearby emitting the steady thump of a diesel engine and associated smells. This provides power to the aircraft while it is on the ground. Aircraft have batteries, but you don't want to run them flat; it takes a lot of juice to run an aircraft. The gas turbine unit (GTC) on the aircraft may already be running. They have a distinctive whine that cuts through other noise, and of course there is the smell of burning jet fuel. Heady stuff!

The first time you stand in front of an aircraft to marshal it, you feel terrified and exhilarated beyond measure. As part of the start, or see-off crew, you will be responsible, in conjunction with the aircrew, for the safe starting and seeing off of the aircraft. A see-off crew is typically three people: a 'man 1' who will control the outside of the aircraft, liaising with the aircrew and the rest of the see-off crew; a 'man 2' who will be in charge of the fire extinguisher, ready to pounce at the merest hint of fire during start up; and a 'man 3' who will be there for safety, to keep an eye out for anything else that may cause a problem. The aircrew do a walk-round check before settling themselves into the cockpit. Once their pre-flight checks are complete, they signal that they are ready to start engines. They may be in direct contact with the man 1 via intercoms or may just be using hand signals. The aircrew fire up the GTC, and then, when they have enough power, they start the first engine, normally the port side. This is because main entry and exit on an aircraft is on the port side, and for multi-crewed aircraft the captain sits in the left-hand seat so that they have a clear view of everything. Single- or tandem-seat aircraft aren't quite so complicated. On multi-engine planes the see-off crew keep going until everything is turning

SQUADRON LIFE

Houchin GPU connected to a Victor bomber. (Tony Lamsdale)

and burning – a lovely phrase to indicate that all the engines are working. Once everything is running and all the pressures and systems are right, the aircrew indicate they are ready to move. At this point, with the aircraft running on its own power, the GPU needs to be unplugged.

The aircrew pass the signal to the see-off crew, who unplug the power cable and stow it away. The aircrew request permission to taxi from Air Traffic Control. Then it's chocks away. The aircrew signal to the man 1, who passes the signal on. (Arms down, fists clenched and thumbs sticking out. The arms then move from the centre to the outside of the body to form an inverted V, with the thumbs on the outside. This is easier to do than to write about!) The see-off crew remove the chocks and move away from the aircraft. When everyone is clear the man 1 gives the aircrew the thumbs up. The aircrew flash the taxi lights when they are ready to start moving. At this point the man 1 raises his arms above his head. The arms are used to give directions such as come forwards, move backwards (some aircraft have reverse), go left and go right. The speed of the arm movements controls the speed of the aircraft and man 1 is in control, albeit briefly, of a multi-million-pound aircraft. Once the man 1 has safely navigated the aircraft from its stand out onto the taxiway, they pass control to the aircrew with a cheery wave, then rush off to the crew room for a much-needed brew.

Of course, before the aircraft taxis there are many hours of hard work completed by multiple trades. This work is rarely mentioned – at best a brief paragraph or passing comment, a footnote at the end of the first chapter before the exciting account of the trip to target, engaging the enemy, and tea and medals back in the mess. How do you know when a pilot walks into a bar? They tell you! How do you know when an Armourer walks into a bar? You won't know because you'll have gone to bed hours ago. While the pilots are in the bar, the Armourers have been busy downloading the unused weapons, making the aircraft safe, and getting it ready for tomorrow.

It all starts with ops. Ops determine the daily flying programme based on need. Live operations take precedence, followed by training requirements, aircraft testing and AOB. A list of needs is passed around the squadron the day before: the number of aircraft, fuel load, weapons load, plus any other requirements. Traditionally, each section writes all the details up on its ops or aircraft state board, often referred to as the 'plastic brain'. Usually this is a white board, neatly lined, with a list of all squadron aircraft by tail number down the left-hand side and various headings across the top to indicate the state. Priority aircraft are at the top. Depending on how the squadron is organised, the Armourers may be working out of the same area as the other trades or, in the case of Kinloss in the 1980s, have their own line office and aircraft state board. The rectifications (recs) controller is in charge of keeping the aircraft state up to date, chasing up the teams working on the various snags and jobs and fending off the aircrew who are impatiently waiting for their aircraft.

Does all this still happen? Are state boards still hanging on walls? Do people really still use magnetic labels or write on the boards in chinagraph pencils? The answer is yes, some still do. The reason being that they are easy to read and update; not having to rely on technology can have its advantages. Of course, modern systems are also in use. A lot of aircraft record-keeping is now online, and this allows the modern version of the state board to be shared around units or different sections on the camp or squadron. You can even project it onto the wall for all to see. It must be said that the modern way helps prevent the aircrew constantly chasing the recs controller, and the other big advantage of an electronic board is that people cannot move things about in a fit of fun. It may be that, back in the day when an Armourer was getting posted or perhaps slightly disgruntled, or even just in need of a jolly good chuckle, a board could be rearranged to bear absolutely no relation to the actual aircraft state. On discovery of this, the recs controller would spend many happy hours reorganising the board to reflect reality.

Tony remembers his days at Kinloss in the late 1980s:

> Working on the line at Kinloss was the best job. We worked shifts of three days, three nights, and six days off. Every other off shift you had to be within an hour of camp and contactable. (This was sketchy because it was before mobiles, but it worked.) Shifts ran from 7 to 7, so the day shift would turn up about 6.30 ready to make a brew and get the gen from

the off-going shift. Often when you turned up the other shift would be out finishing off jobs, probably seeing off aircraft or working any snags found when the aircrew did their walk round. It wasn't uncommon for an aircraft to be redeployed, so you might have to change loads or add extra stuff. It was all part of the job. There was immense pride in the off-going shift about not leaving jobs half finished. I've known people be out several hours after their official finish time so they could complete a job. A good on-going shift would get folk out to tricky jobs to help the off-going shift. We all worked together to get the job done. That's the way it was.

Not all shifts were as nice as Kinloss. At some bases people worked days, evenings and wrecks, wrecks being the work on broken aircraft that had to be done to get them ready for the next day. Wrecks work could go right through the night. There are many variations of shift patterns. One of the worst is recalled by Tony:

Not long after I got to Kinloss I got nominated to do gate guard. It was a two-week duty, and you did something like three hours on shift, six hours off, then three on and nine off. You did this for seven days, then you had twenty-four hours off and started again. It was so bad because you hardly knew where you were and forgot mealtimes to help orientate you. You went to the mess before you started and whenever you finished to get a meal. Until you've eaten a roast for breakfast you have no idea of the real meaning of confusion.

Looking at the state board gives you an idea of the shift you are going to face – how many aircraft you need to load, see off, and see back in. If you work on fast jets it will be a matter of how many trips or sorties are planned for the day. They may only be gone for an hour, then back for a splash of fuel and more bombs. Larger aircraft could be gone for some time. Nimrods from Kinloss were always gone for a minimum of five hours, unless it was an air test. During the Cold War, their role was patrolling the seas looking for Russian submarines or trawlers that were trying to sneak down between Norway and Greenland into the Atlantic. It was a constant game of cat and mouse, with each side trying to gather intelligence on the other, and at the same time show force and presence; more politics than anything else.

The start of any shift begins with a brew and a chat with the off-going shift to get the gossip. Next would be the routine jobs such as checking that all the tools and equipment were serviceable and ready to tackle whatever the day may bring. Shifts or teams have their own tool kits, partly for safety and partly for scalability (no point in having one toolkit between five teams when there is a war on). Aircraft are complex machines with many moving parts, some of which are delicate and sensitive. Flying controls, for example, may be wires or rods running through bulkheads. You don't want anything stopping the movement of those controls so everything, absolutely everything without exception, is accounted for when working on aircraft.

Let's talk FOD! Foreign object damage, or FOD, can seriously affect aircraft and operations. A loose stone on the taxiway or runway, a strip of metal slicing a tyre, a spanner rattling around in the cockpit – all can be catastrophic and possibly fatal. It is drilled into you from training not to be careless on airfields; there are many reasons, not least of which is FOD. Every trade is taught about it, but the aircraft trades have it drilled into them at every stage of their training. Everything is controlled and designed to minimise the risk.

You are taught to leave everything unnecessary in your locker at the start of your shift. Rings, watches, jewellery, wallets, cigarettes, lighters – all of them go into the locker. You put on your denims or overalls and wear shoes or boots with FOD-free soles. The grooves in the soles and heels are wide, and are designed so that stones and mud don't get stuck in them. You can even get away without carrying your ID card. Being without your ID card is a chargeable offence in normal circumstances, so it gives you an idea of how seriously being FOD-free is taken.

Losing items in the cockpit was something to avoid at all costs, because of the potential dangers involved, but it seemed to happen with great regularity. And very often it was the Armourers who were called in to try and make a plane safe. During the series of interviews we carried out while writing this book, lost items in planes was a topic that came up again and again.

The procedure was that if you knew that there was *definitely* a loose article, you had to do everything possible to find it, otherwise the plane was not safe to fly. Let's say that a nut has gone missing. Assuming an initial search is unsuccessful, the next step would be for the Armourers to remove the ejection seats. When the seats were out, the cockpit would be stripped, as far as is possible. If necessary, you could use an endoscope to look for the nut in any crevices. If the missing nut wasn't found, you'd replace the cockpit fittings, put the ejection seats back in, and the plane would then be taken up for an inverted flight check. The hope was that the missing object would come loose and land on the canopy of the aircraft, where it could be recovered by a member of the aircrew. If it wasn't found, the process would

SQUADRON LIFE

start again – ejection seats out, cockpit stripped, search again. If the object was *still* not found, the station commander would have to make the decision as to whether the aircraft was passed as safe to fly again.

Podge Middleton remembers an incident when he was working on 9 Squadron, deploying aircraft to Turkey and Saudi Arabia, to keep an eye on Iraq. The aircrew at the time carried pistols. The process was that they would sign a pistol out and load a magazine, then at the end of the mission they would return the pistol. But on one occasion a member of the aircrew kept a pistol all day, during which he flew on two different aircraft. When he came to hand his pistol back, there was one round missing from the magazine. Podge and his team had to strip two aircraft, searching for a bullet that they didn't actually know was in either plane. They also checked along the taxiways, and looked in any other vehicles where this member of the aircrew might have been. They never found the bullet.

That's enough of the process when there is potential for FOD to happen; let's get back to the steps needed to prevent such a possibility.

Virtually every job needs tools, so you go to the tool store and draw out exactly what you need, nothing more. Tools are tagged out to an individual, so you hand over your tag or tags and in return are given the tools you need. At the end of the job you return the tools and get your tags back. It's an easy way of making sure things don't get left on aircraft. Shadow boards are used to keep a visual track on everything. The shapes of the tools are cut out, often in dayglo colours, and stuck on a board. The tool is placed over its shadow on the board. When the tool is there it hides the dayglo, and when it has been signed out it is easy to see that it is missing. Tool kits

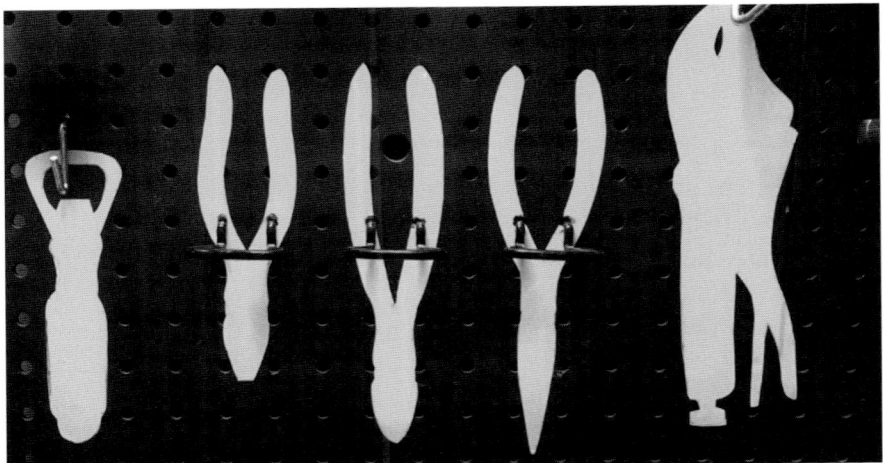

Tool shadow board. (Tony Lamsdale)

are often lined with foam cut to the shape of the tools and then lined with dayglo: it's the same principle.

Why bother, you ask? Well, on a busy flight line with many people coming and going it is easy to miss a spanner. Imagine working on an aircraft at night on an airfield. You may have the luxury of floodlighting, or you may be scrabbling around in the dark with a torch, which would also have been signed out. If you were using a toolkit, as you pack up the tools it is easy to see if anything is missing. On a good day in the sunshine, with nothing going wrong, it isn't so much of a problem. In the middle of a busy shift with ten jets coming and going, the flying programme changing, and the wind and rain slicing horizontally across the pan, having an easy way to check that all the tools are there is a real blessing. It has been known for tools to be misplaced, things left where they shouldn't be. The best outcome is that someone realises and raises the alarm before the aircraft goes flying. This will instigate a methodical and systematic search until the missing tool is found. Aircraft may be grounded, there may be raised voices, tea break may even be missed – but the priority is finding the tool. Someone will be shouted at and possibly be called some unpleasant things but, let's face it, keeping quiet in the hope that it will turn up could have disastrous consequences.

FOD is such a serious business that any vehicles operating on the airfield must have FOD-free tyres, regular FOD patrols will be carried out, and lots of things will be swept. Teams of people have been known to sweep the runways. And why not? Why risk a multi-million-pound aircraft (and the crew) for the sake of a little tidy-up?

The ethos of being clean, tidy and organised is drummed into you from the moment you join up. It is all about taking care of yourself and your kit so that when you are needed to do a job, you are ready. Operating under extreme conditions is only possible when certain things are habit. It allows you to focus on the other, more important things.

Once everything is checked and ready to go, it's a matter of starting on the first job of the day and working through until everything is done or your shift ends. Jobs are allocated based on priority, and also availability of skills. Tony remembers:

> The first job on the line at Kinloss (after a brew) was checking that the tool kits were ready. They were kept in the tool store. Each shift had two kits, each a mirror image, and enough for two teams. Each shift was eight people – two SNCOs, two JNCOs, two JTs and two SAC/LACs, which equals two four-man teams.

SQUADRON LIFE

Nimrod bomb bay, looking from the aft (back) of the aircraft. (Tony Lamsdale)

Most loads on a Nimrod needed a four-man team. One of the SACs would go and check the tools, then sign the kit list, and the other would go and check the jacks. To load a Nimrod you needed jacks to hoist the carriers and whatever was fitted to them up into the bomb bay.

The jack was a hydraulic hand pump. It had a reservoir, a pump mechanism and a handle. When you pumped the handle, the ram came up. It had a mushroom-shaped head which fitted into a pintle in the bomb bay. Once the head of the ram was in the pintle, you pumped the jack and it retracted the ram, raising the carrier up into the bomb bay. You used two rams, one each side. We had loads of jacks to use. You needed them because they were always going wrong. The jacks were kept in an area in the hangar. They were up off the floor on a pallet. There was a big drip tray filled with chicken sh*t (absorbent pellets), because the jacks were always leaking oil. There were two pallets, one for serviceable and one for U/S jacks. There was also a drum of hydraulic oil so you could top up the reservoir.

You also had to check out the vehicles. We had a couple of Land Rovers (110 series) and a Bedford flatbed truck. You needed the truck to carry a full load of sonobuoys and flares to load a Nimrod. On day shifts, the first job was usually doing all the BFs. I used to love this job, and was often first out to crack on with it while the others sat and had another brew. The SAC usually did all the running around, but I didn't mind. You'd get a list of aircraft that were due to take off and would go around to each making sure they were ready to fly. You checked that they had the correct load for whatever they were going to do (usually SAR) and that all the armament systems were working. You have to remember that the jet may have been loaded the day or night before, and that other people may have worked on it since the last Armourers finished.

The line at Kinloss was massive so you had to drive to get places, otherwise you'd never get anything done. Our hangar was a little drive away from the line. NLS (Nimrod Line Squadron) were based in a hangar outside the line, so could walk. These were all the other trades: riggers, sooties and fairies. Once you'd gone round and checked all the aircraft you needed to, you went to the line office to sign all the paperwork. Each aircraft has its own book (the RAF F700), and any servicing was recorded on the RAF F705. It was quite a responsibility to go and check an aircraft and say it was fit to fly from an armament perspective; I was 22, and so proud to be doing the job.

As described in Chapter 3, Nimrods were heavily involved in search and rescue (SAR) duties. The Nimrod can be on station quickly to conduct searches of the sea effectively, and its advanced equipment allowed it to co-ordinate operations. SAR aircraft would carry specialist kit to support the role. As well as marker flares, the Nimrod used to carry a life raft and two supply containers in the bomb bay, which could be dropped next to a struggling vessel. These items were fitted and dropped in the same way as a bomb or torpedo, and once they hit the sea the life raft would deploy automatically. The supply containers would float, and were attached to the life raft by ropes. Once the survivors got into the life raft, they could pull the supply containers in and have a picnic.

Working on aircraft involves learning everything related to your trade as well as all the other trade jobs you may be required to assist with. In time, most of this knowledge becomes part of you, but in the first few weeks of working on a new aircraft it can be a bit overwhelming. One technique was to carry pocket books or guides to help you remember

SQUADRON LIFE

the important things. The following pictures show Tony's pocket book from his time working on First Line Armament Servicing (FLAS). It's just a pocket photo album with some handwritten notes and photocopied pages.

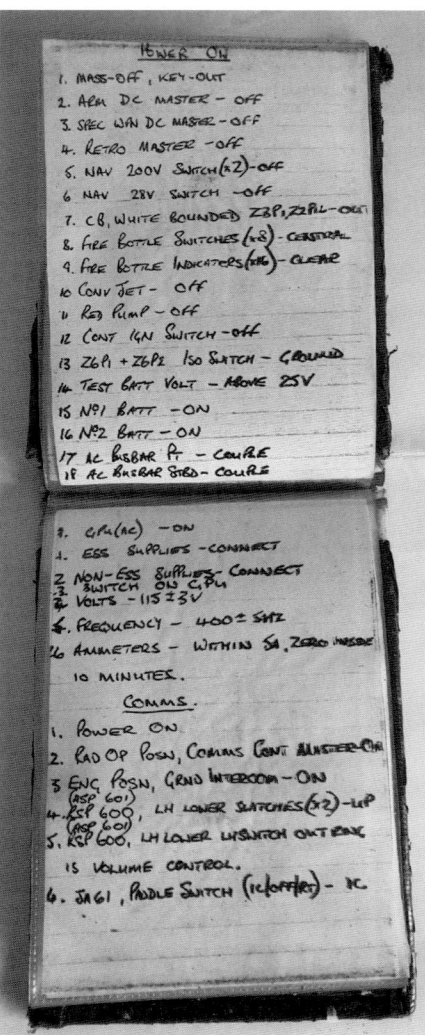

Above left: Nimrod power on. Page showing how to apply power to the aircraft, with all the vital switches to check. (Tony Lamsdale)

Above right: Nimrod Bomb Bay Load stations. Pages showing the bomb stations and the possible loads. (Tony Lamsdale)

THE RAF'S ARMOURERS

Smaller aircraft such as Tornado, Harrier or Eurofighter represent a different set of challenges, and the weapons fitted depend on the role. Fighter/interceptor aircraft are armed with cannon and missiles, whereas those designated to bombing roles are kitted out to carry whatever bombs have been deemed appropriate for the destruction of the target. In modern times it is possible to direct 1,000lb bombs to within a metre of the target using lasers, a far cry from the early days of the RFC when 25lb bombs were dropped over the side of the cockpit by the pilot.

Before anyone does any work to an aircraft it must be safe from an armament perspective. An aircraft with any explosives fitted will have signs placed in front and behind it.

There will also be signs in the cockpit. A visual inspection of safety pins can be carried out when approaching the aircraft and, if ejection seats are fitted, the various safety pins must be fitted. Another important thing to check is that the master armament safety switch (MASS) is set to 'safe'.

BFs are the typical starting point for the day shift. If a jet has already been loaded and fuelled by the previous shift, it will be a matter of

Danger aircraft armed sign. (Mark Bean)

SQUADRON LIFE

Armed sign and MASS green flag, Tornado. (Mark Bean)

Tornado MASS. (Mark Bean)

ARB Tornado. (Mark Bean)

walking round to check everything is still as it should be. Things like tyre pressures, fuel loads, oxygen levels – all need to be checked. Another important consideration is damage – has anything happened since the jet was last checked? When an aircraft is parked up and put to bed it will have bungs, blanks and covers fitted to critical components to stop them getting damaged, or prevent things crawling into places like the engine intakes or exhausts. All of these bungs, blanks and covers are coloured

red to make them visible and they will have small flags fitted to them with 'remove before flight' printed on them. All the bungs, blanks and covers are removed and stowed, and the visual checks carried out, before power is applied to the aircraft. At this point the armament kit will be in the 'safe' condition, which means all electrical and mechanical safety devices are fitted and any pins will have the red flag attached; these all need to be checked.

Now it's time for the liney to look in the cockpit to make sure there are three greens. Three greens refers to the visible check that the undercarriage is down and locked. Most aircraft have three points of contact with the ground; there will be two sets of main wheels and either a nose or tail wheel. These wheels retract during flight to make the aircraft more aerodynamic, so when they are extended there needs to be a visible indication they are down and locked. Also, most armament systems have a WOW switch that acts as a circuit breaker for the electrics. 'Wheels down' means the system is interrupted so that no power can go to the things that go bang. After all the safety checks are carried out the liney will apply power to the aircraft and start to check all the other systems.

It is amazing how many things can break when an aircraft has been parked up overnight. Systems that worked fine the previous day suddenly develop faults. The logical answer is that this is caused by all the stresses and strains on the aircraft during flight, but we all know it's the gremlins. Each aircraft has its own procedures, and once you have done it a few times it becomes second nature. Your eyes are constantly scanning for problems. Is that a leak? Does that panel look loose? It's a habit that, once learned, never leaves you and carries over into civilian life in things like scanning the car as you walk back to it from the supermarket.

By the time the aircrew arrive, the jet is ready and waiting for them to kick the tyres and light the fires, and the see-off crew are primed and ready. For an aircraft fitted with an ejection seat, the liney will help the aircrew strap in then assist with the removal and stowage of the seat pins. The pins are stored in the cockpit because if the jet lands away from base, the pins will be needed to make the seat safe. The same is true with the other armament pins and safety devices. Once the aircraft is powered up the liney will go and remove the pins and stow them somewhere safe. Aircraft have stowage points for the pins, bungs, blanks and covers, so it's a matter of putting things away and making sure any panels are secured. Thumbs up to the crew and it's time to get airborne.

SQUADRON LIFE

A TR service is much more about refuelling, rearming, and checking for damage, then getting the aircraft on its way again. A hot or operational TR is frantic; it's basically getting it all done as quickly as possible, and the aircrew may remain in the aircraft. The AF is more in depth, with the first job being to refit the armament safety pins to make the aircraft safe to work on. Once all the other jobs are done the bungs, blanks and covers are refitted and the aircraft is put to bed.

The picture shows a Nimrod with some of the bungs, blanks and covers fitted. It was taken by Tony at the Yorkshire Air Museum, Elvington, and brings back many fond memories.

Nimrod with bungs, blanks and covers fitted. (Tony Lamsdale)

Armament safety pin fitted to a pylon. (Tony Lamsdale)

THE RAF'S ARMOURERS

So what about previous generations of Armourers? What was their experience of squadron life?

After training, Bill Lanfear was posted to Leconfield, which had been a key strategic airfield during the Second World War. During the war no fewer than seven RAF squadrons were stationed there, and there was even a Polish squadron that helped out during the Battle of Britain. By 1954 Leconfield was a central gunnery school, and Bill worked on Lincolns. He has some vivid memories of his time there:

> Lincolns had three turrets – one in the nose, one mid-upper, and one in the tail. The mid-upper turret had two 20mm guns, and the front and rear turrets had two Browning .5s. We would arm them all up, and off they'd go.
>
> There was a range over towards Bridlington, on the coast, and I got the chance to fire a 20mm gun there that was set up on a stand. Very powerful! One time I went up in the aircraft with the armament officer – I always enjoyed flying, unlike some of my mates – and he let me have a go at firing the Brownings. I was told to fire towards the sea, to avoid any possible mishaps.
>
> On another occasion, to celebrate Battle of Britain Day, there was a simulation bombing raid. I sat in the tail turret, with a load of smoke cartridges and a couple of signal pistols. There was a sliding panel in the middle of the tail turret, so I opened the panel and fired off smoke cartridges to simulate flak.

Shortly before Bill arrived at Leconfield, there had been a major incident involving one of the station's Lincolns. It had been shot down by Russian MiG fighter planes over East Germany during a training exercise. There were no survivors. This was an instance when the Cold War threatened to become distinctly more heated.

In May 1955, the 'Dambusters' film, which recreates the true story of the 1943 'bouncing bomb' raids on German dams, was released. This provided an opportunity for the RAF to indulge in a bit of promotional activity, and Bill recalls being despatched with several colleagues to the foyer of a cinema in Hull where the film was being shown. There they chatted with the filmgoers, including lots of attractive young women who referred to them as 'the Brylcreem boys'.

In late 1955 Bill flew up to Kinloss where he continued to work as a turret Armourer, but this time on Shackleton aircraft.

SQUADRON LIFE

So what exactly was it like being a turret Armourer? For the most part, Bill remembers it as a rewarding and trouble-free job, particularly when working on the Lincolns:

> For the mid-upper turret, there was a big hole in the fuselage, and the turret fitted down into the hole. They were rather nice, the turrets. BAC made them, and they were beautifully made. They had tanks down at the bottom to catch the spent shells. There was a round drum, a BFM (Belt Feed Mechanism) that fitted on the top of the 20mm guns, and you fed the ammunition into the gun itself.
>
> The mid-upper turret was all electric. The tail turret was hydraulic, with hydraulic motors. It was all part of the turret, not like the Lancaster, which had hydraulic pipes running through the fuselage to power the motors. We had to set up the guns, and put the gunsight in. Line it all up using a board set about 100 yards away to harmonise the guns. I think we used to pace out the 100 yards.
>
> They were quite big planes the old Lincolns, similar size to the Shacks (Shackletons). The Lincolns had Merlin engines and the Shacks had Griffon engines with contra-rotating props. They put Merlin engines in the Wimpys (Wellingtons) you know, as an experiment.
>
> We always had to polish the Perspex on the turrets to make sure the gunners could see out. We used this liquid polish, sort of a white-grey colour.
>
> One of the main jobs at Leconfield was arming the guns, hundreds and hundreds of rounds. They had any amount of trainee sergeant gunners in those days who all needed to practise so we would spend hours prepping the ammunition. An aircraft would tow a drogue and the gunners would be shooting at the drogue. We would dip the 20mm rounds in coloured paints. The paint had a hard surface but if they hit the drogue the round would leave a coloured mark behind. Each gunner had their rounds dipped in a different colour, so you knew which of them had hit the target. The ammo used to come already belted up so if we had to dip the rounds we would have to take them out of the belts, dip them, then put them back into the belts. We would spend hours and hours dipping the rounds in the paint. Once they were re-belted we would load them back into the guns. The belt feed mechanism was an evil thing. It had a massive strong

THE RAF'S ARMOURERS

Armourer Sgt Bob Francis (kneeling) and a colleague checking ammunition belts in a posed picture. Bob survived the War. (Dick Lindsay)

spring in it. It would take your finger off if you weren't careful. You had to use a cocking tool, sort of a metal hook, to pull the breech block back to get the first round lined up.

Occasionally something would go wrong. Bill rarely worked on the Gloster Meteor fighter aircraft, which ceased production in 1955, but remembers being on duty crew when the Meteors landed one day:

> One of the pilots said to me, 'I've got a stoppage in Number 4 gun.' I had a look, and the breech block was forward, and the shell was up the spout. There was a civvy there and he was saying, 'Hurry up, I want to go home for tea.' And I said to him, 'If this thing goes off it'll cut you in half, so I wouldn't be in too much of a rush.' Anyway, I didn't know what to do, but I did know there was a Master Armourer there. I knew him so I went and fetched him. We turned the aircraft around between us so it was facing in a safe direction and managed to point the gun into a pool of water. There was always a pool near the hangar. We managed to disarm it. I just pulled the breech block back and took out the round. So everything was fine.

SQUADRON LIFE

Bill's National Service ended in 1956, when he was demobbed as an SAC. Little more than two years as an RAF Armourer, but so many memories.

Brian Polson spent several years working at RAF Gaydon in Warwickshire, the first UK site for the 'V bombers'. Brian worked on Valiants, which were actively involved in the Suez Crisis in 1956. Brian recalls that the Valiant was 'a bit of a pig to work on':

> You had to load munitions through the top of fuselage, which involved putting a gantry over the top of the aircraft to give you access to the bomb bay from above. You wheeled the bombs underneath the fuselage on a trolley and then winched them up from above into position. We had a mock-up of the gantry which we called the 'cock-up', which we used for practice loading.
>
> One day we were loading practice bombs and one got stuck. As we were trying to sort out the problem our squadron leader, who was a bit of a tartar, turned up, so I explained that we had a problem. We used throat mikes to communicate, and he asked me if he could borrow mine. He got on the radio and asked for the flight lieutenant, who was in charge of the loading, to explain the problem. The FL replied, 'Don't stand there like a prick, get round here and give us a hand.' He clearly didn't realise it was the squadron leader on the radio. Within two weeks the FL had been posted to another base; that was the sort of bloke the squadron leader was.
>
> I also worked with Flight Sergeant Bill Williams, who was a dour Cornishman from Redruth. He had worked on Lancasters during the Mau Mau crisis in Kenya. During the crisis he was taking a lorry-load of live bombs from the bomb dump, and they all fell off. Everybody did a runner apart from the FS, who went round and defused all the bombs, making them safe. He separated all the fuzes and then went to air traffic control to tell them he had sorted the problem. They awarded him the British Empire Medal – the military equivalent of an MBE – for that. A long time later, the same squadron leader asked Bill to come to his office. He called him in and told him he didn't deserve the medal, that he should never have been awarded it. Bill requested that he and the squadron leader go to the group captain's office, so that the comment could be repeated in front of witnesses, but he declined. Not long after that Bill was reposted.

THE RAF'S ARMOURERS

More recently, when Martyn Mander was transferred to Marham in the early 1980s, at the time when the airfield was very quiet as a result of many of its activities being transferred to Germany, Marham had the Victor OCU and two operational squadrons (55 and 57) and also 100 Squadron Canberras, whose role was target towing.

Life was pretty quiet for the Armourers. There was an armoury where the majority of them worked, and a small bomb dump to hold the fire bottle carts and starter carts for the Canberras. If a job needed doing, such as pulling a seat for maintenance, they would put a team together from the armoury and go and do it. Martyn recalls:

> For the Victors we had an old Bedford truck, the RL I think. I was one of only a couple of Armourers on camp who could drive it because I had my HGV licence from when I was in Germany. You needed the truck because the Victor was a big aircraft. If we had to fit or remove the fuel tanks from under the wings, you needed the truck as it had the jacks fitted to it. I would drive the truck and position it under the wings. The jacks were above the wings and attached to the tanks by dropping the connectors down through. The tanks would be raised or lowered using jacks which pulled the tanks up from above. Even the seats were a bit of a faff because you needed one of the big access platforms, the giraffe, because it was the only thing tall enough to reach. We had an A-frame on the end of the giraffe to hoist the seats in and out. You were really high up and had to clip yourself onto the giraffe in case you fell.
>
> Fitting and removing the seats from a Canberra was also interesting as the main seats had to come out through the access door. You had to remove all the kit and then you had a chance of manoeuvring it out. I think the rear seat came out though the rear canopy. You had to remove the canopy then you could lift the seat out.
>
> The jobs were few and far between because the people who had been there longest grabbed all the work they could. The newbies didn't get much of a look in.

There are times when planes and their pilots have to be on standby, ready to leave at very short notice. Ever since the RAF was formed, its role has been defence of the United Kingdom and its dominions. During the Cold War, aircraft were on standby to intercept 'enemy' aircraft or shipping entering UK territories. QRA aircraft would be on standby 24/7, ready

SQUADRON LIFE

to launch at a moment's notice to investigate potential threats and, if necessary, take action to neutralise those threats. In some ways it was a massive game of chicken, with each side often goading the other to provoke a response, to test reactions and ascertain strength or technology in use.

In current times, the threat comes from different places, but the readiness remains constant. It isn't always about a threat either. The RAF has provided search and rescue cover for many years in the form of its Air Sea Rescue helicopter and the maritime patrol capabilities of aircraft like the Shackleton, Nimrod and Poseidon. The RAF has also stepped in to assist with recover and supply following national and international disasters; for example, in 2019 RAF Chinooks delivered vital materials to shore up the flood defences in Doncaster. The stations that are home to these squadrons provide 24/7 support to ensure that the squadrons and personnel are able to perform their duties. Messes provide food, the station fire service are on standby for aircraft landing and taking off, and the duty Armourer is ready to issue weapons and sometimes ammunition.

When Tony was stationed at Lyneham in the 1980s, there was always a duty Armourer because there were always people coming through Lyneham who needed to store weapons. Being a duty Armourer meant being on call twenty-four hours a day, and you would generally be in the role for a full week. At Lyneham, there were no special sleeping facilities for the duty Armourer. You opened the armoury for work during the day, did all the gash jobs, then locked up in the evening after everyone had gone home. If you were lucky, you got the chance to eat your tea before you got called out to accept or issue a weapon. Of course, you might not get called, or you could be in the armoury all night, grabbing some kip between jobs. Either way, you had to be ready to get the place opened and ready for business at 7.30 the next morning.

In contrast, Brian Polson's experience as a duty Armourer at Gaydon was very different. It was at the time of the Cold War and there was always the potential of terrorist activity. Brian was one of three duty Armourers on call. There were two bunks, so two people could sleep while the third was on active duty. One curious memory that Brian has of that time is the fact that while they had weapons with them, they had no ammunition. Perhaps the idea was that if some enemy intruder infiltrated the armoury, pointing the guns at them might be an adequate deterrent.

Squadron or line work is always interesting, and although a lot of the tasks can be repetitive, you have to keep focused because aircraft can be nasty and bite hard. Complacency is one of the biggest enemies, so you develop a system of approaching each job as though it is the first time you have done it. It is so easy to miss something because you see what you expect to see, not what is actually in front of you. It's wise to rely not just on sight; sound, touch and smell are also really important. Taste less so because it's considered weird to lick an aircraft; also, they contain some very nasty chemicals. As you approach an aircraft to start your work, you are constantly looking for things that are out of place, missing or unusual. You scan the area around the aircraft to make sure you have all the kit you need (chocks, Houchin, fire extinguishers, etc.), and look out for debris, and puddles of fluid that may indicate a leak. The sooner a problem is spotted the sooner it can be tackled. Aircraft that have just flown have been subjected to incredible stresses and the possibility of being struck by something during flight, such as a bird.

Bird strikes are common and can cause catastrophic damage. The main threat of bird strike is during either landing or take-off. Airfields employ many strategies to prevent bird strikes, including having noise-generating units positioned around the airfield to scare birds away. Airbases can also use birds of prey, either fake or real, and also people hired specifically to control the birds, known as the Bird Control Unit (BCU). If a bird is ingested into the intake of a jet engine the damage can cause the engine to fail, so one of the most important flight checks is to look for signs of a bird strike. Dents, scratches, blood smears and dead birds (obviously) can indicate a problem. During a TR or AF servicing someone will have to inspect each intake to look for signs of damage. Some aircraft are easier than others. For example, a Jet Provost was low to the ground and the intake could be inspected easily. A Nimrod required a ladder, a torch and, if you were lucky, someone to hold the ladder while you climbed it and crawled into the intake to get a proper look. Other jets required a more lithe or acrobatic approach. Tony recalls checking the intake of a Buccaneer during his training at Cosford:

> The Bucc was a lovely aircraft to look at, but to check the blades you had to crawl head-first down the intake with a torch. Not so great if you were claustrophobic. The routine was always the same. First you had to inform all the other trades working on the aircraft that you were going to inspect the intakes. You would need a safety man, and also have to make sure power was off, or at least that no one was in the cockpit fiddling with switches. It wasn't unheard of for some fun-loving pranksters to wait until someone had crawled into the engine then press the engine ignitors button. While there was no danger of the

SQUADRON LIFE

engine actually starting, the noise of the ignitors 'cracking' could be heard in the engine and cause heart failure at the very least. Oh what fun!

Each aircraft is different, and some are easier to work on than others. Fast jets tend to be smaller, so some of the tasks can be completed quicker, whereas an AF on a Nimrod could take a couple of hours. Working on a Nimrod involves a lot of running up and down the access steps and crawling around on your hands and knees in the bomb bay. A lot of people say the Harrier was quite low to the ground, so there was lots of bending down to do jobs. People develop favourites. It might be the aircraft they first worked on, or that the squadron was brilliant. Sometimes it comes down to the environment.

While researching for this book, we asked the Armourers community which aircraft people liked working on and why. The questions were posted on a Facebook group and the responses were overwhelming. In less than twenty-four hours we received over 150 responses. The passion with which people wrote their responses was evident. Memories (mainly good) were rekindled, and the banter was prominent along with the slang. They say that you may leave the service but the service never leaves you, and that is so true.

The first thing that jumped out was the number of different aircraft types people have worked on, and many worked on multiple types, which underlines the flexibility of skills.

In no particular order we have Wessex, Lynx, Sea King, Puma and Chinook (all rotary wing); Shackleton, Lancaster, Short Sunderland, Strikemaster, Javelin, Lightning, Victor, Vulcan, Canberra, Hunter, Buccaneer, Bloodhound, Phantom, Jaguar, Jet Provost, Gnat, Hercules, Tornado, Harrier, Hawk, Nimrod and Typhoon. Slightly less common aircraft included F-111s, classic Hornets, L-159, and one Armourer who worked on Sea Vixens (clearly harbouring aspirations of a life at sea!).

The majority had nothing but kind words about their chosen aircraft. There were a few foibles highlighted, which indicate that a particular aircraft may cause Armourers discomfort or trouble, but nothing fun is ever simple. The following comments have all been taken directly from the responses and give fascinating glimpses into the aircraft and the world of the Armourer:

'I found the Bucc better to work on for a variety of reasons. Just seemed easier and more straightforward than the GR4.'

'Phantoms were awesome, the very best to work on and brilliant dets. Hercs at Lyneham were also good fun but Pumas at Benson were dogsh*t. Couldn't get away fast enough.'

THE RAF'S ARMOURERS

'The best? Phantoms I think, bloody awful design (Armourers always had to remove something for somebody) but good dets and the gun was a real Armourer's toy! The worst? Not really an aircraft, but did 18 months on Bloodhounds and hated it! Constantly loading and unloading as kit went U/S, 5 Armourers with 45 ground fairies and baby officers who did not know their arse from their elbow but were "Intercept Officers" and supposedly in charge. Couple that with a Sqn Ldr who was posted in on promotion (ex helicopter winchman) and did not have a clue! Still look back on it with a smile though!'

'Jags were an awesome aircraft to work on, but still enjoyed working on the Nimrod and the Tornado.'

'Phantoms were definitely the best. The worst would be Jet Provost, seats only, what a pain.' This led to the following response: 'Nappy pins holding the leg restraint pin in. Parafab change not too hot either lol.'

'Just loved working 1st line whatever the aircraft They all have their foibles & good points! Nimrod, Jaguar, Chinook, Tornado, Canberra.'

'Vulcans. Loved almost everything about them except the filthy oil around the ARD bay. I blame "engines" for that.'

'Hunter, best plumber aircraft by miles, less than 15 minutes turn round.'

'Nimrod, ohh the detachments, and Phantoms, same as above, but a great bunch of lads as well.'

'Jags, simple to work on and at Lossie when you turned up in winter they often said: "Range closed, go home".'

'PR 9s were a bitch, bent bomb beams and canopy dets.'

'Hunter and Javelin were great. Blue Steel Victor awful, jack up to 27ft position using dreadful trolley, lower a/c, connect to release gear, pump up to carrier then finally hammer in the locking bolt. To load a live missile total time from start 3–4 hours!'

'Hawks were great at Brawdy on Decci shifts. Role changes took minutes. The only thing you had to contend with was the weather and a knobhead FS called John Thomas… Phantoms were a nightmare in the Falklands … Never taken out so many seatpans for dropped articles and then working until the early hours to get everything back up.'

'Hawks by far. Ej. Seats out and in in a couple of hours, all other weapons a piece of cake, unless the jockey leaves the flaps down and you stick your head into the corner while loading the gun.'

'Absolutely love the Harrier. Fabulous aircraft.'

'Vulcan – always stayed dry when loading lol.'

'A FLEM on Tonkas … cause they were the swing wing, angel of death!!'

'Jags, everything was at the right height.' Which prompted the response: 'CBLS on centre line wasn't.' And back at you: 'Better than on the Harrier!'

SQUADRON LIFE

'Hercs K model obvs! Loved a Hot turnaround – got the blood going!'

'Loved getting dirty working on Harrier, Phantom, Lightning, Chinook & Tornado. Timeless memories with many a scar!!'

'Canberras were awful; Hunters were a dream; loved the good old F4 as well …'

'Harriers (metal and plastic) and Hercs – enjoyed working on both!'

'Definitely Nimrod for me (my first tour), although I enjoyed Tornado GR4 (my last tour). Harrier not so much as the Centreline Pylon, for me, was a real pain in the arse!'

'Vulcans swiftly followed by Phantoms.'

'Bloodhound and yes it was an aircraft … it had a 700 anyway.'

'Loved working on 2 AC Jaguars. Very easy aircraft to load, especially the Aden guns, and you could do a double gun change on your own. Shame the Tonka didn't learn from that. The only pain on the Jag was the Centreline ReccePod.'

'My fave was XV Buccaneers. They were not the easiest to load but I was quite useful with an R Trolley even though I was a sprog SAC. Obviously never did any seat work but often saw our guys upside down in the cockpit, but then that is nothing out of the ordinary as we all know.'

'Vulcan not too bad. Had to keep low under a Phantom unless you wanted a scarred skull! Jag was easy. Lockwiring the command ejection selector on the Tornado was a real pig.'

'As a civvy Armourer at St Athan in the early '80s had to help connect up all the hatch removal detonators in a Canberra at Picketston. That WAS a bas***d of a job.'

'Definitely Nimrods. My first posting after mech training. NLF at St Mawgan. The best 2 years of my life 80–82. Just to add, I have no recollection of 95 per cent of it so it must have been good!!!!'

'The mighty Buccaneer.'

'First operational aircraft was F-4 (recessed missile launchers) only as a station OTR team. Worked on Harrier GR3 & T4, Tornado GR1, 3 tours on Nimrod in between that lot and finally Typhoon FGR4 (recessed missile launchers again). I'm with Vince Wolverson and enjoyed them all, just the smell of AVTUR and jet engine fumes to be honest but all had their own "getchas" for lumps, bumps, scratches, stitches as well as Armourers knees and backs. Still do it all again though.'

'Nimrods were the best but the mighty Toom was a close second especially the J as the rear seat pan didn't need pulling on every AF and you didn't get covered in quite so much oily s**t.'

'Loved working on Nimrods, Canberras too. Lynx and Sea Kings were fun except when doing rotor running rearms or hanging mines off the

THE RAF'S ARMOURERS

sacrew (the big hook underneath) when they were hovering above you. The static electricity generated was scary.'

'Buccaneers and Jags. Hated any version of Tornados.'

'Buccaneers without a doubt.'

'Phantom and Harrier great, Jaguar and Shackleton good. Nimrod and Tornado Crap.'

'Shacks, Lightnings, Phantoms, Harriers, Tonkers 1968 to 1990.'

'Jaguar from an Armourer point of view, enjoyed them over Harrier and Tornado. That said overall best time was with Hercs closely followed by Nimrods. Sea Vixens in training were a pain lol. To be fair loved 'em all.'

'Loved every aircraft I worked on, first line ... Vulcan, Harrier, Nimrod, Tornado, Jaguar and Hunter. I guess favourite had to be Harrier, a bitch at times (C/L pylon for a fuel leak). Liked Jags in Oman, along with the Billy Bunters, but it could be strange working Jags one week then Billy Bunters the next week, but all definitely enjoyable.'

'Jaguars were great. Tornadoes not so great.'

'Very easy to work on for all groundcrew particularly as you could do most jobs on your own if necessary even a gun change, exact opposite to Tonka.' To which someone replied: 'Once did a double gun change on my own in 20 minutes.' And someone else recalled: 'Remember going up to Lossie for a course and watching Jerry Fowler load 1000lbers onto a Jag on his own. My own experience was cross servicing at Gut on Jags and Bucks.'

'Harrier Gr 3, T4, Tornado Gr1/1A, Harrier Gr5/7/7A and Typhoon FGR 4/T Mk 3 loved them all.'

'Phantom, Jet Provost, Tornado & Harrier – loved working on all of them. Phantom is my personal favourite and Harrier the least.'

'Lightnings, loved watching 'em stand on their tail and heading for the moon.'

'Jaguars definitely and Phantoms too. Also worked on Vulcans Victors and Buccaneers at St Athan between 1971–73 and found removing/fitting ejector seats in the Buccaneers a nightmare!'

'F-111Gs on an exchange with the RAAF in the mid-90s. The smiley face graffiti on the nuke arm button always amused me.'

'F-4 bloody long nights seats/seat pans out waiting for the fairies to fix the radar or IFF but the best work hard play hard, especially on APC, in parallel Harriers GR3, GR5 & GR7 and not forgetting Tornado GR1, GR4 plus the F3.'

'Definitely tooooms, but I'm surprised my knees are still working!'

SQUADRON LIFE

So no clear winner in terms of favourite aircraft, and there are some big names missing from the list. It's the passion that comes over, and also that Armourers just love working on aircraft. Of course, there are other interesting jobs, but in the main people join the RAF because of the aircraft, don't they? Perhaps it is best summed up by the following: 'Owt with wings (or rotors at a push) is alreet!'

For many the biggest challenge with the greatest potential reward is fixing a snag. There is nothing more satisfying as an engineer than being given a problem, the more obscure or strange the better, and then solving it. Add to that the pressure of fixing the problem so that the aircraft can complete its mission, and you have the perfect scenario to test your skills and knowledge. This is why the constant training is so important; being able to complete a task almost automatically, but still being aware enough to spot something amiss, is the goal. The line is very fine indeed, because not paying enough attention can lead to serious errors, injuries and possibly even death; but spending hours on something that could be done in minutes could have just as big an impact.

Another interesting aspect is rank versus experience. People are familiar with the military hierarchy, and that orders are key and must be carried out quickly and efficiently and, in the main, without question. Often the orders are issued by the senior person present. It stands to reason that they have the most experience, therefore know the most. All of this is perfectly reasonable; however, from the start of your Armourer training, you are encouraged to look, question and shout if you see something that looks wrong. No point in following orders blindly if someone gets killed just because the person issuing the orders is a higher rank than you. You might be able to see something they can't. Working on an aircraft line can be fast-paced and noisy. There are many distractions, and you need more than one pair of eyes to see everything that needs to be seen. You build trust with those around you, and that trust is two-way; you must trust and be trusted, irrespective of rank. During training you are taught to ask questions and not let rank get in the way of calling out a problem. No one should be afraid to question something they believe is wrong.

Even experience isn't a definitive measure. For example, a Tornado GR1 had different processes to a GR4, so while some skills transfer directly, others need to be learned on the job. Tony recalls an event on the line at Kinloss:

> As an SAC, I had been working on the line for about a year. There were a lot of changes on our shift, and we ended up with a new C/T as our shift boss. He was a great bloke, just

back from RAFG and incredibly experienced with aircraft; he must have had a good fifteen years' service on me to be a chief and had worked in so many different places. Just the sort of career I was looking forward to. Thing is, he had never been to Kinloss or worked on Nimrods, so it fell to me to take him round and show him the ropes. I was the most experienced person on our shift because of all the changes. Sure we had the training cell, and they did a great job, but you cannot replace seeing the job first-hand. We spent the day together doing AF/BFs, prepping loads and all the other shift jobs. Basically, he did an SAC's work for the day. I told him how it was, and he asked loads of questions. At the end of the day he thanked me, and that was that. I guess during our time together that day we had both learned a lot about each other, and to be trusted in that role was something that has stuck with me ever since. It's testament to the training you are given.

Working on a line means working with lots of other trades; aircraft need constant care to keep them ready for action and also to tuck them up at night. Riggers, sooties and fairies are the other main aircraft trades – not as important as Armourers of course, but still useful. The line or squadron involves all these trades working together in harmonic unison, always fuelled by tea and banter and all with one common purpose: get the aircraft ready, then back for a brew. From its earliest days, this method has served the RAF well. The technology has developed and aircraft may look slightly different, but the work ethic is still the same – work hard, play hard. During conflict the pace increases and the adrenalin flows, but the role of the military has always been the same: be ready for anything.

Although teamwork is critical, occasionally you rather wish that one of your teammates had chosen a different career. Podge Middleton had such an experience with another member of his squadron:

In the mid-1980s my Man 2 in the team was a bit of a character. He was a ninja freak – unarmed combat and suchlike – and a bit of a military cabbage. About that time, when an exercise kicked off you always got guns but never got blank ammunition. Whereas intruders in the exercise did get blank ammunition. People were getting a bit pissed off about this, so much so that the OC Arm started to carry a cap

SQUADRON LIFE

gun. So we thought, if OC Arm can do something like that, why can't we?

One day during an exercise, Man 2 brought in a riot baton with him, in case he had to take out an SAS man in the HAS. It was a riot baton you could only buy in Germany, and it had CS gas in the end of it.

As you went into a HAS, on your right was a gun rack, so on this exercise that's where we put our rifles. And Man 2 put his baton there too. So we went off and did our job – loaded up the aircraft with weapons for the sortie. And while we were sorting out the paperwork, in came the crew. While they were waiting for us to finish, the navigator walked over to the gun rack, saw the baton, and picked it up. Then he says, 'What does this do?', presses the switch and gases the pilot. The pilot was coughing, and his eyes were streaming, and the navigator's saying, 'Oh my God! What have I done?'. Man 2 goes over and says to the pilot, 'It's alright Sir, it's only a very mild form of CS gas.'

Each HAS had a cabin where all the paperwork was held. So the pilot goes into the cabin, picks up the phone and calls the 'Squadron Warlord', the executive officer responsible for mission planning, making sure crews are trained, etc. The pilot didn't want to make anything of it, because he knows that his crew had been fiddling around with something they shouldn't have been, so he just says, 'Sorry boss. We'll have to delay the launch for a few minutes. I've just had a whiff of CS.' The next minute we've got the police turning up, an ambulance turning up, the immediate reaction team turning up – all outside the HAS. And next thing my Man 2 gets carted away.

Surprisingly enough, not much happened afterwards. If it was OK for the OC Arm to carry a cap gun, what was wrong with my Man 2 carrying a CS baton? In the end, it was all brushed under the carpet.

Being in the RAF gives you an enormous sense of pride, a feeling that you are part of something bigger and rather special. Being on a squadron magnifies that feeling – proud of what you do and proud to be a part. Every squadron has its own crest and a motto. These were displayed everywhere around the squadron buildings, often on the aircraft and also on the uniforms. The crest would be made into cloth patches that could be sewn onto flying suits and overalls so that the wearer would instantly be associated with their squadron. In later years, Velcro was used for the badges because during conflict you wouldn't want to wear anything that gives the enemy any unnecessary details; the Geneva Convention says that all a captured service person has to reveal is their name, rank and service number.

It is not uncommon for people to create unofficial badges, T-shirts, artwork; you name it and it's probably been done. These unofficial designs not only identified the wearer as belonging to a squadron, but also to a specific trade or having taken part in a deployment, exercise or detachment. For example, the line Armourers' badge at Kinloss, worn on their overalls, had an image of a Nimrod in flight, the union flag in a corner, and their name and the word 'Armourer' proudly embroidered. Any Armourer who worked (or had previously worked) on the line could wear the badge. They would have to buy it for themselves. Normally someone on the squadron or section would take the lead in designing the badge, and ordering in stock. They would sell them through the tea bar so that any profits would help fund a social event, and when people joined the squadron they could buy one straight away.

The following picture shows a couple of badges Tony acquired during his time:

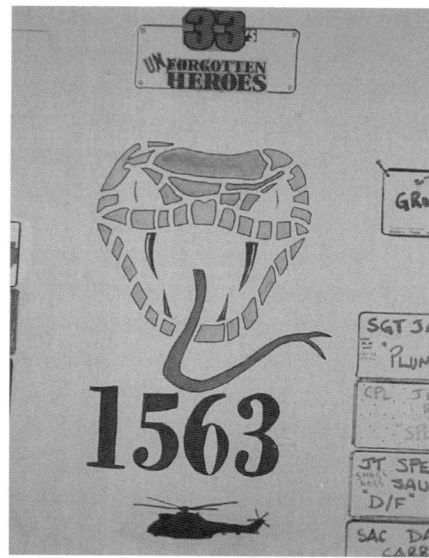

Above left: Overall badges. (Tony Lamsdale)

Above right: 1563 Flight Pumas in Iraq. Squadron wall art. (Mark Bean)

SQUADRON LIFE

Above and below: Armourers' badges. (Mark Bean)

Small bomb containers (SBCs) getting prepped. (Dick Lindsay)

Loading small bomb containers with 4lb incendiary bombs. (Dick Lindsay)

SQUADRON LIFE

Ready for loading. (Dick Lindsay)

Carrying the .303 ammo out to the aircraft, RAF Kirton 1940. (Dick Lindsay)

THE RAF'S ARMOURERS

Getting the guns ready to load, RAF Kirton 1940. (Dick Lindsay)

Belts of .303, RAF Kirton 1940. (Dick Lindsay)

SQUADRON LIFE

Loading the .303, RAF Kirton 1940. (Dick Lindsay)

Winner of best dressed Armourer, Nick Snowdon replete with a belt of 30mm next to a Vampire. (Dick Lindsay)

THE RAF'S ARMOURERS

Above and below: HAS art, Tornado GR4 squadrons, Kuwait, 2002. (Mark Bean)

SQUADRON LIFE

Buccaneer in a HAS. (Bob Worthington-Harris)

Putting a 1,000lb bomb on to the Hunter. (Bill Morton)

THE RAF'S ARMOURERS

CBU and 1,000-pounder on a Tornado. (Mark Bean)

See-in crew waiting for the jets to return, Cold Lake. (Mark Bean)

SQUADRON LIFE

Y loader and 1,000-pounder with 117 tail unit. (Mark Bean)

Y loader and Paveway IV, 617 Squadron, Cold Lake. (Mark Bean)

XIV Squadron Tornado loaded with 5 x 1,000lb bombs. (Mark Bean)

Chapter 5

EOD

'Prep the pigstick, this is a nasty looking bugger and I'm going to smeg it!' Not your everyday sentence, and even an Armourer wouldn't utter those words regularly unless they were engaged in the disposal of bombs. In fact, some Armourers would never hear it issued in anger in their career unless they were 'chosen' to join the ranks of an Explosive Ordnance Disposal (EOD) team. It would be impossible to document the history of Armourers without discussing EOD, which is also known as bomb disposal; the terms are interchangeable and represent a very niche and skilled branch of the Armourers' trade.

The first bomb that failed to detonate created a need for someone to go and 'deal' with it. It's just like dealing with fireworks. If you have ever set off fireworks in your back garden, the chances are that at some point one of fireworks failed to do what it was meant to: the Catherine Wheel that refused to spin, the Roman Candle that issued no light, or the rocket that didn't shoot skywards. The advice for dealing with malfunctioning fireworks is to wait, then wait some more, and once you have waited a long time, approach with caution and a bucket of water. Drop the offending article in the bucket of water then dispose of it safely. Clever people have two buckets of water, the first one to throw over the firework, and the second one to put the thing in.

Imagine the same problem but magnified. Think of an airfield that has just been bombed by enemy aircraft; think of 500lb of high explosive wrapped in a steel case that has been dropped from a great height. It is now sat there, partially buried, right in the middle of the entrance way to a vital building, the fuel store perhaps. It sits there with an air of malevolence and the threat of detonation amidst the chaos of rubble, broken glass and steam pumping out of fractured pipes. Not nice, and it certainly limits the use of that area because you can't have people running around nearby, which in turn means you cannot access the fuel stores. And what would happen if the bomb went off? Let's not go there.

The history of bomb disposal stretches way back into the mists of time. The Royal Army Ordnance Corps were the go-to regiment for many, dealing with all the unexploded cannon and artillery shells that littered the battlefields and training grounds. If they didn't happen to be available, enthusiastic amateurs were always on hand. One tale from the First World War recounts that 45 Squadron RFC, while serving in France, had a hole in their runway. On investigation it was found that the hole was caused by an unexploded British anti-aircraft shell. Members of the investigation team were not experienced in dealing with unexploded bombs (UXBs) and the team was most likely made up of willing volunteers from the camp, probably ground crew because shovels and manual labour were involved. In this case a little bit of shovel work and a very gentle walk carrying the shell somewhere safe for disposal solved the problem.

By the end of the First World War bombing raids were commonplace, and during the Second World War rapid developments in air power led to the ability to deliver death and destruction on a grand scale. Air raids on both military and civilian installations, and the number of mines being laid out at sea by the Allied and Axis forces, caused problems that needed specialist personnel to sort out. All three services saw the need for action and started creating teams of specialists to deal with the increasing quantities of UXBs. The Royal Navy took responsibility for dealing with all things nautical: torpedoes, mines etc. The RAF took on the task of UXBs dropped by aircraft (hostile or friendly) especially around RAF stations, and the army picked up the rest.

RAF Armourers were already well established as a trade and highly trained in the world of explosives, so it was natural that they would move into the busy area of bomb disposal. It didn't take long for specialist courses to be set up at stations around the country. One such station, the RAF Armament School at Manby in Lincolnshire, started running week-long courses in unexploded bombs. This was very early in the war and nothing was known about German bombs, so pupils were given instruction on the bombs and pyrotechnics used by the RAF instead. All the graduates must have left brimming with confidence and eager to take on their first job! There is nothing like a war to stimulate change and, in some cases, improve collaboration; it was not uncommon for members of the army or navy to attend RAF courses and vice-versa. Also common were cross-service postings that could see, for example, a naval engineer working with their RAF equivalents. This working across the services promoted the advance of knowledge, working practices and technical development – something that is still true and practised today.

The response to the need was rapid, and by September 1940 188 RAF armament NCOs were training in bomb disposal. They were deployed around the country at eighty RAF stations and were supported by mobile teams. The 'X stations', as they were known, provided rapid response teams to deal with the ever-increasing number of UXBs.

War has always caused some civilian casualties, people in the wrong place at the wrong time, but during the Second World War the emphasis changed significantly. The Luftwaffe targeted industrial areas, and the proximity of houses and civilian infrastructure meant the population was on the front line. When you enlist, an unwritten part of the job description is that you may be shot at, bombed or killed in an unpleasant manner. This is not something the civilian population had signed up for, and the dread of a raid, the routine of blackout, sleeping in shelters and constantly listening for the wail of the siren takes an immeasurable toll on morale. The dropping of bombs on an area populated by civilians is as much about fear as death and destruction.

The working environment for the bomb disposal teams was pressured, to say the least. One operative, Flight Lieutenant Charlton, was awarded the George Cross. His citation from the *London Gazette*, dated 21 January 1941, reads as follows:

> Flight Lieutenant Charlton is responsible for all work in connection with enemy bombs in an area comprising the greater part of two counties. Both by day and night, during recent months, he has dealt with some 200 unexploded bombs. He has successfully undertaken many dangerous missions with undaunted and unfailing courage.

This single-handed mission in Wiltshire and Gloucestershire, during September and October 1940, involved dealing with about three live bombs per day.

Flight Lieutenant Charlton was not the only one working long hours at a relentless pace in life-threatening situations, using equipment that was constantly evolving against weapons that were evolving just as quickly. The heroism of all involved saved countless lives and untold destruction of vital equipment and infrastructure.

In April 1943 (the RAF seems to have a fascination with April for key events), six bomb disposal squadrons were formed and overseen by their own wing. The squadrons saw service in many theatres of war, including Normandy, and one squadron, 5131, continued the tradition right through until its disbandment in 2020.

An RAF EOD team was normally three people. Man 1 was in charge, and was either a snec or an officer. The remaining two members were drawn from the ranks and had specific jobs. They were there to support the man

THE RAF'S ARMOURERS

1. Their duties included prepping the kit, discussing the job and acting as a 'sounding board', organising comms, safety and security of the area, driving, and first aid. As a team, each member was trained to deal with all these aspects, however it was the man 1 who made the approach to the UXB. They called it 'the long walk', so the more the others did, the less the man 1 had to worry about. The structure was the epitome of teamwork; the more you worked with people, the better you knew them and could anticipate things. Even down to making the perfect brew. Your EOD journey started with training, and the EOD training was some of the best you would ever receive.

Man 1 would attend the 8B1 course at the Defence Explosive Ordnance Disposal School (DEODS). The DEODS course was intense and covered a lot of theory as well as hours of practical assessment. To pass the course you had to complete the written exams and the evaluation.

DEODS also ran 8B3 (Man 2 Cpl) and 8B4 (Man 2 SAC) as well as pre-deployment High Threat and Mine Clearance courses. Everyone who served on 5131 would have attended one of the DEODS courses depending on their rank and role. The station EOD man 1 would attend DEODS then go on to attend AEOD. Most station EOD staff would do their AEOD course, which for many years was run at RAF Wittering, with regular forays to RAF North Luffenham to practise EOD techniques. The AEOD course was very intensive and lasted for four weeks. It started with theory and covered subjects such as the history of explosives, and the difference between an explosion and detonation. As a matter of interest, the difference boils down to rate of burn, or for the chemically and physically clever, the rate at which material creates gas as it burns. An explosion has a burn rate up to 300m/s, whereas a detonation is between 3,000 and 9,000m/s. Physics, chemistry and thermodynamics were covered as part of the process of learning about explosive substances and their characteristics.

This subject was also covered in the 8B1 course, but in much greater detail. Other subjects covered included the making of explosives and methods of delivery (rocket, bomb, mortar, etc.) and recognition of different ordnance ('It's a bomb' doesn't really help much when it comes to working out how to make it safe). Recognition was a massive subject and included how to identify different fuze types, as well as extensive research on Warsaw Pact weapons (our main antagonist for many decades) and chemical warfare. Demolition methods, EOD equipment, incident management and communications procedures were also key elements of the syllabus. Throughout the course there were endless opportunities to put the theory into practice. Some operators also went on to complete the tracked vehicle driving course, which allowed them to drive the Spartan or Scimitar (CVRT) armoured vehicles sometimes used by EOD teams.

EOD

EOD CVRT with crew. Ade Thorne is in the upper turret. (Ade Thorne)

At the end of training you were able to deal with all manner of UXBs, including old items uncovered by members of the public, items inadvertently dropped by aircraft on training sorties, range clearance and improvised explosive devices (IEDs). RAF EOD teams were also trained to deal with ejection seats and miniature detonating cord (MDC), which is fitted to aircraft canopies to assist the ejection process. A crashed aircraft represents a significant hazard to the public, a military one more so because of the equipment it carries. Tony went on the AEOD course in 1993:

> I did a lot of training in the RAF, but the AEOD course was the best. Initially I didn't want to go, but choice didn't factor into things so off I went. From day one the pressure was on to work hard and learn. The instructors were all great and really knew their stuff. They were friendly but tough on you. They recognised those who were grafting, and really supported you throughout. You learned so much on that course and came away stuffed full of great info. More importantly, you felt like you had really achieved something. I absolutely loved it.

THE RAF'S ARMOURERS

The two main EOD roles were a posting to 5131 Squadron, which meant you were either a full-time operative responding to callouts or attached to the training school, or a war role on your station as part of an airfield EOD team. If war broke out, keeping aircraft flying was critical and every RAF station was a potential target for bombing. To counter the inevitable problem of UXBs stopping operations, a station would have Armourers trained to deal with whatever came their way. Operatives had their primary duty, such as working in a bay or small arms, but during conflict would form up into teams of three and be ready to deploy with whatever they were tasked with.

During the Cold War every station held regular exercises, at least two every year. This was to test the operational capability and iron out any issues before the team had to face the real thing. These exercises were when the station EOD teams had their fun. Sometimes teams from 5131 would deploy to stations, especially during a taceval (tactical evaluation), and if it all kicked off for real then 5131 would be leading the way to the conflict to support whichever squadrons were deployed. Keeping aerial superiority in battle is key, and you can only do that if you can keep your airfield open and operating.

The equipment used varied from state-of-the-art, ground-breaking and revolutionary, to things that wouldn't look out of place in a museum. Kit such as the 4021 Locator and the Wheelbarrow, a remote device for inspecting and rendering safe UXBs and IEDs, were definitely in the first category. You could also find yourself wrestling with mine detectors, trepanning gear and steamers, all from the Second World War; sometimes the old methods really are the best. The nature of the job meant that nothing was left to chance, so kit was doubled up. If you needed one you carried two; if you needed two you carried four. There's nothing worse than getting set up for something to fail then finding you don't have a spare; you can't pop into your local hardware shop to get another. Of course, 5131 Squadron had absolutely everything available to it and was at the forefront of testing new equipment and techniques. The station teams were equipped based on operational needs and who was in charge of the inventory. The more imaginative inventory holder could have a very well-equipped section, and never an eyebrow would be raised as long as the equipment could be produced at inspection time, or a record of its demise produced. Some of the front-line flying stations, typically in Germany, would have almost as much kit as 5131 because it wouldn't be sensible to start transporting kit to Germany after the expected attack from the Warsaw Pact. It was all about being ready.

A fairly typical set of kit for an airfield EOD team would provide everything needed to deal with the more common types of munitions used

Ade Thorne showing off his Wheelbarrow. (Ade Thorne)

by aggressors. A team would carry some form of locating device such as the 4021 Locator or the Second World War Mk4 Metal Detector. The former was a neat bit of kit and with practice could tell you not only where an object was, but also its depth and potential dimensions; this enabled the operators to provisionally identify the UXB before they even saw it. The latter was great because by the time you got it out of the box, assembled it and started it working, the bomb would have gone off, thereby saving you the trouble of any serious sweaty moments. The Mk4 did absolutely wonderful service during the Second World War and subsequent years, and will have saved countless lives, but technology moves on and, with the best will and most dedicated training in the world, deploying 1940s gear in the 1980s and 1990s could leave the operator feeling somewhat like a living exhibit in a museum. That said, if the Mk4 was all you had and there was an airfield full of UXBs all hidden in soft mud, then you used it and were thankful. Spades and shovels were common hand tools because if you found something buried, you needed to be able to clear away the debris and soil to get to it. Pickaxes and sledgehammers were carried for the same purpose. There would be empty sandbags, big containers of fuller's earth for dealing with any potential chemical weapons, boxes of NBC gear (suits, gloves and boots), plastic bags (large), blue roll, miles of bodge tape, binoculars, miles of black and tan cable, batteries, pens, paper – and the list goes on.

A key part of the EOD kit was the means to render UXBs safe. This required different types of explosive devices such as PE, detonation cord and cartridges to operate the pigstick and Rocket Wrench. You also needed detonators and miles of electrical cable. Twin cable twisted together, known as 'black and tan', was the cable of choice, and each team would carry two cable drums full (at least 150m) and probably two spare rolls. You also needed an electrical power supply to initiate the carts or detonators. The Shrike, a multi-circuit unit capable of generating about 400V, was the method of choice from the 1980s, and each team would carry two (one for use and one spare).

Render-safe (the hopefully self-explanatory phrase) gear would include the pigstick, a stainless-steel tube that fired a jet of water powered by an explosive cartridge. This was particularly useful for dealing with IEDs or IEEDs, the collective names for terrorist devices, because firing a high-powered jet of water cut through cables and disrupted the circuits, ideally without initiating the device, and potentially enabled the gathering of intelligence (components used, methods used, etc.). The Rocket Wrench was a wonderful invention and useful for removing nose and tail fuzes very quickly. Two opposing steel tubes, like a Catherine Wheel and a central clamping mechanism, worked to extract a fuze from a UXB at high speed. The Rocket Wrench was powered by two explosive cartridges that imparted spin. The forces unscrewed the fuze from its pocket, and cleverly placed bungee cords provided pulling force to withdraw the fuze once it reached the end of its thread. These are examples of remote render-safe procedures. This approach was ideal because while the man I had to approach the weapon and attach the Rocket Wrench or place the pigstick, they were able to withdraw and fire the items remotely, which was by far the safest way. The more traditional method was to approach the UXB with a bag full of tools, all non-ferrous, and a slightly sweaty pair of hands. The tool kits used now bear a remarkable similarity to those used during the Second World War, and for good reason; contents have been proven to work countless times. Tools would include screwdrivers, mallets, measuring tapes, drifts, punches, hand drill, bodge tape, pencils, chalk and a stethoscope. More on this later.

The range of techniques for dealing with UXBs is varied and often depends on factors such as location, the age of the device, how the device has been armed, potential damage, and operational pressures. A UXB on a runway is easier to deal with than one next to a hospital because the one on the runway can be blown up in situ; all you have is a crater to fill in and you're back in the business of flying aircraft. The logistics of evacuating a hospital are horrendous, so it is likely that an EOD team will have to render it safe and then remove it for disposal.

Many station EOD teams were equipped with armoured vehicles such as the Scorpion or Scimitar to allow them to deal quickly and efficiently with UXBs in remote or uninhabited areas such as the airfield. The 30mm Rarden cannon dealt very effectively with a UXB. The team would roll up all nice and safe behind the armour plate, then locate the UXB and identify it, often without even getting out of the vehicle. Assuming it was high explosive (HE) or incendiary, and not a biological or chemical weapon, then it would be a case of loading the cannon and smegging it! Why not smeg a chemical weapon? Well, you have to be certain of consuming all the contents completely, and firing a 30mm cannon shell does introduce an element of chaos in that respect. Better to 'bag it and bin it', that is, deploy the team in NBC gear and deal with it in a different way. After removing or disarming the fuzes, you might be able to puncture the shell casing using a shaped charge and burn the contents in a more controlled manner. Sometimes the best method is to leave things well alone until later. A UXB on the edge of an airfield with no one around could be cordoned off and left until the immediate threat of attack is over.

If the UXB absolutely has to be dealt with because it's near a vital installation, then the team have no choice – the UXB has to be made safe. As many people as possible would need to be evacuated, and clearly defined cordons set up. This is as much about the safety of the team as the surrounding population; you don't want grandad wandering up to the bomb and asking for a light just as man 1 is extracting the fuze. It could be a tad distracting, and anyway, smoking is bad for you. The team need to be adept at co-ordination and communication. They must be able to liaise with all the other agencies on the scene and clearly state what is needed. The EOD operatives would be considered the experts and in control of the situation. This avoided enthusiastic amateurs butting in and ruining everyone's day. The AEOD Reference Guide issued to station commanders contained the following stark message:

> **REMEMBER:** UNIT EOD OPERATORS ARE A SCARCE COMMODITY AND USUALLY ONLY MAKE ONE MISTAKE. CARE SHOULD BE TAKEN WHEN ASSESSING ANY PARTICULAR INCIDENT TO ENSURE THAT THE PRIORITY GIVEN DOES NOT PLACE PERSONNEL OR EQUIPMENT AT UNNECESSARY RISK.

Once the team (notice the use of the word 'team' throughout; irrespective of rank the team would function as one, with each member knowing their role and looking out for the others) have controlled the area and gathered the local intelligence (the time the UXB was dropped, number of suspected UXBs, etc.) they would formulate a plan. This involved the man 1 approaching the device – the long walk. The man 1 might choose to wear a bomb suit, assuming one is available. This is a heavily armoured suit designed for safety, not speed or comfort. If you think that wearing a face mask in public is inconvenient, try doing your job wearing a suit that can weigh around 80lb and a full-face shield.

Having completed the long walk and arrived at the UXB, the next step for the man 1 was to identify it and work out a plan for rendering it safe. They might find that the UXB was making a noise. For example, a ticking noise might indicate that a timer was working. This is where the stethoscope could be used to listen, placed gently on the UXB near to the fuze; it might be possible to hear if anything was happening. Of course, bomb sites tend to be chaotic places. There may be the sound of water running from a burst pipe, gas or steam escaping, or even the sound of falling masonry and debris. This was another reason for clearing and controlling the area around the UXB; it limited the chaos slightly.

In terms of identification, an amount of digging might be required to uncover the UXB and reveal its markings. Assuming the markings were still legible, books would be consulted and, depending on the scenario, the man 1 may be in communication with their man 2 – but radios have a nasty habit of emitting electrickery (a term used by Armourers to refer to pretty much anything relating to matters of electricity), so they would have to be careful to avoid setting the thing off. Formal identification of the bomb and any fuzes would lead the operator to the correct procedure for removing the fuzes and thereby rendering the UXB safe. Remember that 1,000lb of HE is perfectly safe until you introduce a more unstable compound that can detonate. The fuze contains the means of detonating the HE; remove the fuze and the biggest threat from the bomb is the damage it would do if you dropped it on your foot. Unless, of course, it is a really old unexploded UXB. That is a totally different ball game because the chemicals in explosives degrade over time and can become very unstable. Even more unstable than your favourite auntie at Christmas after a few glasses of sherry.

Digging out is a mucky business. (Ade Thorne)

Back to removing the fuze. Assuming you have correctly identified it and its mechanisms, you may decide to unscrew it using the tools you brought with you. First you would have to break the friction lock of a very fine screw thread; the fuze would have been fitted by a highly professional Armourer using the proper tools in a safe environment. The fuze would have been torqued in place, then the bomb would be fitted to an aircraft, flown an unknown distance, and dropped at height and speed to land where you have found it. All of this makes for a very unhappy bomb. The easy way to remove it would be the hammer and chisel technique – surely enough force will get the blighter moving? Don't fancy that? Thought not! The sensible operator opted to use the specialist spanner, assuming they had one, and as little force as they could get away with. Gently, gently, all wearing 80lb of gear. Assuming you could break the friction lock and start unscrewing the fuze, all you now needed to do was continue until the fuze could be removed from the pocket. Oh, and you had to be careful you didn't allow the fuze to touch the side of the pocket as you lifted it clear in case it went bang. It's not uncommon for fuzes to have anti-handling devices such as mercury tilt switches or even timers to prevent them from being removed. Also, it is impossible to tell with any degree of certainty what damage has been done during impact, so even a fuze with no anti-handling devices could be sat there, all innocent-like, until someone starts to tamper with it.

Once the fuze has been removed, it is placed in a strong metal box and removed to a safe place for later disposal. The bomb itself may well be left where it is or, given that it is now much safer to handle, could be removed somewhere safer and disposed of like the fuze. Occasionally there may be reasons why the fuze cannot be removed. It might be too damaged, unreachable or have anti-handling devices fitted. If you cannot remove the fuze, you have to remove the explosive. There is a technique developed during the Second World War for just such an event. The man 1 would drill a couple of holes in the bomb, known as trepanning, and then use steam to melt the HE and extrude it. The steam would be fed into one hole and the 'melted' HE extruded out of the other. This was not a job to rush. It could take hours to safely steam all the HE out of the UXB, and all the while the team would be in danger and the area around the UXB would be out of use.

Dealing with UXBs is a stressful and highly pressured job. The skill of the operators is exceptional, and their safety must be a priority. The photograph opposite is taken from the AEOD Reference Guide that was issued to station commanders, to remind them that reading the book does not make them an expert.

EOD

'Knowledge of the guide does not make an instant expert'.

Illustration from the AEOD Reference Guide. (Tony Lamsdale)

It might sound like an obvious statement to make, but think of the pressure a CO would be under where UXBs are involved. The station and its operations are their sole responsibility, and during a war or even an exercise scenario the adrenaline can flow. It wouldn't be the first time someone had issued an order to solve one problem and then very quickly caused themselves another, much more serious problem. 'Just pop along and get rid of that FAB250 will you please, Chief,' may sound innocuous, but not if the FAB250 in question is a Warsaw Pact weapon that has been dropped by a MiG, landed on the runway, and bounced along for about 500m before coming to rest right next to a fuel store that holds the station reserves of Avgas.

To further complicate things, the biggest threat in the Cold War was dealing with NBC (nuclear, biological and chemical) weapons. Nuclear weapons destroy large areas, and the subsequent fallout means the area is unusable for years. It is possible to survive a nuclear strike, but if you do, you have to be able to survive the fallout, too. Chemical and biological weapons don't cause the same damage to infrastructure, but the chemicals released can remain on surfaces or in the air for a period of time. When those substances come into contact with skin or are ingested the results can be fatal. Staying safe means being able to operate in NBC gear. The suits, boots, gloves and respirator can all provide limited-time protection from all the nasty stuff, provided you know what you are doing. A lot of EOD training involved being fully dressed in NBC gear because nothing beats wearing the kit and putting the theory into practice. Getting dressed properly takes on a whole new meaning because the consequences of an ill-fitting seal or glove could be fatal. Everyone was taught NBC drills as part of their basic training, including how to spot the effects of the different chemical and biological hazards, and how to deal with them. Tablets and injections were the order of the day. Decontamination was another technique practised endlessly, because practice makes perfect, or at the very least, familiar. That familiarity with the process meant that when it came to doing the job for real, there was an element of instinct that could make the difference between life and death.

Sometimes it was easy to become a bit blasé about the nuclear threat. In the early 1990s, Derek Binnie was working at the nuclear site at RAF Brüggen in Germany – also referred to rather euphemistically as the Supplementary Storage Area (SSA). He had been given the job of putting together the new Manual Handling Assessments document. One day during Weapons System Training, in Derek's words 'a QA from hell', he was about to take charge of a convoy at building 331 and was waiting for the Police Building Guard to arrive. A nuclear scientist from Aldermaston was observing the process, and was standing waiting with Derek. To break the slightly awkward silence, Derek decided to indulge in some idle chat:

> For some reason I started talking about risk assessments, and chose lifting, with an example being the weight of the SA weapon transport trolley towing arm. He rebuffs with, 'Oh, that's interesting. I've just carried out a risk assessment on the possible effects of a nuclear accident at Aldermaston and how it may impact the Reading area.' Suddenly the fact that an SA towing arm weighed 80lb became less important … I think I came back with, 'Looks like it might rain.'

The importance of EOD training has been discussed earlier. As a member of an AEOD team, you would continually be undertaking additional training to keep your skills fresh and current. This training could take various forms, including team get-togethers to go through all the kit, checking and cleaning everything. It could be a theory session where you get the books out and go through bomb and fuze recognition or render-safe procedures, or it could be more practical.

A lot of the sessions involved drawing explosives from the bomb dump and spending the day on a range or at a designated area on the airfield. Of course, you had to warn people if you were going to blow things up, so written permission would need to be sought from the station commander, and Air Traffic Control had to be informed. You'd also let the RAF Police and the station fire section know. To be honest, you could often end up with quite an audience because people are fascinated by things that go bang. A typical session might involve making shaped charges from tubes of steel filled with PE with a copper disc on one end. Some gash steel plate imitates the skin of the bomb – it was best to use that rather than raid the stack of 1,000-pounders from the dump. If you were lucky and had a drill bomb with fuze pockets you could practise using the Rocket Wrench. Even stocks of life-expired pyrotechnics or misfired rounds provided an opportunity to practise demolition.

Handling PE, det cord and fuzes required concentration and attention to detail – the more practice the better. Wiring in the det was the key part of the job, and all the team members were taught this as part of their training. It was important that everyone on the team could carry out all the tasks, partly so that they could keep an eye on each other, but mainly because if the man 1 was 'taken out' for any reason, the team could carry on with the task and not have to wait for a replacement or abandon the operation.

You shaped and placed your PE on the object to be smegged using a pencil to make a hole ready for the detonator. Then you would prep the black and tan by stripping the ends of the outer sheath to expose bare wires. You tore off strips of bodge tape to seal the connections and stuck them on yourself, somewhere handy; you always ended up covered in bodge tape! And you needed to make sure you had enough slack cable to create snatch loops. At this point it was prudent to clear as many people from the area as possible. Whoever was wiring up the det needed to stay and there might be one other, possibly the instructor or someone to help pay out the cable on the way back to the firing point. Once everything was set up and the area cleared, you got the det out from its container. Think of the det as a metal cigarette, with two thin wires coming out of one end. You held it like a cigarette (between your index and middle finger, for the non-smokers), and always towards the end with the wires. If it did happen to go off you might not lose your fingers if you held it properly. Next job was to connect the wires on the det to the black and tan. You would twist bare ends together, seal with bodge tape, and put in a snatch loop or two of black and tan. Once the wires were connected, you would insert the det into the hole you created in the PE. You laid out the cable carefully and made sure it was secured around a stake or held down by a sandbag, because if you tripped on the way back and pulled the cable, having it secured meant you wouldn't pull the det out of the PE. You would then withdraw to a safe distance, usually 100m unless you had some serious concrete and steel to hide behind. You paid out the black and tan as you withdrew and then got back to the firing point. The team would check the area to make sure no one had wandered into the firing area (you'd be surprised). The Shrike would be connected, final safety checks carried out, then the Shrike would be primed while shouting 'Priming', then 'Ready' and finally 'Firing, Firing NOW!'

In an ideal world there would be a large bang, and everyone would sit back thoroughly relaxed and happy with a job well done. Of course, you would still need to check the firing point to make sure everything had gone as planned. Sometimes you didn't get the large bang; not only was this very disappointing, but you also had to work out what had gone wrong. It could have been a loose wire, so you would start by checking the Shrike and connections. Then you'd get the binoculars out and look along the firing cable. Had it snagged? Did everything look OK by the UXB? Worst case scenario, it's the long walk *again*, but this time you would be approaching a UXB to which someone had attached some extra explosives. Generally, you'd find it was a loose wire. In training you were taught to put 'snatch' loops in everything, so if a wire was caught the snatch loop would take up the extra pressure. It cannot be emphasised enough how much thought and preparation went into every job. It was check and check again, talk things through with the team, and then triple-check again.

If you had been unlucky enough to experience a misfire, then it was prudent and strongly recommended that you waited a suitable amount of time before approaching to find out the problem. It's highly unlikely that the det was smouldering and would go off, but you never knew. Operators have been killed returning to misfires too soon, so caution and a strong brew calmed the mind and allowed thinking time for the operator and 'soak' time for the explosives. Sometimes a second set of charges would be prepped near the UXB, so you could just place them, pop the det in, and withdraw quickly with minimum fuss and time. There were so many RSPs to choose from, and the UXB and the circumstances would dictate which you selected. The operators were specialists, and as such had the authority to make their own decisions based on all the factors.

Alongside military UXBs, the threat from terrorists was ever present. Bombs planted at military or civilian targets that are designed to cause maximum disruption even if they don't go off, cause untold disruption, panic and fear. Letter bombs, car bombs, and bombs left in bins, pubs, clubs and shopping centres; all are designed to kill, maim and devastate. Bombs can be made relatively easily with nothing more than a basic knowledge of chemistry, and perhaps electronics if you want to be even more devious. Plastic explosive can be bought, stolen or manufactured. Add to that an ignition device and a handful of scrap metal (nails, screws, ball-bearings etc.) all stuffed inside a food tin or similar, and you already have something deadly. The bomb could be initiated by a crude timer or some sort of anti-handling device, or it could be remotely fired by wire or a mobile phone.

A key part of EOD training covered how to deal with IEDs or IEEDs, and there were specialist training courses for both the man 1 and man 2. 5131 Squadron regularly attended call-outs to suspected IEDs, and station EOD teams were expected to be able to deal with any suspect devices found on camp. From the late 1960s through to the mid-1990s, there were unprecedented attacks on military and civilian people and property, both at home and overseas. The military response to the threat included an increased number of trained EOD operatives, more equipment being deployed to stations, and increased training for all personnel in how to protect yourself, look for anything suspicious, and take control of a potential terrorist threat. Car bombs, mortar attacks and even a letter through the post could pose a threat. You were trained to look out for unexpected letters, anything that may be a little stained or greasy-looking, and watch out if you could smell marzipan because unless mum had sent you a Christmas cake, chances were it was a bomb. For those that don't know, plastic explosives can emit a faint marzipan-like odour. Another unpleasant trick was sending chemicals through the post so that when the unsuspecting person opened the letter, they could be covered in a powder containing something unpleasant such as anthrax. As you can imagine, there were many false alarms, and completely innocuous objects were disposed of, sometimes by being blown up, just because they were 'suspect'. Better that than opening a letter bomb.

The need to deal carefully with any kind of suspicious package could occasionally result in an elaborate practical joke. Ade Thorne recalls being called out to investigate a suspicious device, featuring several protruding wires, that had been sent to the station commander at Cosford at a time when terrorist activity was taking place. Ade and his colleagues headed over from their camp and after taking all necessary precautions they started to investigate the suspicious device. They soon discovered that it was actually a penis enlarger, with additional wires attached. Why it had been sent to the station commander remains a mystery.

The method for dealing with anything was standard, and the initial approach was the four Cs: *confirm* – make sure it is suspicious and not just some sandwiches left lying around; *clear* – get everyone out of the area; *cordon* – put up a cordon of 100m at least to stop people going near the device; and *control* – gather evidence, maintain the cordon, and call EOD.

If the suspicious object was on a station then the local team might attend, and chances are that the 5131 people would be deployed as well, but they could take a while to arrive. The initial action was to gather intelligence from witnesses. What was the item? And where was it? With luck, the team would have a Wheelbarrow, a remote-controlled vehicle, with tracks similar to those of a tank, which is about the size of a wheelbarrow. This could be manoeuvred to the object and its camera used to relay images back to the team. The Wheelbarrow also had a couple of pigsticks mounted on it to disrupt the device. Ideally it would approach, gather the evidence and deal with the item. The same is true of the man 1 if the approach needed to be done manually. Good as the Wheelbarrow was, sometimes you couldn't get it into the right place. In a perfect world the disruption would render the device safe without setting it off; this would keep all the evidence intact for forensic analysis.

Sometimes the EOD team would decide to give the public a bit of a show. Ade Thorne was part of a team that was called out to deal with a suspected sea mine on a beach at Sutton on Sea. Ade describes what happened next:

> There was a big crowd watching from a distance. The beach was all cordoned off. So off we went – the long walk down to the device. The chief took out a little penknife, looked more

EOD blues and twos rapid response. (Ade Thorne)

closely, and said, 'I think it might be a f***ing colander.' To be fair, it did look a bit like a sea mine, only smaller.

Someone asked, 'So what are we going to do?'

The chief replied, 'Two pounds of PE should do it. Go back to the van and collect it, and bring the 4C detector too. We need to look like we're doing something.'

So we went back to the van and told the cops that we weren't quite sure what it was but that we were dealing with it. We stuck two sticks of PE under it and set them off. It nearly hit f***ing Mars, it went that high. A pile of debris came down, then I went out with the locater and did a quick scan, then gave them a thumbs up. We walked back up the beach, and were greeted with a massive round of applause.

Of course, it's always best to ensure that any kind of suspicious device is destroyed, if there is any element of uncertainty about its true identity. The EOD mantra is: 'If in doubt, take it out.'

Another of Ade Thorne's EOD team memories involved weapon testing. After his fitters course, he was assigned to the JP233 trials team; JP233 was a new airfield denial weapon, and Ade was one of the early testers. The trial involved putting the weapon on a rig, fitting some SNEB rockets behind it to simulate the airspeed of the JP233 as it hit the runway, jacking it up, then firing it off.

As the junior member of a three-man team ('man 3'), Ade was responsible for the Wheelbarrows. In the case of JP233, two Wheelbarrows were used, one on each side of the weapon. Each Wheelbarrow had cameras fitted to ensure that the remotely armed fuzes were correctly set up. Ade's job was to check that the JP233 fuzes had been armed, after which he had to pull a cable and move the two Wheelbarrows to a safe location, as quickly as possible. Ade and the other team members, including his boss, would then shelter in a bomb-proof metal hut 100m away. The hut was located in the middle of a large concrete pan, with a massive embankment all the way around it. Meanwhile, the senior officers and scientists responsible for JP233 were waiting safely in an underground bunker. Ade describes what happened next:

At the very first live firing there was one hell of a bang, and our whole shed went back about a foot. The legs were snapped off my chair. I fell out of the hut and saw all these concrete slabs coming down. I quickly got back inside, and we watched the two TV sets in the hut. The initial shock wave had already passed, but we could see smoke coming over which immediately enveloped the hut. And all we could hear on the speaker was an ever more frantic: 'EOD? EOD?? EOD???'

The boss leaned over and said, 'Don't answer them. Give them a few minutes to sweat.'

There were more increasingly concerned utterings of 'Come in EOD. Come in EOD.' I think they genuinely thought they might have killed us. The boss still didn't answer, but as the smoke began to clear he staggered out of the hut waving his arms, coughing and calling out, 'Yeah, we're OK. But maybe 200 metres away next time.'

Garron Clark-Darby had a similar beach-based experience to that of Ade, but with a different outcome:

At Chivenor armoury it fell to the small-arms staff to do any local area bomb disposal work. If it was something nasty, like a present from the IRA (still very active at that time), then we would have called out the army team, but if it was World War Two stuff and the like we would just look it up in the reference books and deal with it.

One day we had a call from the local constabulary to say that a wooden box had been washed up on nearby Saunton Sands, containing what looked like plastic explosives. I was not directly involved but the boys rushed down there, and sure enough the broken box did contain what looked like severely decomposed plastic explosive. You could still see the individual sticks with their wrappers of greaseproof paper, exactly like we had on our own Nobel 808s.

The beach was being evacuated when one of the policemen pointed to the writing stencilled on the box and said, 'That looks like Greek. Why don't I write it down and ask the people at the Greek restaurant in Barnstaple what it means?' He duly did this, while the Armoury team busied themselves erecting a taped cordon, sure that they were going to have to carry out a boyishly entertaining controlled explosion on the beach to destroy this hazard. Eventually the policeman returned looking very sheepish. It turned out that the words on the box actually said, 'Best Cypress Figs'.

But occasionally Garron did get to blow something up:

> The Exmoor area had been used for military training in both wars, so quite a lot of bits used to turn up from time to time, some still live. Also, locals would collect the remnants of the old cast-iron 'Livens Drums' and any shell cases, and sell them for scrap.
>
> One day we had a call from a scrap yard in Bideford to say that they had found what looked like a complete shell in a skip among a load of remnants of other stuff, so off we went. Sure enough, there in the skip was a badly corroded but still very live 3.8in high-explosive howitzer shell, dating from World War Two or earlier. We knew we couldn't blow it in the skip, especially as it was right next to their little office hut, so we very carefully carried it right to the back of the scrapyard and blew it up there. There was a short lull after the explosion, and we all stood up from our sheltered positions. Then suddenly it started raining nuts, bolts, bits of broken glass, and oily fragments of metal, all of which had been thrown up by the blast and had to come down again. We were well and truly, and painfully, covered in crap.

Clearing ranges wasn't a glamorous job, but it was something that had to be done. Using a military range for weapons practice is a common occurrence and the main way our armed forces remain ready for operations. There are a number of ranges around the country, and all are Crown Property and as such are looked after by either the military or private contractors. The ranges tend to be in remote locations, for example Otterburn in Northumberland or Salisbury Plain in Wiltshire, and the public are not allowed to access them. Red flags are flown to show when a range is 'live', that is, being used, but the public are never allowed access even if the range isn't being used. The RAF ranges are used for bombing and gunnery practice. Sometimes practice bombs, and sometimes live weapons, are dropped. A practice bomb is smaller but designed to simulate the behaviour of a full-sized bomb when dropped from an aircraft. On impact they can emit smoke or flame to mark the hit. Using practice rounds is cheaper and safer than using the real thing. Also, because they are lighter, more can be fitted to aircraft so the crew get more opportunities to practise on each sortie. Of course, whether dropping live or practice stores, the area must be made safe after flying has ceased. The range needs to be searched for

THE RAF'S ARMOURERS

Left: Range clearing could be a mucky business. (Ade Thorne)

Below: Holbeach range recovering a CBLS and 3kg practice bomb. (Ade Thorne)

Above: Heavy-duty lifting gear. (Ade Thorne)

Right: Old school. (Ade Thorne)

any unexploded ordnance and cleared of the rubbish such as the remains of the practice bombs. The recovered ordnance is collected together and disposed of safely by the EOD team; usually it is burnt or blown up at the range. This gives the team the opportunity to practise their demolition skills but often involves trudging around muddy, cratered areas in the cold and wet.

Garron Clark-Darby recalls his experience of range-clearing:

> Each time an aircraft dropped a practice bomb or fired a rocket that didn't go off, the Range Officer would make a little Chinagraph pencil cross on a laminated map. When the map was suitably full, he would call us and we would drive down to Pembrey Ranges, which were just the other side of the River Towy estuary from Pendine Sands, home of the Welsh land speed records. We went in our wonderful green Land Rover, suitably armed with wellies, shovels and a packed lunch, as it would be a long day.
>
> That Land Rover is worthy of mention here, being probably the slowest motorised vehicle I have ever driven. It was a short wheelbase diesel, as required for bomb dump use, but with a lockable metal body and doors for security, and with red-painted wings for Bomb Disposal duties. It did have a blue light on the roof, which made us feel very important, but sadly it was the type that just blinked feebly rather than going round and round like a proper one. It is also pretty pointless having a blue lamp to enable you to carve through the holiday traffic when a) there was no siren to go with it; and b) given the slightest gradient even the pensioners on bicycles would overtake us.
>
> Anyway, using the woefully inaccurate map we would wander about the dunes for hours and attempt to locate all the still live (but now damaged or bent) bombs and rockets which we would nonchalantly pick up and place in a big pit we had just dug in the sand. When we had all of them (or thought we had enough, or it started to get dark, or started raining – whichever came first) we would apply some Nobel 808s and a No. 8 detonator to the pile, retire a safe distance, and set the lot off. All of which was very noisy and really good fun for little boys like us. It was made even better when the trips were overseen by a small, wizened Polish warrant

officer from the base, named Ted Plusa. He was old enough to have really fought against the Nazis, so each time we were applying the plastic explosive to the pile of bombs he would have us imagine we were blowing up another bridge to stop the German tanks crossing. A truly great character, just one of many I was fortunate enough to work with over the years.

Sharing a station with the army could lead to some interesting outcomes. Back to Garron Clark-Darby, now stationed at Upavon in Wiltshire. As at Chivenor, it was the army's responsibility to deal with the nasty stuff in terms of unexploded devices. But sometimes it was the RAF Armourers who were called in:

> Being on the edge of Salisbury Plain, one of the biggest army training grounds in the UK, we were always having bits and pieces, such as blank ammunition, handed in to the Armoury by locals who had found it when walking. It just went into the box for disposal (or our private use) later.
>
> One Saturday morning the duty RAF policeman was approached by a local farmer who, in his own words, 'had found some bullets on my land'. He was asked why he hadn't brought them in, and he said the policeman would have to go with him and take a look. So they headed off in the police Land Rover. When the policeman arrived in the field, there in the middle was a stack of green wooden boxes, each with yellow writing saying something like: 'Shell HE 105mm, Qty 1 Off'.
>
> It turned out that an artillery gun team had deployed on that site in the middle of the previous night, presumably during some army exercise, and in the rush to leave had left all their ammo behind. So we put the boxes in our little ammo store and waited for the Royal Artillery to collect them.
>
> The problem came later, when it transpired that the young officer in charge of the gun team had realised that they had lost their ammo, and that he had 'cooked the books' to cover it up. This was fine until the boxes subsequently reappeared, and apparently his all-too-brief army career took a sudden downturn.

Above and left: RAF Wittering EOD Memorial. (Mark Bean)

EOD

Sadly, especially for those in the RAF who trained in the arts of EOD and performed many of the tasks described in this chapter, at the time of writing all responsibility for bomb disposal has been removed from the RAF. Not only has 5131 Squadron been disbanded, but there are no longer any airfield EOD teams. All EOD work within the armed forces is carried out by the Royal Engineers (RE), Royal Logistics Corps (RLC) and the Royal Navy. However, the need for clearing ranges hasn't gone away, and there are insufficient military EOD specialists to do the job. Instead, civilian firms are being employed to clear the ranges. And guess what? They're hiring ex-RAF Armourers with EOD skills to help them.

Bomb disposal badges. (Mark Bean)

Chapter 6

Bay Work

This chapter covers a wide range of different roles or jobs that are just as vital as working in a bomb dump or on a squadron or line. Pretty much all armament kit is specialised, complex and potentially critical in terms of safety and mission, so its preparation and maintenance are highly important and require skills and experience.

Think of a bay as a building or area that specialises in preparing and maintaining specific equipment. Everything needed to support the equipment in question is gathered in the bay to ensure that it is ready to perform its primary role. Carriers, ejection seats, armament ground support equipment (AGSE), missiles, launchers ... the list goes on. All this kit requires somewhere to be stored, maintained, repaired and prepared for use.

Anything fitted to an aircraft is subject to enormous stresses during flight. Take-off, landing and high-speed manoeuvres generate g-forces that can test components to their limits. If you don't believe this, take a look at the wings of the next aircraft you get onto when you're going on holiday. The wings and fuselage will be held together by rivets, and chances are there'll be a few missing! Don't panic though – everything should be fine. During flight there are extreme temperature and pressure changes, all of which can stress components. Over time things can become loose and may fray, crack, distort, twist and corrode (although hopefully not all at the same time). A lot of money is spent on preventative maintenance, flying hours of components are monitored, and the manufacturers of the equipment will specify the frequency of maintenance to ensure that problems are spotted before they cause an issue. Even something simple like a loose wire rubbing against a metal bracket could cause a fire, which is never good on an aircraft. The consequences can be disastrous, so regular checks are designed to spot any issues before they become serious.

Perhaps the most complex and safety-critical piece of equipment is the ejection seat. Since the formation of the RFC, getting pilots and crew away

BAY WORK

from doomed aircraft was a point of much discussion. War is a wonderful way of speeding up the development of new ideas and ground-breaking solutions to problems, and towards the end of the Second World War the ejection seat was born. The company at the forefront of this new equipment was Martin-Baker; they are still in existence today, and still very much at the forefront of this life-saving technology.

An ejection seat is a highly complex and technically advanced bit of gear with many components, each of which performs a vital function in the operation of the seat. In many ways the seat represents just how technically skilled an Armourer needs to be. Precision, discipline, engineering skills, technical acumen, experience and responsibility all come together to keep the seat ready to save a life.

Any station that operates aircraft fitted with ejection seats will have a seat bay. The personnel assigned to work in the seat bay will undergo specialist training courses to gain a qualification (Q) to work on the seat and its associated components. Rocket motors, parachute packs, drogues, canopy breakers, barometric devices, harness systems, firing handles, guide rails, oxygen systems and leg restraints are just some of the components fitted to a seat. All need to work together in perfect mechanical, electrical and explosive harmony, and this requires skill to maintain. Seats are prepared in the bay ready for fitment to the aircraft. They undergo hundreds of checks. Tolerances are checked using precision gauges and tools, functional tests are performed, and the results are recorded. Individual components have their own Engineering Record Card (ERC) carrying their life story from manufacture, with every service and modification faithfully recorded. Every ERC exists in a physical format, although for some modern aircraft, such as Typhoons, all of the data is now entered online. For older aircraft and equipment, there is a mix of paper and digital. Each check is carried out by a qualified specialist in strict accordance with the procedures set out in the AP. The work is then checked by a more senior person and is subject to even more scrutiny. Only when everyone is happy is the seat declared serviceable and ready to be fitted to an aircraft.

The fitment is typically performed by the squadron Armourers, but not always. There are more checks and recording; absolutely nothing is left to chance, and you will never meet an Armourer who doesn't take this job seriously and give it 110 per cent. It doesn't get any more serious than working in a seat bay.

Martin-Baker have a policy of continuous testing and development. They even have their own aircraft to carry out trials.

THE RAF'S ARMOURERS

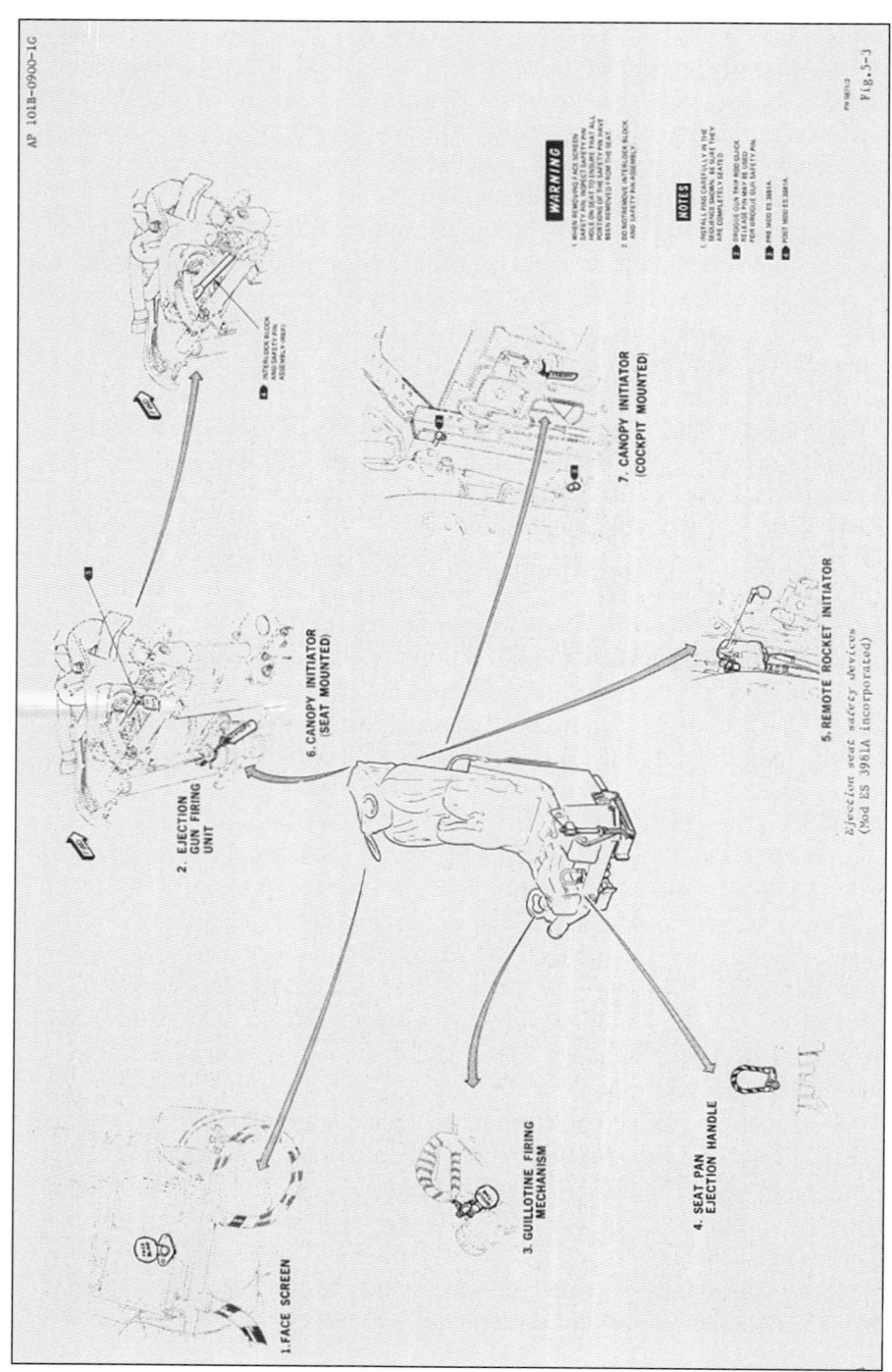

Mk7 seat pins, Air Publications picture. (Mark Bean)

BAY WORK

Ejection seat safety is paramount and all seats have safety pins to isolate certain key components until the aircraft is ready to fly. The diagram shows the pins and their locations for a Mk7 seat.

It's not all hard work; there is always time to relax a little. The second photo below shows a Mk10 seat stand converted to a sailboard.

Martin-Baker test plane, test seat in the rear. (Mark Bean)

Ejection seat stand sailing. (Mark Bean)

THE RAF'S ARMOURERS

Bob Worthington-Harris worked in a seat bay at Leeming airbase. He really enjoyed the job, and said it was interesting, highly technical, and you were always very aware of how critical the work was. Bob describes the processes involved:

> You would have a seat come in on a Monday morning, and you'd strip it down to its last component. So you'd have a drogue gun and BTRU [Barostatic Time Release Unit], and you'd strip those off. Then you'd do the same with the seat pan and linkages. Make sure everything's tickety-boo. Then you'd take off the back of the seat, and finally the components. When the seat's been completely stripped down, you'd clean and degrease it. You'd have a barostat in the bay so that you could recreate the air pressure, and you'd test the BTRU three times to make sure it was working properly. Then you'd put everything back together and perform a series of checks. Basically, you followed the guidance in the manual. We worked on two seats: the Tornado and Hawk. They were very similar but had critical differences. So you had to make sure you followed the steps for each type really carefully. There was a lad I used to work with who wound me up. You'd do all your lock wiring and he would come along and check it. If it wasn't right he would cut it off with snips and you'd have to start again. He wouldn't say anything, just cut it. It wound me up but that was the way things had to be, it would have to be done right. The worst part of the job was putting all the information into the LiTS system on the computer afterwards. That was a nightmare – not what Armourers are trained to do!

Role equipment is common on flying stations. The role bay is responsible for the maintenance and servicing of all the role equipment fitted to aircraft. Items such as pylons, carriers, release units and launchers are all classed as role equipment. Depending on the nature and amount of work on a station, the role equipment work may be completed in one place or may be separated by equipment type. For example, Kinloss didn't have a role bay, it had a carrier bay. This was because the major role equipment was carriers. A flying station with lots of squadrons flying the same type of aircraft is more likely to have several bays dedicated to servicing specific equipment; there may be a pylon bay, a release unit bay and a launcher bay. As with all things military, the right to make things up as you go along always takes precedence.

Hanging anything underneath the wing or fuselage is not as simple as tying it on with string and hoping for the best. There are some very important things to consider such as the flying characteristics of the aircraft. Military aircraft are designed to be adaptable, so fitting different equipment can give you almost endless flexibility that enables you to respond to a variety of different mission requirements. Adding external fuel tanks can greatly increase the operational range, bombs give you the ability to strike a target (air-to-ground), and air-to-air missiles give you the ability to defend yourself and attack hostile aircraft. It's a lot like Lego – the possibilities are endless.

Launchers provide the interface between an aircraft and a missile. For example, in the case of the Sidewinder missile, its launcher, the LAU-7/A, provides a complete launching system including a rail which carries, retains and launches the missile. It also provides electrical and coolant services to the missile whilst it is attached to the aircraft. It has a number of safety devices to keep the missile attached until the pilot actually wants to fire it – a key factor in not shooting down anything you shouldn't.

Whatever you fit (often referred to as 'stores') needs a way of being securely attached to an aircraft during take-off, flight and landing. Every aircraft will have its own Release to Service document that details what can be fitted, and where to. Not everything fitted needs to come back – bombs are a classic example – however, ensuring that an aircraft returns with the pod carrying the latest expensive electronic equipment avoids a potentially career-limiting conversation. The weight of the item to be fitted, and whether it needs to be returned, are key areas to be considered. Also important are what, if any, connections to the aircraft are needed. An external fuel tank will need to be coupled into the fuel system for the engines, otherwise all you are doing is taking some avgas for a jolly. Another consideration is the ability to jettison the attached equipment in an emergency. While it is always preferable to return with the external fuel tanks, having the ability to get rid of them before an emergency landing is better than pranging the kite (aircrew term for crashing!) carrying an extra few thousand litres of fuel. Essentially there are two options when it comes to jettison capability; they are selective and emergency. Selective allows the pilot to specify a specific store or station to jettison, and emergency is 'get rid of everything, NOW!' Not all aircraft had both types; a lot depended on the age of the aircraft and other considerations such as capability.

The most common equipment used to fit stores to aircraft are pylons and carriers. Pylons are normally fitted externally to the wings or the fuselage by riggers, whereas a carrier is designed to fit into a bomb bay, or in the case of the CBLS, onto a pylon. A carrier will be fitted by Armourers and the stores may already be fitted. Both pylons and carriers are designed to be strong enough to bear the weight of the item they are carrying as well as the forces generated through flying. Once fitted they become a structural

THE RAF'S ARMOURERS

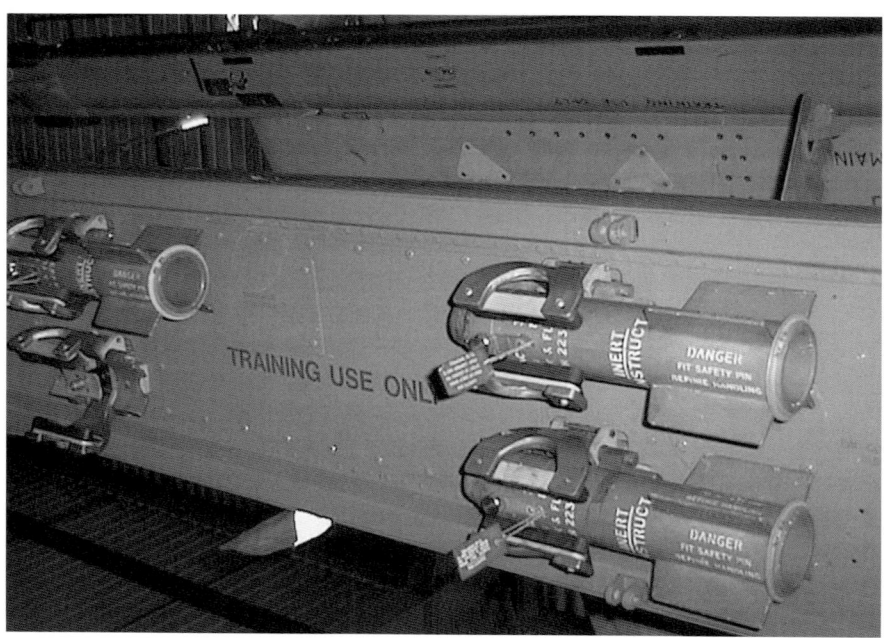

CBLS from below. (Mark Bean)

CBLS loaded. (Mark Bean)

BAY WORK

part of the aircraft, so are typically bolted in place or secured and locked in place using other mechanical methods. For example, carriers fitted into the bomb bay of a Nimrod were located onto a pintle and secured by a locking pin screwed into place. The carrier or pylon acts as an interface between the aircraft and the store so provides the necessary connections between the equipment and the aircraft. It may also include ways of preventing the equipment moving during flight; this is known as 'crutching'.

The release unit is typically fitted into the pylon or carrier in the servicing bay, which makes it easier to make the electrical and/or mechanical connections. It comprises a number of components such as jaws, electrical connectors and, if it utilises explosives in its operation, pistons. The release unit provides a mechanism for mounting the store to the pylon or carrier and may be mechanically or electrically operated. Since the advent of fast jets (have you ever seen a slow one?) it will utilise explosives to ensure that whatever the pilot is wanting to get rid of actually leaves the aircraft.

In some ways it is harder to describe the function of the various components. The best way is to describe how a bomb is loaded onto an aircraft, so here goes. A bomb is prepped in the bomb dump. Part of the prep will be fitting suspension lugs, some electrical leads, and cables. The bomb is then towed to the aircraft line. The riggers will have fitted the pylon to the correct place on the aircraft, secured it, and made all the connections. An Armourer will have fitted the ERU to the pylon. As with all things, there may be exceptions or differences between aircraft or stations. For example, Armourers fit the pylons and ERUs on Typhoons. When the bomb arrives it is taken off the trolley using a loader of some description and is positioned under the pylon. It is then hoisted up to allow the lugs and jaws to mate. An Armourer rotates the jaws to engage them in the lugs. The bomb is now attached to the aircraft with the weight being supported by the pylon through the jaws of the release unit. Once the store is suspended by the jaws, a pin is inserted through a hole in the mechanism to ensure that the geometric lock is properly engaged and stays that way. We don't want any nasty accidents. Next comes the crutching. This ensures that the bomb doesn't wobble in flight, which would not be a good thing. Crutches are nothing more than an adjustable bolt with an articulated 'foot' or disc of steel on the end. There would be four crutches, two each side, which are wound down evenly onto the surface of the bomb. Once secured they are tightened using a torque wrench. If they are too loose the bomb will wobble, too tight and the bomb may not release. Once the crutches are tight it is time to make the connections and, if used, fit the explosive carts. Using explosives to release a bomb became really important with the development of jet aircraft. In the good old days, a bomb could be fitted just as described

THE RAF'S ARMOURERS

HDERU locking mechanism closed. (Mark Bean)

and, at the appointed time, be released by the crew. Gravity would take effect and the bomb would fall to the target. Jets flying at the speed of sound need a rapid way of 'pushing' or ejecting the bomb away from the aircraft, and this is where explosives come in. An explosive cartridge, when fired, creates gas and pressure. This pressure can be harnessed through a cylinder to operate a piston that pushes the bomb away from the aircraft. It's a beautifully simple system and very versatile. Different-sized throttles control the amount of thrust imparted to the store when the carts are initiated. The chambers that house the carts are interlinked in case one cartridge fails to fire. The size of the throttles used depends on your aircraft and what they are carrying. Releasing stores in this way ensures that they are pushed down into the airflow and away from the aircraft. Thrust and airflow cause the connections between the stores and the aircraft to be broken. 'Why would the bomb be connected to the aircraft?', I hear you ask. Well, it allows the crew to finally arm the bomb when they are ready to use it. This is much safer than finally arming it on the ground. Since the inception of Paveway, you can also use connections to pass guidance information prior to release. We really have got very clever with our weapons.

The importance of role equipment cannot be overstated. Nor can the importance of its maintenance. The forces exerted on this equipment are

BAY WORK

considerable, and wear is common. As much as technology has real benefits, nothing wears quicker than electrical cable in flight.

Working in the bay may not be seen as exciting, but it is every bit as important as being a liney, and a whole lot warmer! The job can be technically demanding and make use of all the mechanical and electrical skills learned during your mechs, DE's or fitters course. Drilling out worn rivets, rewiring connectors and gauging tolerances are regular occurrences, and all this brain-draining work needs to be counteracted with regular tea breaks and Uckers. Tony remembers his time in the carrier bay at Kinloss:

> I went to the carrier bay for a few months before I went on my fitters course. It was a good idea to get some experience working in a bay as the move to JT means more responsibility and working at the next level. Working in a bay is more relaxed and structured than on the line. You don't need to rush around so much, and it could be a bit repetitive, but the lads were great.
>
> I spent a lot of time cleaning the carriers when they came back to us. Anything fitted to an aircraft gets covered in dirt, oil and general crud, even if it's in the bomb bay, so the first job was to get rid of all the muck so we could see what we were faced with. Once the dirt was off we would remove the release units, then they would go off to another part of the bay for checking.
>
> I worked my way around the different jobs getting experience of everything, always working with someone else, usually a JT, as most of the jobs needed a fitter, not a mechanic. There was a lot of wiring, and this was always an area which needed careful checking. The protective sheathing could wear through so most of the time we replaced this as a matter of course. Sometimes you had to fit new plugs or connectors, so I got the chance to practise my soldering. That helped when I got to Cosford because soldering is a major part of the FTJ.
>
> There were lots of specialist products used to maintain the carrier. The stuff we used for cleaning and painting the carriers was lethal. Trichloroethylene is nasty stuff and so is Suncorite. You daren't get it in your eye or on your skin; it could really burn, so you had to watch yourself. During training there were some particularly nasty training videos shown on the aftermath of getting burned by this stuff and tales of Armourers who fell into the big baths full who didn't emerge alive.

We were fairly self-contained in the bay, had our own tea bar, and used to go for nights out. Every now and again we would host the weekly Armourers beer call – that could get messy. We also got heavily involved in the regular Armourers 'It's a Knockout' competition, because we had the space and tools to build the games. They were fun days!

Ade Thorne remembers being the victim of an elaborate practical joke while he was doing gun bay work at Kinloss. One of his colleagues was working on a harpoon carrier in the middle bay, and while this guy was away Ade sneaked in and drilled 'SFC' in one of the tiles on the floor. He then returned to his own bay, happy to have left behind a lasting tribute to his favourite team, Southampton Football Club. He thought no more about it, until half an hour later someone came in and asked, 'Have you been down by the harpoon carriers?' 'Er, yes. Why?' 'Because there's loads of water on the floor.'

So Ade followed him into the middle bay, pushed his foot down on the SFC tile, and his heart sank when water spurted out from the holes. Within ten minutes the whole of the bay was covered with water – what Ade didn't know was that this was the result of dustbins full of water being emptied over the floor. Next thing Ade got a call from the training cell next door: 'Has your water gone off? We've got no water.' This was followed by a number of similar calls. It turned out that someone who was in on the joke had turned off the water main, so no one had any water. By now Ade was starting to panic, but at the same time he couldn't believe that his 'SFC' was the cause of such chaos. After all, he'd only drilled down a couple of inches.

He then noticed that, out at the back between the bay and AGSE, there was a JCB digging a trench. Maybe that was the culprit? So he walked over and spoke to the driver. But even the JCB driver had been tipped off. He told Ade that it wasn't him, and that the water main ran all the way down the bay but was only an inch or two beneath the surface.

So Ade sprang into action. He returned to the middle bay and started to try and fill up the holes with araldite. While he was scrabbling around on his hands and knees, Ade's chief walked on with the station commander. 'Thorne, what the f*** are you doing?' A question to which there was no easy answer.

Ironically, all of this happened exactly a week after Ade had been promoted to sergeant.

Back to bay work ... Aircraft that have guns fitted would have a gun bay to support them. It would probably be very close to or part of the armoury because you have to be very careful with guns, even very big ones like

BAY WORK

a 27mm Mauser or 30mm Aden gun, the two most common guns fitted to aircraft. Some aircraft have very specialist installations. The Hawker Hunter had its four Aden guns and ammunition in a pack that was fitted in a bay underneath the fuselage. The whole pack could be loaded by the Armourers in less than five minutes (sometimes).

Bombs are typically transported on trolleys and loaded using winches, hoists or loaders; the AGSE bay will look after all this. Well, they would have back in the day. Now the GSE bay looks after it all because Armourers cannot be trusted to service anything dangerous like a trolley. The S-type trolley, or to give it its proper name, Trolley Weapon Transporting Type S, is the most common type of bomb transportation. It's a flatbed trolley with four wheels and a steering towbar, which allows for greater manoeuvrability. It is easy to work on and maintenance is straightforward: check for lumps, bumps, cracks and damage, correct operation of all components, grease the axles and pivot points, make sure the brakes work, repair the paintwork and make sure the safety items (brake handle) are painted red. Job done! Other kit is more complex and may include a motor. The Y loader is the most basic bomb loading kit; nicknamed 'the shopping trolley', it has wheels that go where they want and a hand pumper hydraulic mechanism for raising and lowering the stores. A step up is the R loader; it is not self-propelled but does have a motor that powers the hydraulic lifting mechanism, so in addition to all the checks mentioned above you need to maintain the motor and hydraulic systems. Some of the kit serves more than one function. The W, or Wendy loader, is self-propelled and is great at loading weapons, but can also be involved in Formula 1-type races where

Armourers on a VAP-60 loader towing a toolkit. (Mark Bean)

F1 Armourer style, Tucson. (Mark Bean)

S Types in the Afghan desert, 2010. (Mark Bean)

BAY WORK

Armourers compete fiercely to be the quickest around the pan/dump, or any space suitable for the chaos and carnage of racing. The current crop of Armourers use the VAP-60, another motorised weapons loader, to race (and load weapons). Successful competition (and loading) required the driver of the Wendy to have one long leg (the other being of unspecified size) to reach the pedal. Design improvements to the VAP-90 mean you now need a short leg instead.

Tony remembers his time in AGSE at Kinloss:

> I spent a couple of months working in AGSE before I went on my fitters course to broaden my experience. At Kinloss we had F types (low, long trolleys for getting in the bomb bay), S types for general work, K types for the buckets of sunshine, and jacks that were used for loading the carriers into the bomb bay. We also looked after the Spartan and Scimitar tracked vehicles used by our station EOD teams. They were fun.
>
> I worked with one of the best, a lad called Corporal Jeff Poole (Bonz) who was the most cheerful bundle of Armourer you could ever wish to meet. A larger-than-life character who knew his way around all things Armourer and specialised in all things entertainment. Every Friday afternoon we used to fire up one of the tanks and go for a little pootle around to make sure it was working. You can have a lot of fun in a tank, especially with Jeff driving and a beach nearby.

Not all stations need large buildings or sections dedicated to a specific role or function. Some stations amalgamate the various roles within an area but have dedicated personnel to perform the different functions. One such example was RAF Lyneham. The Armourers at Lyneham were all based in the armoury, however there were a number of different roles within the one building. The busiest section was small arms, closely followed by the explosives accounting desk and the aircraft bay. The aircraft bay was where the fire bottles and parachute release units were serviced. Fire bottles are operated by an electrically operated fire extinguisher cartridge (EOFE cart), a small but potent little piece of equipment whose only purpose is to spring to life in an emergency. If the pilot (or crew) get an engine fire warning alarm while an aircraft is running, they need to take urgent action. An engine fire is a bad thing and can cause all sorts of nasty problems if left unchecked, so all aircraft are fitted with a fire suppression system. The system comprises one or more canisters of fire suppressant which is fed to the engine bay through pipes. On getting the alarm, the pilot will activate the fire bottle system. This sends an electrical impulse to the fire bottle cartridge, which then explodes, rupturing a metal disc that contains the fire suppressant. The suppressant is released into the engine bay, smothering the fire. This allows the aircraft to land safely (we hope).

Tony describes how he moved from working in the carrier bay at Kinloss to doing similar work at Lyneham:

> I was nearing the end of my fitters course when the flight sergeant came to see me. He wanted to know if I would like to be posted to Lyneham on completing my fitters course. He gave me twenty-four hours to think about it. During one of the breaks I got the Armourers telephone directory out and found the number to call Lyneham. I can't remember who I spoke to, but they assured me Lyneham was OK – fairly quiet and no trips away. There was loads of work in small arms, lots of bullets to count and the fire bottles and PRUs (whatever they are) to service. The Hercs weren't armed other than with a Very pistol, so no Armourers working on the line.
>
> Lyneham ticked all the boxes as my wife had been posted to RAF Upavon, which was about 20 miles from Lyneham, and we already had a house on the quarters. Also, because Lyneham was fairly quiet it would be good to have an 8-to-5 job for a while and settle into normal life again. At that point we had only been married for a couple of years and had spent a good deal of it apart. Kinloss had taken me away a lot, and so had my fitters course. I opted for Lyneham thinking that was me sorted for a couple of years. By then I would be out to Germany, so back at the sharp end – maybe sooner if I was lucky. Things didn't work out that way though.
>
> I arrived at Lyneham in May '92. I drove onto camp and got lost looking for the armoury. I pulled up outside this old prefab type building and asked a chief if he could tell me where the armoury was. 'You've f***ing found it!' was the reply. The chief was a very straight-talking Scotsman who happened to be in charge of the armoury. It was a great set-up (apart from the building, which was very old and tired). There was a chief and sergeant, four corporals, three JTs and five SACs. It was a small set-up and we all worked from the same building but

BAY WORK

with different jobs. The SACs worked in Small Arms, the accounting for the dump was managed by a couple of JTs, I worked in the aircraft bay and we each worked for a corporal and a sergeant, and a chief oversaw the whole thing.

My posting was to the aircraft bay, where I was responsible for the maintenance of the fire bottles (cleaning, servicing and replacing the EOFE carts) and the parachute release units fitted to the Hercs. I also helped out the guys on the explosives desk, counting stocks of ammo, keeping the buildings tidy, issuing ammo and whatever else needed doing. To be honest, it was so small and close-knit we all pitched in wherever was needed as it gave us a bit of variety.

Every few weeks we did a week of duty Armourer, which could be a pain. Lyneham was a busy camp, with loads of people coming through every week either going out to or returning from deployments like the Gulf, Falklands, or wherever. Whenever someone was carrying a weapon, they would need securing in our armoury while they waited for their flight, so you were always getting called out to issue or receive guns. It wasn't a sleeping duty so you carried a pager for seven days, and whenever it went off you called Eng Ops to see what the job was. If I knew it was going to be a busy night I would often sleep on the chairs in the crew room rather than have to keep driving to and from home. It was easier for the lads who lived on camp, but still a pain-in-the-arse duty. You also had to open everything up, make all the teas, keep the whole section tidy, and count the guns at the end of every day.

We all plodded along for about a year, very nicely thank you. I was on the list for Germany and getting near the top, and we had a plan to get my wife posted out there at the same time. Being married in the forces was not a guarantee of being together, and we accepted that, but there were ways you could improve your chances of at least being in the same country.

Then it all kicked off in the Balkans. Before I knew it we had a Herc based in Zagreb flying food into Sarajevo three or four times a day as part of the humanitarian aid mission. The Hercs were soon modified to carry chaff and flare, which are explosively initiated; queue the Armourers to fit said items. The powers that be soon worked out they could send one Armourer to support the Herc in theatre, and they could also support the Ground Engineer. GEs are experienced SNCOs, usually either sooties, riggers or fairies who have undergone special training to qualify them in other trades. A GE would go with every Herc to look after it down route. If the job was big enough, they may take other trades, but often they worked alone. Technically, the Armourer in theatre had to be a corporal, however because we only had four, they opened the job up to the JTs. If you were sent out they made you acting corporal (unpaid) while you were away. That took up the rest of my time at Lyneham until I left the mob in July '99. In fact my leaving do was extremely quiet because nearly everyone in the armoury was away somewhere.

This account is fairly typical of life in the forces. Things changed, and never more so than in the 1990s when there was a significant restructuring of the armed forces. Large numbers of personnel were made redundant, people were given the opportunity to re-trade, functions previously performed by service personnel were outsourced to civilian companies; camps were being shut all over the world and, more significantly, the threat changed. For four decades we had been preparing for major conflict with Russia while fending off other threats from terrorists such as the IRA. In the 1990s we were at peace with Russia, but were drawn into conflicts such as Bosnia, Afghanistan and Iraq. The pattern hasn't really changed since the 1990s; continued scaling back of locations and personnel. More work has been outsourced and yet there is still a need for skilled Armourers so recruitment continues. The work in bays may have reduced dramatically but the RAF still needs people to understand the technology that is fitted to aircraft. It is one thing to fit it but another thing entirely to understand it by stripping it down to its elemental components and becoming intimate with its inner workings. That understanding can be transferred directly to snagging on the line, which in turn can help diagnose problems significantly quicker.

Like many jobs, working in a bay is not for everyone. Bay work can feel very far removed from the front-line squadrons; working regular hours can be boring, especially after the frenetic pace of a squadron or line job. What cannot be underestimated, however, are the skills needed and knowledge gained while working on kit. The experience and knowledge that can be passed on from the old sweats to the young bloods is vital, and the most important aspect is the eye for detail. Bay work involves having real pride in what you do – not accepting even the smallest mistake, going back and re-lockwiring a bolt because you didn't like the last twist you put in the lockwire, double-checking the torque settings, or doing a final electrical test, just to make sure.

Chapter 7

Small Arms

Before we start on the detail, let's clear up what the term means. The term 'small arms' refers to weapons carried by service personnel, as opposed to something like a 30mm Aden gun, which most definitely cannot be fired from the hip.

Like a well-known spread made from yeast extract, and not unlike bay work, working in small arms either appeals to you or it doesn't. As an Armourer in the RAF there is a strong chance that at some point in your career you will end up working in a station armoury. That said, there are many Armourers who have managed to evade this particular aspect of the trade either by luck or through knowing the person on the trade desk at the RAF Personnel Management Centre (PMC).

Small arms work is exactly like working in a bay. The chances are it will involve steady start and finish times, and there will be a duty Armourer whose job it will be to open up and lock up and do all the gash jobs in between. The size of the station determines much of the daily routine. In the early 1990s, RAF Upavon armoury had about four Armourers and fairly flexible hours, whereas 20 miles down the road, RAF Lyneham was much livelier, with numerous comings and goings of guns throughout the day and night.

The station armoury is where the guns are stored and maintained, and within its walls the dark art of weapons servicing takes place. As such, it will be one of, if not the, most secure buildings on site. Typically, a weapons storage and servicing area is built of reinforced concrete, with steel doors and the minimum number of windows (if any). It is designed to repel bombs, rockets and mortars – as well as the challenge of having Armourers working within it on a daily basis – with the security of its contents being paramount.

The keys for the armoury are treated with reverence, and access to them is strictly controlled by means of a list maintained by the senior Armourer on camp and OC Arm. The list is shared with only those who need to know its contents. A need to know is the underlying principle of security within the military; only tell those who need the information based on operational requirements, and everyone else can suffer in blissful ignorance. In addition to the keys only being available to those who are on the list, further security measures ensure that opening the armoury is no easy task.

The keys are held either by the RAF Police or the Station Guardroom, and they are only produced when the requestor shows their RAF 1250 (identity card) and their name is checked on the list. After identity is established the recipient of the keys has to sign for them. Once signed for, the keys need to be removed from the key safe; only authorised people know the combination. The combination is changed regularly and comprises a series of digits that have to be 'dialled' into the safe. The movies make it look easy, but at 7 a.m. on a cold morning when the duty Armourer is suffering from sleep deprivation, getting the safe open can be an insurmountable problem: five left, four right, three left … Oops, too far … Start again! Further pressure can be added by people in the queue behind you; the guardroom can be a busy place in the morning.

Once the keys have been removed from their hibernation, the duty Armourer needs to proceed at once to the armoury and start the unlocking process. The RAF Police or guardroom staff also have an alarm panel in their building and will be looking to see that the station armoury alarms are deactivated properly and within a timely manner. Anything else could indicate a problem and mean a visit from the RAF Police to make sure all is well.

Arriving at the building, the duty Armourer needs to unlock the outer door. Once inside the outer door, they'll secure it behind them. They then face the second door, which will also have some sort of security, most likely a key code or similar. The idea is that, even if someone steals the keys and opens the outside doors, they cannot progress beyond that point. The Armourer opens the second door, heads to the alarm panel, keys in the code to deactivate the alarms, and breathes … From the moment you insert the first key, you have a specified amount of time to gain access and deactivate the alarms. There may even be other steps to perform. Let's just say that whatever time is allocated, it will always flash by in an instant.

The security of weapons is a serious business, so no step is too far, although there does come a point at which you may feel that opening the armoury is more bother than it's worth. The biggest threat is the weapons being stolen by terrorists. There have been times when terrorist organisations have seemed to be bold enough to try anything, so precautions are very sensible. In addition to the threat of terrorists, organised criminals would very much like to gain access to a neatly stockpiled and very well-maintained collection of guns. This is why the main stores of guns and ammunition are never kept in the same building. Small, ready-for-use quantities are issued

SMALL ARMS

for specific purposes such as armed patrols or training, but everything is very tightly controlled.

Even when you're safely inside the armoury there are further controls: more locked doors, keys locked in safes, and bolts all contribute to keeping things secure. Doors to access the servicing room or bay and gun store are kept locked at all times and only opened to allow authorised people to enter or leave. This makes the armoury a very relaxed place because snap inspections lose the element of surprise when the visitor has to bang on the door and ask to be let in. The cards can be cleared away and evidence of purposeful industry can replace the green baize in an instant. The Armourer is nothing if not adaptable and responsive in a crisis; years of training produce lightning-quick reactions and unflappable calmness.

Typically, the gun storage (gun room) and servicing room are separate. The rooms may have trembler switches on the walls and ceilings, all linked to an alarm system. The gun room won't have any windows and it may have only one door. There is a good chance there will be a metal hatch or hatches to issue and receive weapons. The hatch system is an ingenious way of opening up a space big enough to allow a weapon to pass through, but not a person. The opening would be about 24in square and roughly 4 to 5 feet high. The walls are thick, so there is a metal hatch on the inside, with either sliding or hinged doors, and another hatch on the outside. The doors on the outer hatch are hinged to open inwards. The intervening space creates a handy ledge that can be used to keep the paperwork to record the issue or receipt of the weapons and associated equipment.

The process for issue and receipt of weapons is pretty much the same. The Armourer waits for the person to arrive and announce their presence by knocking on the hatch or, if they are observant, ringing the bell. The Armourer then peers through the spyhole in the hatch to check the area. Assuming there isn't a horde of terrorists outside, the Armourer opens the hatch and greets the person with a cheery hello, because customer service is a very important part of Armourer training. There may even be an exchange of banter. Once the introductions have been made, the transaction can commence.

The 'customer' produces their ID card and presents it to the Armourer, who checks their name against the planned issues/receipts for the day. No name on the list, no gun. It may sound harsh, but with good reason. Assuming the name is on the list, the Armourer then gets the customer to complete the paperwork. They will add name, rank and service number, then date and sign for a specific weapon identified by its type and station serial number.

THE RAF'S ARMOURERS

The Armourer retrieves the weapon from its place in storage and 'clears' the weapon. Clearing is the process of proving the weapon is unloaded: check that the safety catch is applied, check no magazine is fitted (remove if present), and expose the working parts by sliding the moving parts to the rear using either the cocking lever or action. This clear sight into breech and barrel shows that no rounds are present. The working parts are held to the rear by the retention mechanism so the customer can see it is 'clear' for themselves. The weapon is handed through the hatch butt first. The customer takes charge of the weapon, ensures it is clear, and then releases the working parts to close the breech and release the action by firing it off (nothing to worry about because it's not loaded!). The final act is to reapply the safety catch.

Handling weapons safely is one of the first things tackled during basic recruit training and is practised annually by all RAF personnel, culminating in live firing on the range. That said, handling a weapon once a year doesn't always ensure that accidents don't happen. Weapons drills are learned through repetition but, like any skill, their effectiveness can diminish over time. Unlike the army, RAF personnel don't carry weapons as a matter of course, only when there is a pressing need. Generally, it's better not to have a weapon about one's person.

It is worth noting that one of the biggest crimes in the military is a negligent discharge (ND), that is, a weapon being fired or pointed at something it shouldn't be. During weapons training it is not uncommon for someone to have 'a bit of a moment' and point a gun at someone, or drop it. Most people have a healthy respect for guns, which is great, but some people are afraid of them, which can cause problems. There are many stories of loaded weapons being pointed randomly around the range, across the firing point or worse, and sometimes even discharged. An ND will involve arrest and, if you are lucky, being marched in to see the CO without your hat by the SWO followed by a lengthy and lively 'discussion' that culminates in a limited career. If you are unlucky someone got hurt or worse, and the consequences could include military prison. So, drills like 'clearing' a weapon are vital; they give everyone on the same side the slim chance of surviving the annual live firing.

Safety and security are the two abiding principles of weapons handling. Operating from the station armoury is all well and good, but sometimes even the RAF deploys armed to the teeth. Exercise Purple Star in 1996 was one such example. Tony takes up the story:

> There were two of us from the Armoury and we took about thirty SA80s and a similar number of Browning 9mm SLPs. These were to be issued to the aircrew when they were flying

SMALL ARMS

on ops. The idea was to make it as realistic as possible. After we arrived, we were allocated an ISO container to store the guns and the rest of our kit. The thing was double-locked, and all the guns were chained up inside so that it was all fairly secure. The keys were kept with the ops office, which was always manned.

On the first day of issuing weapons the crews nominated to fly that day lined up outside the ISO. My oppo was sat in front of a desk and was handling the paperwork. My job was to get the gun, clear it, and hand it over to the recipient once they had signed for it. The crews were all going to draw out SLPs, standard aircrew weapons, but there was a shortage of holsters, so we hadn't been able to bring any. This squadron leader turned up, and as I handed him the pistol he asked for a holster. My oppo replied: 'I'm sorry sir, we don't have any.' The squadron leader responded (in a haughty and confrontational voice), 'Well what am I going to do with this, put it in my pocket and lose it?' To which my oppo said (in a bright and cheery voice), 'I suggest you put it in your bag and take good care of it, sir. You don't want to explain losing a pistol in your care to the CO!'

Armourers 1, aircrew 0.

The armoury in Iraq as pictured is a great example of how to deploy in style.

Working in small arms isn't the most exciting role as an Armourer, and the environment can be claustrophobic. Gun rooms don't have windows,

The Armoury in Iraq. (Mark Bean)

and often the servicing bay can be bleak and dismal. That doesn't mean to say you can't brighten things up a little though. Recruitment is diverse, and people bring many skills with them into the military; sporting prowess, musical genius and artistic flair are all commonplace in the crew room. The latter skill can be exercised in a variety of ways: painting images on the noses of aircraft, designing T-shirts and squadron badges, and adorning otherwise drab walls with artwork designed to transport you somewhere else. Even the simple image of a window looking out onto a green field (virtual reality has been around for longer than you think) is better than whitewashed concrete walls. There aren't many sections that don't have a budding Picasso or Dali, and those that don't paint can purchase the services of one for the price of a crate of beer. Crew room art is infamous, and often coupled with gizzits from around the globe. Flags, uniform, number plates, street signs and weapons (we are Armourers after all!) can all lift the mood of a room and make it a more pleasurable place in which to spend time. The only limit is your imagination, and Armourers have particularly wild imaginations.

There is an unwritten rule that you never leave an Armourer with time on their hands. Your typical Armourer is best kept busy, otherwise beware. If an Armourer is working on a mundane or repetitive job such as servicing weapons, there is a strong chance their mind will wander and seek to spice things up a little in the interests of mental agility and entertainment. The obvious antidotes to boredom are games such as Uckers and cards, but don't dismiss the fun that can be had in the gun room with the lights off. One of our contributors remembers:

> Working in the armoury was boring. It was all servicing pistols and the SA80 – very repetitive. All of us could service a weapon blindfold and do a bloody good job, so you often flashed through the daily quota really quickly. We played a lot of cards. We had a baize cloth and a deck of cards stored in the bottom of a toolbox. The door into the workshop was always locked from the inside so no one could drop in unannounced. We'd get the cards out and play for pennies or matches for hours. Sometimes we would mix things up and play cricket – on the basis that exercise is good for you. You'd go into the gun room and mark a wicket on a wall. An old gun stock serves as a bat and a ball made out of bodge tape is perfect. In our armoury we kept night vision goggles so we would all put on a pair then turn out the lights. It was pitch black in the gun room. We'd use an alley between racks as the wicket and the

SMALL ARMS

batter would defend the stumps to the death. The only rule was don't get caught, and I don't mean by catching the ball. Trust me, night vision cricket is a lot of fun!

One more interesting, or perhaps more challenging, job involving small arms would be a posting to an RAF Regiment squadron. The RAF Regiment was formed during the Second World War to meet the need for defence of RAF stations both at home and overseas. The role had typically fallen to the army, but apparently there was a war on and there weren't enough troops to go round. The RAF Regiment quickly grew to become many squadrons whose primary role was ground defence of airfields and installations, typically those on or near the front line.

During the Cold War, when Germany became the front line, members of the RAF Regiment were stationed alongside the front-line squadrons at places like Laarbruch, Wildenrath and Brüggen, the latter being the home of the Harrier squadrons. Because of their versatility, the Harriers would deploy into forward-operating bases. They could set up virtually anywhere and operate from tented hides using PCP runways or roads to land and take off. Defence of these deployments required troops and ground-to-air weapons such as the Rapier missile. It fell to the RAF Regiment, AKA 'rock apes', to provide the skills. Now rock apes are adept at weapons handling. It is a core skill, whereas most people in the RAF, once they have passed out of basic training, only handle a weapon once a year. The rock apes are also very good at marching. For 70 years their elite band was the Queen's Colour Squadron (QCS), and they were the ones seen parading on ceremonial duties at places like the Royal Albert Hall and the Cenotaph. Of course they are now the King's Colour Squadron (KCS), and are likely to remain so for a very long time given the line of succession. All joking aside, they really are outstanding to see. The rock apes are much maligned and ridiculed by all the services, however their role is vital in that they are expected to defend RAF stations against ground attack, so each squadron is trained in all aspects of fighting including infantry combat, using armour such as light tanks, and artillery. All of this means they need an Armourer (or two) permanently attached to a squadron to take care of the guns.

Everyone who joins the military is taught the basic care of a weapon, including how to clean it, and the rock apes are more proficient than most because they use them all the time. They even develop quite deep knowledge, but they aren't trained as engineers, so when it comes to proper servicing or repair, you need a qualified Armourer – someone who can use the gauges properly and carry out repairs to the required standard to ensure that the

THE RAF'S ARMOURERS

weapons work properly when needed. A posting to a rock squadron is not for the faint-hearted because not only are you expected to be on top of your game servicing the weapons, but you are also expected to be extremely fit and wear green a lot. This can come as a bit of a shock to most Armourers. Fitness is something you had when you joined and is developed to a heightened peak during training, but once you get through training, tabbing miles and doing assault courses is best left to the professionals. To survive on a rock squadron you have to be battle-fit, so these Armourers deserve respect for their endurance and, at the end of their tour, a nice posting somewhere quiet where they can recover and regain the proper levels of fluid and fat intake.

During his time working in the armoury at Brize Norton, Martyn Mander had an interesting insight into the types of small arms that ended up being used by 'unofficial' military sources – in this case guerrilla forces in Rhodesia, shortly before it became Zimbabwe in April 1980. These guerrilla groups included Robert Mugabe's African National Liberation Army and Joshua Nkomo's Zimbabwe People's Revolutionary Army. In December 1979, the Lancaster House agreement was signed following negotiations involving the UK government, Mugabe and Nkomo. As part of this agreement, a ceasefire was imposed, and the guerrilla forces were encouraged to hand over their weapons – this was known as Operation Agila. Martyn takes up the story:

> As part of Operation Agila, camps were set up in Rhodesia where the guerrilla groups would come along and hand over their weapons, which were then piled up in big heaps. All those weapons were then shipped back to Brize Norton, where they ended up in the armoury. We had AK-47s, some made in Russia, others in China. The Chinese ones included a long stiletto-type bayonet. We had fixed ones and folding-butt ones. And we had PPSH 40 submachine guns, which dated back to the Second World War – they were a kind of Russian machine gun with a drum magazine. We even had muskets; the African guerrilla fighters would use whatever they could get hold of. There were so many different types of weapons, and some of them were really classy – the kind of thing you want to take home and put on your wall.
>
> An additional complication was that some guys were trying to smuggle guns out of Rhodesia, a nice AK-47 they'd picked up from the camp. Mostly they'd realise at the airport that taking a gun on board might not go down too well, so they'd leave them behind – so there would be stacks of guns in the

SMALL ARMS

airport toilets. A few did try to smuggle them on board, but they'd get nobbled.

Anyway, the first thing we had to do at the armoury was to write down the serial numbers of all these weapons. There was no room on the racks, so they were piled up on the floor of the armoury – all these classic guns, some of them *really* old. We wondered whether they might have been stolen from the walls of ancient colonial properties!

One day these two blokes appeared – they had long hair and beards, and moustaches. They were wearing boiler suits. They knocked on the door of the armoury, told us their ranks, and said they were from the SAS. And that they were expected. After a few phone calls we let them in. They asked where the weapons were, so we took them into the gun room. Then they started picking up the weapons, examining them, and saying, 'Yep, we'll have this one. And this one …' They picked out everything they wanted, threw them into the back of a 4-tonner, and off they went. Basically, they took the pick of the litter. So we were left with all the remaining stuff and had no idea what to do with it.

A few days later we were told to start gathering these guns together, log them on a clipboard, and take them over to the station workshops, where they would be destroyed. My job was checking the serial numbers against the list – a sort-of formal record of destruction – while the general equipment fitter (GEF) was responsible for the cutting up itself. So we took them over on a trolley, laid the guns out, matched the serial numbers with the numbers on the clipboard, and got out a gas axe. The bloke in charge said, "Cut them there, and there". So that's what the GEF did. He cut each gun into three pieces, then tipped all the pieces into a metal skip. This went on for several days, there were so many of them. As an Armourer it made you cry, seeing all these weapons being destroyed. I never did find out where they all ended up.

Martyn's experience with confiscated weapons was not unique. Some years later Bob Worthington-Harris had some come into his possession.

Working in small arms is a Marmite job for certain, and is most definitely not for everyone. Some enjoyed it and managed to make a career out of it, but this was rare. It was more normal for people to try and avoid small arms at all costs, but if you did get an armoury posting you made the most of it and had what fun you could. As we have seen, there was fun to be had and, like everything, it depended on who you were with and to a lesser extent, where you were.

THE RAF'S ARMOURERS

Above and below: Confiscated weapons. (Bob Worthington-Harris)

Chapter 8

Detachments

A detachment, or det, is where you to travel to a possibly far-off and exotic part of the world to take part in an exercise, do some training, recover a broken-down aircraft or even take a truckload of torpedoes for servicing. In fact, the list of possibilities is endless. A lot of the time you go on a detachment as part of a team.

From an RAF perspective, the ability to perform the operational objective from a squadron or unit perspective is paramount – this was certainly the case during the Cold War. If your wartime role is putting aircraft in the air to perform a vital function such as air defence, reconnaissance or attack, then you need to ensure that your squadron or unit is able to meet its operational requirement. Training in the RAF is continuous and built into everyday life, however there comes a point at which something more real is needed.

One of the biggest limiting factors in the UK is the weather, and it is not uncommon for training sorties to be abandoned because the conditions don't meet the requirements. This is not a wimp-out or an excuse to have a quiet day in the tea bar; the weather is a genuine reason to abandon training because the quality of the exercise would be impacted to the extent that it's rendered pointless. It costs a lot of money to put an aircraft in the air, so spend the money wisely and don't risk valuable personnel or equipment on a pointless exercise. A classic Armourer trip back in the day was to an Armament Practice Camp (APC) so the aircrew could get down and dirty firing their guns. Belize and Cyprus were favourite places for APC because of the weather and ranges. These days UK ranges are used more. Although sadly for the Armourers, some training can now be done online.

Detachments can be very large events that take a whole squadron or a large force of station personnel away from their main location for a period of time. They might also be much smaller, such as an individual going somewhere different to work for a period of time, possibly to cover absence or to cope with extra work. Another variation is a long-term detachment somewhere, for example Belize, to support operations or exercises.

THE RAF'S ARMOURERS

An important aspect of being in the military is being able to respond to situations quickly and being ready to move at a moment's notice. Service personnel always keep kit handy should they need to travel. A bag packed and ready to just pick up, containing spare uniform, passport, books, camera, travel plugs, tea bags and wash gear – all the essentials for one or 100 nights away. You never know when the call might come, and turning down a det is not the done thing. When you join the RAF you 'sign your life away on the dotted line'; that is, for the career and all that it offers, you must be prepared to go where you are needed. Some of those places will be peaceful and lovely, and some won't. Normally dets are worked out on a rota. You all take turns and take whatever comes along when it's your time. Sometimes things come out of the blue, so the good shift bosses or snecs will balance things out. If someone puts their hand up for a less-than-desirable trip, or can go away at short notice, that will be factored in when something more exciting comes along.

Detachments can be glamorous and take you to far-flung and exotic corners of the globe, such as the Far East or possibly the west coast of America. Equally, you might find yourself in the middle of Sennybridge Training Area in Wales or Machrihanish, just north of the Mull of Kintyre. There is nothing wrong with either place, in fact both are beautiful; however, most people join the RAF because of the promise of travel to far-off destinations. The RAF has operated from many different locations across the world throughout its history, so the opportunities for travel have always been there. Tony remembers:

> I grew up in Somerset and family holidays were a trip to Torquay. I was lucky and did go to Italy on a school skiing trip, but when I joined the RAF at 21 that had been my only trip abroad. I wanted to travel. I wanted to see other parts of the UK and also the world – that was one of my main reasons for joining.

Deploying a squadron takes a lot of planning, so for about a month before a squadron detachment everyone will be busy putting all the kit together and getting it ready to be shipped out. Most fast jets cannot carry a lot of luggage, so the transport fleet will be booked to load all the equipment such as Houchins, bomb trolleys, bombs, tool kits and spares, as well as the personnel. There is also the opportunity to use equipment from other NATO or allied countries. Because some detachments are regular events, such as Red Flag (see below), the RAF has kit stored at each host base; every little helps (to keep the travel costs down!). Often the squadron or

DETACHMENTS

station sends an advance party for big detachments. Their official role is to liaise with the locals to make sure there is enough storage for the weapons and equipment, and that squadrons have been allocated space to operate on the airfield. Their unofficial role also includes checking out the local hotels, bars, clubs and restaurants, so that when the main force arrives the out-of-hours activities are already planned.

Given that the RAF is a military force, detachments are often focused around operations, weapons and weapons training, Red Flag is one such detachment. Red Flag is the code name given to a multi-national exercise held annually and involving different aircraft from the UK, US and other countries, to test their ability to collaborate and deal with threats from around the world. Elaborate scenarios are written to define the threat, and it is up to the collaborating forces to work out their strategy to neutralise the threat and return the world to peace. Given the expense of bringing together all the resources required to run the exercise effectively, it makes sense to hold it somewhere with enough space and far enough away from civilians so as not to scare them witless. Predictable weather also helps, weather that won't ground the air forces of the world because there's a bit of fog. Nevada is just the place. The US military has 4,500 square miles of testing ground there (roughly half the size of Wales), and it's peaceful – well, until the bombing starts. And best of all is the weather; it's the desert, so hot and dry. The exercise is based at Nellis AFB, which just happens to be right next door to Las Vegas. So Vegas makes a handy place to quarter the troops while they're on exercise – what an excellent plan!

With the Red Flag advance party already in situ and the beers ordered, the transports can be loaded and the fast jets can start their journey. Fast jets have limited range so may well stage over somewhere to break up the trip. From their base in the UK they might land at Goose Bay in northern Canada. Goose Bay is handy because it's a short(ish) flight across the Atlantic. The base is run by the Royal Canadian Air Force, and the UK, German, Dutch and Italian air forces have wings there. The jets can land and take on fuel, and the pilots can have a rest and set off the next day fully refreshed and ready. Alternatively, instead of rest they can hit the bars on camp; notorious watering holes and a great way to start a detachment.

Another detachment similar to Red Flag was Rum Punch. It was the opportunity for the kipper fleet, based at Kinloss, to deploy and practise dropping torpedoes. You couldn't just 'drop the fish' in the English Channel, so somewhere suitable was needed such that the local fishing fleet wouldn't get sunk. Rum Punch was a detachment to Florida using Homestead AFB as a base and dropping torpedoes in the offshore ranges. Typically, the torpedoes were not fitted with explosive but carried electronic gear that enabled the torpedoes to be tracked, and airbags that would deploy and float the torpedoes to the surface so they could be recovered, and the data analysed. Civilian engineers from Marconi, the company which made the torpedoes, had the job of monitoring the exercise, recovering the torpedoes, and analysing the data. Sadly, the airbags didn't always work, so a few 'fish' would sink to the bottom of the oggin, never to be seen again, but those that were recovered could be reused – recycling before it became so popular.

Like Red Flag, there would be an advance party and the usual loading of kit and personnel on the transport fleet. Also, because the Nimrod could carry more than just the aircrew, some groundcrew would hop aboard and be treated to a maritime patrol around the North Atlantic for a bit before heading across the pond to Goose Bay, or Bangor in Maine, to grab fuel and hop down to Florida. Maritime patrols are not exciting; they consist of searching the seas (and skies) for suspicious activity and monitoring anything found. The Cold War game of 'see and be seen' led to low flypasts of trawlers, with the RAF planes flying in close formation with Soviet aircraft while each side could take pictures and wave. It was also an opportunity to play cards; lots and lots of games of cards helped the groundcrew pass the time. The beauty of a Nimrod was that it had a galley so you could make a brew and settle around the mess area to play gin rummy, whist, pontoon, or whatever took your fancy.

All the time your mind would drift to the eventual landing in Florida; you were hot and tired – flying always does that to you. You had the seemingly endless taxi to your pan and then ... Look, there was the advance party waiting for you! A miracle that they'd extracted themselves from deep discussions with the hierarchy of the host base – or left the bar. They would bring some steps, and before you knew it the aircraft had stopped, the chocks were in place, and the power was off. The lineys on board would have already started their AF checks and be debriefing the crew, because once those doors were open, you'd be lucky to see the crew until the next day. Finally, the door was opened, and you were hit by the heat and the smell of somewhere foreign, full of exotic promise. It was time to put the aircraft to bed and hit the hotel to freshen up and sample the local fare. Tomorrow was another day!

The size of the detachment determines how many people go. A squadron deploying a few aircraft needs enough groundcrew to cover the work of looking after the jets, AF/BF/TR, and fitting whatever kit was required, armament or otherwise. There would be at least one of each aircraft trade, so they had good technical coverage and an experienced snec to oversee and over-sign all the work. Depending on how much flying there is, they

DETACHMENTS

may even have more than one team so they could run two shifts, especially if it's a longer trip (more than a few days) or if there is going to be lots of flying. If there is just one team, the hours are flexible, you work when you need to, and the jets are always ready. If there is no work, your time is your own. If there are shifts, then typically you do twenty-four hours on and twenty-four off. It means that the off shift gets the chance to have a day off and can explore the area. One of the perks of going away is experiencing the local delights (and not just the bars and clubs).

The first day of any big detachment usually starts with a slightly sore head, a leisurely breakfast because the travelling days are long and exhausting, and a briefing from the advance party. Some of the frequent fliers will have been before (many times) so you don't have to listen too hard, although some of the information can be vital. Tony recalls the arrival briefing at Cherry Point military base in North Carolina:

> We all gathered in the briefing room and this US Marine Officer took us through a fairly long slide show about the camp, the local area and all the facilities. The site was so big we had to get a taxi from where we were staying just to get to the main gate. Most of us had a bit of a hangover, but we all woke up at the end when he started talking about the local wildlife. Cherry Point is pretty much surrounded by swamp so there were mozzies, spiders, lizards, crocs, alligators and snakes. He went into great detail about the million ways you could die and all the characteristics of the various nasties. The one that stuck with me was the last one discussed. He put a picture up of a snake and said, 'This is a cotton mouth. It's belligerent. It will come looking for a fight!' and that was it, a brief 'Thanks for your time and enjoy your stay' and he was gone. Welcome to North Carolina!

Not all detachments take you to exotic places, but every single one was a different experience in terms of work and had the potential to be a lot of fun. Tony recalls some of the trips he made in his career:

> My first ever trip was from the bomb dump at Kinloss down to somewhere near Glasgow. I was the escort for some torpedoes that were being returned for servicing by the navy experts. There was me and an MT driver who was about 18 or 19. We got lost on the way down and ended up in the middle of Glasgow, which was a big no-no given we were carrying

explosives. We sorted ourselves out and no one was any the wiser, so no harm no foul.

Then came my trip to Sigonella. It was only meant to be one night away, but what an adventure and my second ever flight in my life was on an RAF Nimrod! I walked into the line office one morning and was given four hours to pack.

They were sending a Nimrod to Sig with spares for another one that was broken. We would deliver the spare, wait while the US aircraft was fixed, then fly home – twenty-four hours on the ground, tops. We arrived and delivered the spare, and the other aircraft was duly fixed. We had a night on the town then got up early for the flight home, but our aircraft was bust so we had to wait for a spare to be delivered by another Nimrod. We had nothing to do so decided to have a trip to the local town of Catania. There were five ground crew on the trip: me, a rigger, a sooty, a painter and finisher, and the crew chief (a snec who had done cross-trade training on the aircraft so could over-sign the work of other trades). We jumped into our hire car and headed off, with the crew chief driving. He had been there before so knew the way. We stopped on the way. The sun was shining and there was an orange seller at the side of the road, so we bought a massive bag and a big jug of the local hooch. By the time we got to Catania we were all very relaxed and noisy, apart from the snec who was driving. We wanted to visit the local town but sadly got a little lost. A diversion down a one-way street led to a small altercation with a barrow full of oranges, which ended up rolling all over the road. Eventually we abandoned the trip to town and returned to the hotel instead.

I spent four absolutely brilliant days away in the end, I went to a country I had never been to before (not difficult for me in the '80s), met some fantastic people and saw lots of different things, including Mount Etna. Somewhere in between we did actually fix the aircraft but the thing about dets is you tend to remember (or not) the socialising.

Detachments do mean hard work, in spite of what you may think, although every trip offers the opportunity to have fun – even the short-notice trips when you get called out to solve a problem. However, it's fair to say that some detachments were more fun than others! Tony recalls one of his trips to Scotland:

DETACHMENTS

One that sticks out was a short-notice hop to Prestwick to recover a broken Herc. I was duty Armourer at Lyneham, and around 3 p.m. we got the call to say they wanted an Armourer to replace fire bottles. A Herc had fired its onboard fire suppression system to deal with a suspected engine fire. Once the bottles are fired the aircraft is grounded as the fire bottles have to be replaced and the engine fault investigated. I had an hour to grab my kit and jump on board the Herc with the engine change team. We arrived at about 6 p.m. and cracked straight on with sorting out the problem. The engine was faulty and had to be replaced, so we got on with removing the duff one while a new one was flown up from Lyneham. By the time it arrived we had the old one out and were ready to fit the new one. By now it was around 6 a.m. I had been on duty since 7 a.m. the previous day, and the others had put in similar hours. The Ground Engineer (GE) in charge asked what we would like to do – grab a few hours' kip or get some breakfast and crack on. We were all knackered so wanted some kip. The GE phoned the captain of the aircraft, who was in the hotel bar and had been since we arrived, and told him the plan. But the captain said we had to crack on and fit the new engine as the crew needed to be home. So we pushed on and got the new engine fitted. It didn't go well, and the last panel didn't go back on until about 3 p.m. When a new engine is fitted it must be tested on the ground before flight, which involves firing it up and running it for about an hour or more with the final bit being at full power. This is noisy, and the navy wouldn't give us permission to do the run until the next morning. The captain went mad but there was nothing to be done so we all got to go to the hotel for a meal, shower and sleep.

And this is where things got a little heated. When you travel away you are entitled to rates to cover food and other expenses. The senior person on the trip is in charge of the money, and if you fly that will be the aircraft captain (senior pilot). They always carry money and credit cards, enough to cover food and expenses, and to fill the aircraft with fuel. We got to the hotel and the captain was waiting for us. This was our second night away so we should have been given two days' money. He refused, saying that we were only going to spend one night in the hotel; the other night had been spent on a military base so we weren't entitled. There were about seven of us who had all been working solidly to get his aircraft fixed, and we were not happy. The GE was calm, and politely told the captain that he had serious concerns about the new engine and doubted it would pass its tests the next day, which would mean another day at least on the ground, and that given we had all been working for well over twenty-four hours, we wouldn't be working the next day for H&S reasons. The captain paid us two days' rates and bought us a beer, and we flew home the next day.

But happily most detachments were less stressful, as Tony recalls:

On one occasion I had a trip to Machrihanish from Lyneham. We were there for a few days to test out chaff and flare on the Herc. I love Scotland, and it was just me and Flight Sergeant Wynne Davis, who was SNCO of the armoury at Lyneham. It was a great trip. Workwise, we prepped the chaff and flares together and fitted them to the aircraft. We only did about half a dozen loads, which the crew duly fired off to get some practice. Everyone was happy and we had some lovely free time to explore the area and meet the locals. I did a few EOD trips to ranges including Sennybridge, and I spent about six weeks doing range clearance at Pendine Sands in west Wales.

I also did a hop to Goose Bay from Kinloss. We were doing SAR cover for jets that were flying across the pond to go on Red Flag. Basically, the Nimrod would get airborne and circle the North Atlantic while all the jets transited over. Once they were all safely across we landed at Goose Bay ready to follow them down to Nellis. It was November and freezing on the ground when we landed at Goose. It was about -15°C so we were marshalled straight into a hangar, which is unheard of. We were issued with parkas to keep the cold out and got on with the AF. You couldn't touch anything metal with your bare hands because your skin would stick to it. We got the jet ready for bed then popped off to find our accommodation.

Because the RAF had a permanent presence at Goose, we were in military transit accommodation, which is grim. From memory it was underground, and everything was very old and tired. There were two of us in the ranks accommodation. The crew chief was a snec so he went to the sergeants' mess, and the aircrew were a mix of snecs and officers. We had arranged to meet the crew chief outside the sergeants' mess. Neither me nor the other lad had been to Goose before, so we put on our best going-out togs but wisely wore our military boots because it was cold and very snowy outside. We found the way out of the block and started following directions to the mess. The snow was so deep and it was so cold your breath froze, but never mind, there was a cold beer waiting. A car passed by and stopped, and this lad wound the window down and asked us what we were doing. Apparently no one walks in Goose because it's so cold and people always stop if they see a pedestrian. He gave us a lift to the mess, where we met our snec, and told him about getting a lift. He said we should have used the tunnels and covered walkways to get round. I did point out that we didn't know about them, and he might have told us given we had never been there before.

The night was great. The bars at Goose are lively and we did the rounds. It was an early start so we didn't see the point in going back to the miserable accommodation, so we just kept going. We had to the leave the Bulldog Club when it shut. So the crew chief took us into the sergeants' mess – a bit naughty, but it's only a crime if you get caught. We got there about 1 a.m. and carried on drinking and chatting to folk. A while later the mess manager came up to me and said he needed a hand. He took me to the main entrance door, which was one of those revolving ones. Our crew chief was so drunk he had got into the door and fallen asleep, and wasn't going to be woken. The mess manager knew that me and the other lad weren't snecs, but he was prepared to turn a blind eye if we helped him out with the door situation. Me and the other lad wrestled our illustrious leader from the door and put him to bed. The reward was free drink and a lovely hot brekkie at 4 a.m., whereupon we went and got ready for work and collected our still slightly ill crew chief, ready for work at 5 a.m.

One place Tony didn't go to was Deci in Sardinia, or to give it its full name, Decimomannu. The airfield was used by the RAF, along with many other NATO air forces, as a front-line training facility primarily specialising in Dissimilar Air Combat Training (DACT) on the Air Combat Manoeuvring Instrumentation (ACMI) range. The pilots loved Deci, but for the ground crew it was considerably less enjoyable. In the words of Martin Turner, 'There was a local flea market that actually sold fleas – that's how bad it was.' The best solution, as was often the case, was to have a few drinks.

During one of his trips to Deci, Martin was in bed. He'd had a couple of beers the night before, but nothing excessive. Martin was woken by

Jeff Poole, sadly no longer with us, on a trip to Deci. Jeff is wearing overalls and in the right of the picture. (Tony Lamsdale)

A familiar sign to many an Armourer. (Mark Bean)

DETACHMENTS

the sound of banging doors and shouts of 'Fire! Fire!'. Generally, when that happens it's a false alarm or a hoax, so he turned over and went back to sleep. But the shouting continued, so he got up with the intention of having a word with whoever was causing all the noise. He opened the door and saw one of his colleagues standing at the end of the corridor, waving his arms in the air and yelling 'Fire!' Martin's first thought was that this person was involved in the wind-up, but then he noticed a thin film of smoke in the air. His friend confirmed that this was no hoax: 'No, there really is a fire!'

And indeed there was. So Martin and the rest of the Armourers dutifully followed fire orders – leaving the building as quickly as possible and gathering outside at the designated assembly point, under the watchful eye of an unknown warrant officer. As one of the sergeants, Martin had to tick off his own team members to check that everyone was accounted for – and the numbers didn't add up; he found that he was two people short. By now there was more and more smoke coming out of the building. Martin asked the others if they knew where the missing pair were. 'They're in the TV room, fighting,' was the immediate answer. This was a concern, because that seemed to be exactly where the smoke was coming from.

After moving the rest of his team into the sergeants' mess anteroom (following orders from a grumpy warrant officer), Martin braved the smoke and headed into the building. He probably shouldn't have, but when two of your men are missing you do what you have to do. It was difficult to breathe, but he managed to get to the TV room and popped his head around the door. Sure enough, there were the two missing Armourers, in the smoke, fighting. Martin yelled: 'Quick! Get outside! There's a fire!', or words to the effect. The response: 'Yeah, we know.'

Martin led them outside, still grappling with each other. The grumpy WO was now turning purple, and unleashed a tirade of expletives. In contrast, while the WO ranted, Martin was completely calm and in control – in the way that you only can be when you're thinking, 'This really can't be happening to me.' By now the fire engines had arrived, so Martin led the two pugilists into the anteroom, where he found the colleague who had initially alerted him about the fire taking beers out of the sergeants' mess fridge and handing them round. Not really what you want when everyone is already slightly the worse for wear, but at least they seemed happy.

A corporal from one of the other trades labelled Martin 'The coolest man in NATO' that night – an accolade he was more than happy to accept – and for the remainder of his time in Deci that was what everyone knew him as.

As for the origin of the fire, that remains a mystery to this day.

THE RAF'S ARMOURERS

Detachments and deployments were a great reason to generate something special to commemorate the event. Tony recalls:

> In the mid-'90s I went on an exercise with the Hercs called Purple Star. It was the biggest joint service and multi-national exercise since the airborne landings of the Second World War. We went to Cherry Point Marine Base in North Carolina and took three Hercs. Our fleet was around twenty-seven at the time, so three was quite a decent number given that there would have been at least four Hercs being serviced. Some would be U/S, and the rest would be operational delivering supplies and personnel around the world. The idea was that we teamed up with the Americans to drop paras and equipment into a battle zone – lots of troops and their equipment, all of which would be deployed in order to fight some imaginary enemy. The twist was that we would drop each other's troops and kit, to practise multi-national co-operation. Our paras weren't too happy because they would have to use the American parachutes, which had a bit of a reputation for not being as good as the British kit. The Americans have a much bigger military force than us; their army, navy, air force and marines, not forgetting the national guard, exceed ours in numbers by a significant amount. They also have a lot more kit; we rocked up with our three Hercs and I think about 500 paras. The Americans turned out a reserve National Guard Squadron of Hercs, which had about thirty aircraft!
>
> It took a few days to get up and running, and there were a few false starts. Hurry and get everything prepped for H-hour … Rush rush rush … It's all on … Then, after hours of graft and prepping the aircraft, it would be 'Stand down, it's off until tomorrow.' Anyway, the first day of drops came around and off the paras went for their first mission. We got a couple of aircraft airborne to drop some spam paras and their kit. Aircraft fly off full and come back empty, mission accomplished. Cherry Point is massive - you have no idea how big this place is. Anyway, we were staying in an area out of the way and living in 12 x 12s set up on hard standings; not exactly camping, but too close for comfort. We had a field kitchen as a mess, so you rocked up and queued for your grub with one of those trays that holds everything. The morning after the first drop I was

in line for my breakfast and down the road come our paras; there were at least half a dozen in bandages and a couple on crutches. Turns out the Americans had dropped them right on their kit so they were landing among tanks, Land Rovers, field guns and containers full of equipment.

About halfway through the exercise one of the Herc lineys came up with a T-shirt to commemorate the trip. It was brilliant; the thought that went into the design was amazing. We had already coined a phrase to describe the trip and it was being used all the time. We were calling it a 'rolling goat f***!' which is almost as ridiculous as the trip itself. The T-shirt renamed Purple Star to Purple Helmet and had an image of a large cartoon penis.

Apart from the travel and the fun of visiting different parts of the world (and the social side), the other really enjoyable aspect of a detachment is the work. Even if you are doing the same job as you would be back at base, doing it somewhere different and possibly in better weather is like having a new job.

Exercise Purple Star T-shirt. (Tony Lamsdale)

The chance to wear shorts and no shirt was a distinct possibility and was always taken if the opportunity arose. A detachment was the perfect excuse to brush off the khaki drill (KD) uniform (if you had any); the feeling of digging it out of the back of the wardrobe is akin to getting the swimming trunks and suntan lotion out for the annual holiday to the Costa del Sol. Khaki drill harks back to the days of the Empire and consists of long and short trousers and long and short-sleeved shirts. All were made from a lightweight material and, combined with nylon socks, were designed to keep a travelling Armourer cool and ready for action in the sun. In later years the uniform was rubbish. The older issue kit from the early 1980s and before was OK because it was made of cotton. The newer KD used a lot of man-made material and, rather than keeping you cool, made you sweat even more. In the Far East and Med, where the temperatures could be in the 40s, it felt like you were wearing molten plastic – which was pretty accurate really.

The detachment rules regarding dress are always simple. When in public (hotel, shops and travelling to and from work) try to be smart. At work be comfortable and safe. The rules should lead to a consistently dressed, smart-looking bunch of professionals gathering for breakfast in the hotel before work It's always good to have a plan even if it doesn't always work out! On the pan, those same people could be likened to bronzed sunworshippers, going about their business in very short shorts, socks rolled down to the tops of their desert boots and with bare chests. The more stylish would wear Ray-Bans, and possibly top everything off with a cotton neckerchief tied around the head to stop the sweat dripping into their eyes. Getting sunburn, which leads to time off work, is a chargeable offence, classed as self-inflicted injury – so if you do burn, make sure you can still get to work. Many is the time an engineer has had to find a loose-fitting pair of overalls to wear for a few days after a particularly vigorous tanning session by the pool or on the pan.

Often the work is more varied because you don't have all the resources and personnel to fall back on, so you have to solve problems between you, help each other out, and muck in. It's a chance to do lots of different things and work with different people. Tony recalls:

> I did a lot of trips with the Hercs where it was me as the Armourer and the Ground Engineer to cover all the engineering. Normally the GEs did it all themselves, but certain trips needed Armourers. The Hercs didn't have a lot of Armourer stuff so I always helped out where I could. I learnt to refuel and do all the flight servicing jobs so the GE could get on with snagging. I'd also help with any of the bigger jobs even if it was just making a brew, fetching tools or scrounging kit. In my time I became an expert in wheel changes and engine changes. I was working with a GE once and we had to change a main wheel. He'd never done one before so he got the book out and started working through it. I was able to give him some pointers that I had picked up, and even showed him how to reassemble the anti-skid mechanism on the wheel – he'd put it on backwards. That was the beauty of being an aircraft trade. You all got the same excellent grounding in being an engineer so that you could turn your hand to anything and work with others, combining your knowledge to get the job done.

DETACHMENTS

Overseas detachments also provided you with the challenge of being in a foreign country and trying to get what you need. If you land somewhere that doesn't handle your aircraft type, especially civilian airfields, even getting something basic like a set of steps to disembark can be challenging. You have to be prepared to deal with anything. The classic barrier is language, but most linguistic challenges can be overcome with a smile accompanied by lots of waving and pointing. Pointing is the universal language at any airport.

Although sometimes the language barrier never quite gets broken down. Garron Clark-Darby's Italian experience is a classic example:

> Some of the lads had gone off to the beach and went in search of a bar for a few cool beers. None of them knew any Italian at all so communicated in the time-honoured manner by shouting English words in an Italian accent, in this case 'uno beero coldo'. Unfortunately the Italian word for 'warm' is 'caldo', and the proprietor in question was well familiar with the rumour that the Brits prefer their beer warm, so he served the warmest beers he could possibly find. These were, of course, not to the lad's liking so much shouting of 'mucho coldo' took place, and the beers got warmer and warmer. When one of the other lads arrived, one who did speak a little Italian, he went to the kitchen to explain what was required and found the landlord busy running bottles of beer under the hot tap to make them warm enough for those funny Brits.

The transport aircraft tend to land at civilian airports more than the fast jets, and getting ground servicing for something like a Herc is fairly easy. Fuel couplings are standard, and the Herc has its own steps and uses the common ground power coupling. Toilets on board the older Hercs are primitive; there is a urinal (plastic tray) down the back on the port side by the ramp. The urinal vents to the outside so it's used only when airborne. Next to it is the potty, a metal bucket called an Elsan, which is filled with Rackasan, a blue disinfectant. Privacy is afforded by a curtain that can be pulled around both, should their use be necessary. Some advice – never use the Elsan on a Herc. There are two reasons: the first is that someone has to empty it; the rule is whoever deployed it destroys it. The second and more important is the logistics of use. You have to disrobe the bottom half of your clothes. If you are in a flying suit or overalls, that is not easy in an airborne aircraft that is being buffeted about. You then have to sit on said potty without falling off, while at the same time screening yourself with the curtain – another task fraught with danger and not guaranteed to work. On completing your ablutions there is the matter of cleanliness. The toilet paper (if present) is useless. And finally, there is the matter of odour. If one does one's business, everyone on board knows.

There are tales, all true, of people being so desperate that they have no choice. But it must be a last resort, and all who work on Hercs are told of the poor aircrew member who, following a hard night on the curry and beer, was left with no option. All seemingly went well until the moment when he pulled up his flying suit, and realised that he hadn't pulled it down far enough for the act and had deposited in his suit rather than the Elsan. A cautionary tale.

The later J model Herc pushed the boundaries of human toilet-based comfort with the addition of a proper aircraft toilet behind the curtain. Well, it wouldn't do to spoil the troops too much!

Sticking with toilet-related tales, Tony recalls a couple of incidents:

> Part of the AF on a Nimrod is emptying the toilet. The toilet on a Nimrod is just like on a civvy passenger plane. All the waste is captured in a tank, and when you land you call for the waste bowser or 'boggy truck'. We were in Sig and had just landed. It was my first trip, and the crew chief asked me to sort out emptying the toilet. I found the boggy truck driver. He must have been 80 if he was a day, a lovely chap with a massive smile and not a word of English, which matched my distinct lack of Italian. Anyway, I managed to convey my need of his services and he drove the boggy truck to the front of the aircraft, all beaming Italian smiles with a big cigar firmly clamped in his mouth. It was unlit so not a fire hazard. I lowered the panel, and he took a look and went for his pipe. I was confident at this point, so let him get on with coupling the pipe. It was his after all. Once coupled he gave me the thumbs up, I opened the valve, and he started the pump then wandered back to the coupling by the aircraft. All went well for about a minute, then there was a rumbling and knocking and the pipe disconnected. There was a big spray of effluent, which lasted for what seemed like forever, then it stopped. The spray and mist cleared to reveal the Italian, still with the cigar in his mouth but soaked from head to foot. One small detail that I shall never forget was that he was wearing a smart jacket with a top pocket and there was a turd poking out of the pocket. He mumbled and walked off in a huff to call the airport

cleaning truck. Presumably this had happened before. He bore me no malice, but I couldn't help feeling that Anglo-Italian relations had taken a bit of a knock.

Mind you, having a boggy truck was a luxury. Normally on dets you emptied the toilet into a length of lay-flat plastic tubing. Every aircraft carried a roll, and the idea was that you cut a good length, tied one end, and turned the top of the other end over into a sleeve. You put your hands into the turned-over bit and slid the tube onto the outlet pipe, then your oppo would open the valve and the toilet would drain into the tubing. Wise people always cut a really long length of tube because when the toilet was empty you had plenty of pipe spare to tie up. Inexperienced lineys were always given a short length of tube which filled straight away, at which point your oppo would walk away leaving you with a tube of s**t, both hands holding the pipe in place, and no way of closing the outlet. It never happened to me. I clocked that trick early on. But I've seen it done; it was horrible and also very funny.

The most bizarre thing I ever saw involving an aircraft toilet involves a serviceman who had been away from home for a while and was returning to his new wife. We all knew how much he missed her because he had talked about her non-stop for the whole det, and as we got close to coming home he started focusing on how to perform his husbandly duties properly and ensure she enjoyed the experience. His phrase, repeated incessantly for about two weeks before we went home, was 'and the second bang is my kitbag hitting the floor!' Accompanied with a big smile and pelvic thrust, it got really tiresome. He became increasingly worried about a build-up accruing in his reproductive system during the trip away, so on the flight home he decided to relieve the pressure build-up manually. He took himself off to the Elsan at the back of the Herc and pulled the curtain around him. Everyone knew what he was up to and one of his mates decided it would be funny to catch him 'in flagrante delicto'; well, we were returning from Italy. His mate waited for a suitable time to elapse then moved down the aircraft towards the ramp. The crowd started following; we were carrying freight and a few soldiers who had been on deployment, so there were about ten people in the back. The mate of the newly married husband got to the screen and pulled it back to reveal the lad in all his glory. To

THE RAF'S ARMOURERS

be fair, there was a lot of ingenuity. He was wearing a head torch to shine a light on the reading material, leaving both hands free, one for the magazine and the other for … well, we will leave it there. The lengths some people will go to to ensure the happiness of their other half is extraordinary. He got a standing ovation, which thankfully he received sitting down, covering himself up with his magazine. I suspect the thought of the incident curbed the passion sufficiently when he returned home.

Enough of toilets, and back to detachments …

Belize, formerly British Honduras, is not an easy country to live in. It's a similar size to Wales, but its total population is a little over 400,000, equivalent to a city the size of Sheffield. The Belize climate is tropical, with high humidity, frequent torrential rainfall and temperatures ranging from the mid-20s to mid-30s. Sixty per cent of the country is covered by jungle, and there are large areas of swampland. There are mosquitoes that attack you from 6 in the morning until 6 at night, and sandflies that take over when the mosquitoes have moved on. Not to mention huge spiders and lots of snakes.

Despite these challenges, Mike Steel was more than happy to be sent to Belize in 1980. He had just achieved promotion to sergeant, and was ready for a change from his role as an instructor. So he duly headed off to Central America. In the end Mike spent fifteen months in Belize, doing three different jobs, so it turned out to be more of a posting than a detachment.

The camp near Ladyville was run by the British Army. There were only four Harrier jets and two Puma helicopters at the base, with a small crew of RAF pilots and land-based personnel. Mike was originally put in charge of the bomb dump.

He soon discovered that the location of the bomb dump had not been very well thought through. It was next to a pool, on a low piece of ground, and every time there was heavy rain the area would flood and any weapons that were being held there would be irreparably damaged. Mike and his team would then have to move the damaged weapons to a safe area, where they would be demolished. Things didn't always go smoothly:

> We had a couple of 10-tonners piled with damaged explosives, which we took up to the range. We blew up the explosives, making three great big holes 30m across, which soon filled with water.

DETACHMENTS

Belize bomb dump, 1980. (Mike Steel)

A few months later we had a lot more to get rid of, so we loaded up and set off. It had been raining quite heavily for a few days.

The main road was nothing but a mud track, and it was even worse when we left the road. The ground was really soft. It wasn't long before the first vehicle lurched sideways, and sank.

We tried to pull it out with the second vehicle, but that sank too, along with the Land Rover driven by Frank, the Chief Technician.

So we had two sunk lorries, sideways on, full of explosives. And eight men, going nowhere. We were only planning to go for the day, so we had no food, and no camping stuff. And of course the radio didn't work.

One of the lads soon became quite ill, and it was pissing down with rain. We were in big trouble. The nearest phone was at the range itself, which was about 3 miles from where we were. So I strapped on two water bottles, took the rifle, and said: 'I'll see you later.' Frank was the chief, so he did what he could to make the guys comfortable, and look after the ones who weren't well.

Belize on a wet day. (Mike Steel)

Belize EOD trip. (Mike Steel)

DETACHMENTS

Belize BD Land Rover. (Mike Steel)

Belize CRV. (Mike Steel)

THE RAF'S ARMOURERS

I walked to the range and made the phone call. After talking to the duty officer, I eventually managed to get hold of an Armourer and explained the urgency of the situation. We weren't going to get out, we had two lorries packed with explosives, we needed tents, we needed food, we were going to be there for the night, and we needed somebody to tow us out.

By the time I got halfway back there was a helicopter overhead. We shot up a couple of flares so they could find us, and the guys in the helicopter threw out a load of food and a tent, and picked up the two guys who were most ill.

We put up the tent, cooked some food, and slept as best we could. Next morning, a couple of tanks came up from another of the camps, and they towed us out.

We carried on up to the range and blew up the explosives, making another two circles. So in the end we had an Olympic sign – five circles, all about 30m across. The pilots loved it. When the sun shone the water would gleam, and they could use the Olympic sign to take them straight onto the range.

Later, Mike moved over to one of the hides at the edges of the runway, looking after two of the Harriers, as part of a team of twelve. The facilities at the base weren't great, but being in Belize had its benefits. It enabled the army to do jungle training, and its position in Central America was highly strategic in terms of keeping tabs on potentially volatile nations such as Guatemala. What's more, when you got out of the camp and into the countryside, there was amazing natural beauty, and the local people were extremely friendly and welcoming.

The fact that the RAF were 'guests' of the army did cause some problems. Mike recalls Armourers wandering around with their socks down around their ankles, missing berets, and hands in their pockets, much to the consternation of the garrison sergeant major, who insisted that the army personnel were always impeccably turned out.

There were around thirty RAF senior NCOs at the camp, and they tended to socialise together in the bar. A round of drinks for thirty cost around £1, so much alcohol was consumed. The favourite tipple was Appleton rum, from Jamaica – a smooth and silky drink that had the benefit of not giving people a hangover, although short-term memory loss was one of its after-effects. The sergeant major wasn't happy that Mike and his colleagues would often drink well into the night, while his troops had to get to bed early in anticipation of early-morning exercises. And he was particularly

DETACHMENTS

unhappy about the empty bottles that would frequently be left as evidence of the previous night's excesses.

The RAF cook came up with a clever solution. He brought along a very large teapot, which would hold the contents of several bottles of Appleton's. Milk (mixers) and sugar (ice cubes) would be added to the teapot, and the crew would enjoy a highly civilised but increasingly drunken teapot party.

When the garrison sergeant major was about to leave the base and be replaced by a Coldstream Guardsman, the RAF team invited them both to join their teapot party – to bid farewell to one and to welcome the other. A great time was had by all – so much so that both the sergeant major and his replacement were so hung over the next morning that they missed their formal parade. They were not amused.

One aspect of life in Belize was that many of the missions were not merely exercises. For example, British forces, together with the local security forces, played a significant role in suppressing the rampant local drug trade, including raids on ships that were believed to be carrying illegal drugs.

On another occasion, reports came in of a civilian aircraft from El Salvador that had landed with a suspected bomb on board. One of the army EOD staff sergeants suggested blowing up the plane in situ, but with a potential bomb and a large fuel load on board, the Armourers' Chief

Mike Steel with his oppos Frank and Manny, and the infamous teapot. (Mike Steel)

Technician Frank Jacques and his colleagues persuaded the army sergeant that making the aircraft safe through a controlled disarmament process would be a better solution. Fortunately, there was no IED and the aircraft remained in one piece.

Sometimes an incident would be closer to home, as Mike recalls:

> One of the Harrier pilots had just taken off, and after a couple of minutes we heard 'Bang! Bang!'. Of course we knew exactly what had happened. A parachute in the sky, and no plane.
>
> There was a river a few miles away, known as the Sweetwater Canal, which ran down through Belize City to the ocean. It was quite wide, 25 to 30m, and the aircraft had crashed on the far bank of the river, with its back end in the water. It was armed to the teeth, because it was on its way to the bombing range. No one could go near it until it was made safe. So a Puma helicopter picked me up and dropped me next to the Harrier that was lying in the river. Of course these are South American rivers, full of piranhas, snakes and alligators – things that bite you! So I had to get into the water and try to disarm this aircraft, before anyone else could get to it. They were on their way in a boat, so I had to make it safe. I took the cartridges out of the pylons and disconnected the guns, so that there was nothing that could hurt the guys.
>
> The pilot was OK. He wasn't injured. He got picked up by the Land Rover and taken back to the hide. Another team found the ejector seat, not far from the river, and the plane was lifted clear of the bank with a heavy crane and was shipped back to the camp. That was an interesting morning!

In contrast to the heat of Belize, in January 1999 Bob Worthington-Harris was sent on an Arctic Survival Training exercise in Norway, with a team of Pumas. This was a joint exercise with the Norwegian Army. The purpose of the exercise was for the pilots and groundcrew to learn to operate in harsh winter conditions. Also, if an aircraft went down in the mountains, the groundcrew needed to be able to get to it and survive in the frozen environment. The Pumas would fly over the area, with the crew using RECCO sensors to check for potential avalanches.

Bob remembers the Norwegians giving a demo in which a rescue dog located someone trapped in the snow within a matter of minutes; it was extremely impressive. However, the rescue dogs also doubled up as guard dogs. After the demo the RAF flight lieutenant on the exercise, who was not

DETACHMENTS

very popular, put his head down and reached over to stroke the dog. Feeling threatened, the dog immediately leapt up and took a large chunk out of the flight lieutenant's lip. Apparently those who weren't present, but who had suffered negative experiences at the hands of this officer, responded to this news by asking: 'Is the dog alright?'

It doesn't matter where you go, a detachment is a wonderful opportunity to put into practice all the training and theory; to do your normal job but in a different place. Of course, there is the opportunity to have some fun and experience different places and cultures, but the real benefit is building confidence in the equipment, your team, and your own ability. It makes you better able to face whatever may come along. History tells us that conflict is almost inevitable, and the rapid response of the military is key. The RAF has a long history of facing adversity and the Armourers have always been at the sharp end.

Chapter 9

Conflicts and Terrorism

Throughout its history the RAF has been involved in conflict around the globe. In fact, its very existence is owed to the First World War. Air power is vital in modern warfare. Air attacks can control a battle, keep troops pinned down, and create chaos. Aerial reconnaissance can provide vital information, enabling senior officers to direct resources where they are needed. Air support can bring much-needed supplies, and drop troops behind enemy lines to open up a new line of attack. The very presence of aircraft can deter aggressors from launching an attack. The Cold War epitomised this strategy perfectly – the threat of retaliation on both sides was enough to maintain a fragile stand-off.

Previous chapters have described the training and various jobs that Armourers undertake: the countless hours in the workshop on the FTJ; the repetitive servicing of small arms in the armoury; the prepping of countless bombs, ammunition and missiles; and the loading of jets on the flight line in all winds and weathers. It is all preparation for that day when the squadron or station is ordered to deploy. Often, the RAF is first to respond to a situation. They may be called upon to evacuate civilian or military personnel from an area of hostility, transport the advance troops, carry out aerial reconnaissance, or start to move the machinery of war to the battlefront. In some instances, they may be the only military force involved. For example, targeted strikes by jets or drones can remove or neutralise a threat without the need to deploy troops. The equipment may be different, and the threat may come from anywhere, but the need is still there. Be ready and, if needed, stand and face it.

From the very beginning the Armourers have stepped up to face whatever challenges the RFC or RAF have had to face. From major conflicts through civil wars and insurrections around the globe, when the aircraft are deployed the Armourers are ready to arm them and fit the kit that saves lives.

The rest of this chapter includes memories of Armourers we spoke to who served in conflict zones and wrestled with terrorism over the years. Sadly, we weren't able to talk to any Armourers who saw service in the Second World War, so our stories begin in the 1960s.

CONFLICTS AND TERRORISM

1960s: Borneo

Bill Morton's first overseas deployment, at the age of 19, was to the RAF Tengah airbase in Singapore. At that time, in 1962, Singapore was a British colony. You would have thought that Bill could have hopped onto an RAF flight to the Far East, but that wasn't the case; instead, he boarded the troop ship HMT *Oxfordshire* in Southampton on 18 September and arrived in Singapore in mid-October, after twenty-four days at sea.

He found that the Tengah airbase was on a state of alert because of simmering tensions in nearby Indonesia, including a policy of confrontation against Netherlands New Guinea. As well as UK airmen from 45 Squadron (Canberras), 20 Squadron (Hunters) and 60 Squadron (Javelins), there were Canberra squadrons from New Zealand and Australia. Bill was assigned to the missile site.

The situation worsened in December, following the Brunei revolt, and some of the Tengah aircraft were relocated to the Labuan airbase in Borneo. Aircraft carriers, including HMS *Ark Royal*, started to arrive in Singapore, and soon a number of Vixens and Vulcans joined the aircraft at Tengah. Although the Borneo conflict was never officially declared as a war, by late January 1963 it had become a full-scale confrontation between Indonesia and Malaysia, with Indonesia's President Sukarno taking a leading role in stoking up the hostilities.

Ammo tanks being loaded to a Javelin at Tengah. (Bill Morton)

Boxes of missile components were being shipped over from the UK. The Armourers in the bomb dump would prepare the missile warheads, and Bill had the task of attaching the warheads to the 3in rocket motors. The missiles would then be fitted onto the Hunters from 20 Squadron. With the Borneo conflict raging, it was a hectic time. As one trolley-load of missiles was despatched to the aircraft, another had to be prepared.

Bill remembers some of the military actions. For example, when news came through of Indonesian planes full of paratroopers heading for Labis, in Malaysia, several Javelins were dispatched. One of the Indonesian troop-carrying Hercules aircraft crashed into the sea while being pursued by a Javelin. The remaining paratroopers who had landed successfully were killed or captured during separate operations over the next few weeks.

Of course, there was time for leisure too, and many happy hours were spent in the NAAFI. If the Armourers were needed, they would hear the Tannoy calling them into action. Based on the exchange rate at the time you could buy sixteen pints for a pound, so unsurprisingly plenty of the local Tiger Beer was consumed.

In the early 1960s Singapore was a very different place to the modern city that it is now. In many ways it was more of a shanty town, with wooden shacks rather than skyscrapers. But even then there was a developing culture of commercial trading, as Bill recalls:

> I used to do scuba diving in the water around the islands. On one occasion we went out on a dhow, across to Pulau Tioman, which is now one of the top leisure resorts in Malaysia. At the time there was nothing there – just an American landing strip and some mud huts. We'd been doing our diving, and I was walking along the beach. I saw this house on stilts, and there was a Malayan chap there. He didn't speak English, so I asked him in Malay how many dollars he wanted for six coconuts. He said he didn't want any money, but he would trade me six coconuts for my socks. So he clambered up the tree and brought down six coconuts, and I took off my socks.

1970s: Cyprus

Mike Steel's first overseas posting was to the RAF Akrotiri base in Cyprus. His wife and five daughters (eldest 14 years old, youngest 1) were looking forward to what they thought would be a kind of extended

CONFLICTS AND TERRORISM

holiday, with lots of warmth and glorious sunshine, while Dad did his stuff at the camp.

It didn't quite work out like that. Mike and his family flew in on 14 July 1974. The following day a military coup took place in Cyprus, with the Greek army ousting the president. All hell broke loose, with violent clashes taking place across the island between supporters of both sides. Hundreds of Greek Cypriots died.

Mike describes his family's experiences:

> We'd just moved from our hotel into the residency we'd been allocated in Limassol. We hadn't even been to the shop. We had no food in. So we went out to the local supermarket, and when we came out the streets were empty. We were lucky to find a taxi that took us back home. The fighting was going on right outside our house – shooting all night, bullets whistling all over the place. I'd been under fire when I was in the army, so I was used to it, but it was terrifying for my wife and kids. We had no protection, so what I did was put all the mattresses in the corridor, on the floor and against the walls, and we slept in the corridor, in the middle of the house. It was the safest place for the family. In the morning, there were bullet holes all along the walls.
>
> We sheltered at home for five days, before the UN started moving people up to the camp. The family got split up then. A couple of the kids ended up in one place, my wife was in another, and I was in Episkopi with two other kids. Later, we were taken by minibus to Akrotiri, and as we were driving, people were shooting at the minibus. Bullets were bouncing all around the bus as we drove down the road. The kids were scared out of their wits, and the wife was petrified. It was not pleasant.

A few weeks later Mike's family was flown back to the UK, but even that didn't go well. They were thrown off the VC10 in which they were due to travel home, and instead were packed into the back of a Hercules transport plane, where they had to sit on the floor for the whole of the flight. Perhaps unsurprisingly, Mike's marriage failed to survive the whole Cyprus experience.

1980s: Falklands War

The Falklands War in 1982 saw the British military undertake the massive task of organising and transporting a task force to the other side of the world,

THE RAF'S ARMOURERS

something they hadn't done for a considerable time. The logistics involved were perhaps the biggest achievement and demonstrated just how effective the military can be. The undeclared war started on 2 April 1982, missing the sixty-fourth anniversary of the formation of the RAF by one day. Perhaps the Argentinians thought we would all be hung over! By 4 April the first British vessel was en route, with other ships quickly following. By mid-April the RAF had set up a base at Ascension Island, and the first troops on the ground in the Falklands arrived on 21 April – a fantastic response given the distances involved.

RAF operations included surveillance, air defence and long-range bombing missions using part of the V-force. Vulcan bombers, using Ascension Island as their base, carried out a series of raids, flying 6,600 nautical miles to bomb the Argentinian forces. The Black Buck raids, as they were known, were the longest-range bombing raids carried out at that time. It was a very poignant display of UK military capability, and was carried out on the world stage. The Cold War was still very much happening, and the RAF had demonstrated just how effective they were.

Ade Thorne was in the Falklands when the war was at its height. He wrote a diary at the time, and he has given us permission to include his diary, and photos taken during the conflict, in this book. You'll find Ade's diary on page 256.

Ade wasn't the only Armourer we talked to who served in the Falklands. Jon Eaton also spent time there, although in Jon's case he wasn't there during the actual hostilities. That's not to say that he wasn't involved. On the day that the war broke out, 2 April 1982, he was working on the missile site at Leuchars. It was a Friday afternoon, and Jon had finished for the day and returned to his room. Suddenly there was a knock on the door, followed by an announcement on the Tannoy. Everyone working on missiles were told to report to the guardroom immediately, and Jon and his colleagues spent the rest of the night getting things ready to be shipped out. Their main task was stripping down Sidewinder missiles into their component parts and putting them on palettes, which were then loaded onto Hercules aircraft. Originally Jon had been told that he would be heading straight out to the Falklands, but things changed and the Hercs left without him.

Later in the year, in early October, he did get sent over. He picked up his kit at RAF Innsworth, stopped over at Brize Norton ('halfway house'), boarded a VC10 that flew to Dakar for refuelling, and finally landed at Ascension Island in the South Pacific the following day. He was greeted with chaos. There were Wessex helicopters everywhere, and everyone's kit was piled up and then loaded into nets. Eventually Jon was able to board a Wessex and was dropped off at the MV *Norland*, an old North Sea ferry.

CONFLICTS AND TERRORISM

Once the *Norland* was fully boarded, primarily with servicemen from the Royal Engineers (RE), it set sail for the Falklands, a two-week trip.

Life on the *Norland* had its pluses. Jon shared a cabin with someone who came from the same part of the UK, and he remembers playing five-a-side football on the car deck when the seas were reasonably smooth. The food wasn't great – during the two-week journey braised sheep's hearts were served up on at least five occasions, eaten off a prison-issue metal tray. On-board activities organised by the army included first aid, map reading, compulsory PT, and an overview of the Falkland Islands, with an emphasis on the key areas. Jon also got to fire a general-purpose machine gun for the first time. But it was the natural beauty that he particularly remembers: the flying fish alongside the ship, and the amazing sunsets.

Jon's first impression on arriving at the Falklands was that it was a bit like a cross between Scotland and the Downs. It was barren, and it was windy. But as a country boy, Jon liked it. He felt an affinity with the windswept Falklands environment.

On its route to Port Stanley, the *Norland* stopped off at several ports, including Falkland Sound and Port San Carlos, and dropped off some of the Royal Engineers who were joining colleagues in the more remote areas of the island. When the *Norland* did reach its final destination, those remaining on the ship were moved into their Falklands accommodation. For Jon, this was a ship called the *Rangatira*, which, in a former life, had been a vehicle and passenger ferry in New Zealand. Most of those on board the *Rangatira* were from the army, and entertainment included shows and performances – shades of *It Ain't Half Hot Mum*. It wasn't luxury – sleeping arrangements involved using sleeping bags on bunk beds, and the food was pretty basic – but there was good company, and a bar, although there were strict limits on the amount of beer available to each individual.

Landing craft were used to get you off the ship and across to the jetty in Port Stanley. From there, a fleet of 4-ton trucks would take you over to the airfield. The journey was only 4 miles, but it took the best part of an hour because the road was so full of potholes. After a while, Jon and a few others started running to the airfield instead. Initially they would get their kit taken over by colleagues on the 4-tonners, but some, including Jon, started carrying their kit while running – it was very good for strength and fitness. The runners would invariably get there first and have time to shower and change before the first 4-tonners arrived. They could even get the kettle on and have a brew ready and waiting.

Most of the Armourers, including Jon, worked in the bomb dump. There was also an Armament Control building, an old Harrier-force workshop, in which there would be a couple of chiefs and a flight

THE RAF'S ARMOURERS

sergeant. Attached to the control building was a lean-to tent, which was the gun and role bay for the Harriers and Phantoms; two Armourers worked there. Initially, Jon's job involved charging nitrogen receivers for LAU-7/As. The receivers are steel cylinders which hold nitrogen, which is the coolant for Sidewinder missiles. Jon had a compressor on the back of a 1-ton trailer, which had originally been used by navy divers for filling up dive tanks. There was a little two-stroke engine powering the compressor, and Jon would put the nitrogen receivers in a metal box (if the receiver was faulty and exploded under pressure, the box would contain the blast, maybe!) purge the receivers through if required to get rid of any dirt, repair any that were faulty, and fill them back up again. He did this for two or three months, but the chiefs then decided that they needed to concentrate on maintaining the Skyflash and Sidewinders, so Jon moved across to join the missiles team and remained there for the rest of his Falklands posting.

In addition to the day job, there were other tasks to do and skills to learn. Jon remembers spending a couple of weeks working on barbed wiring to improve security, including incorporating trembler wires that would set off a buzzer if someone tried to cut through the wire.

The locals loved having the British armed forces on their doorstep. It gave them an enhanced feeling of security, and some genuine friendships sprung up. Phone calls were an interesting challenge. They were radio calls, done via cable and wireless, and you were given an allowance of two calls a week. Every call had to be booked. It was so much of a palaver that Jon (unmarried at the time!) made just the one call home, then decided it wasn't worth the effort.

Air mail, 'blueys', was another matter. During Jon's first Falklands trip, one of the stewards who worked in the field kitchen wrote to his mother and said that he'd really like to have a female pen pal. His mother told the *News of the World*, and everything went crazy – a bit like social media going viral. A couple of weeks later, 5,000lb of mail arrived, almost all of it addressed to this steward. Many included suggestive photos of young ladies keen to be his pen pal. Of course, this was great news for all the other young servicemen, who gathered up armfuls of letters and started writing to their new 'pen friends'. It's believed there were several long-term relations and at least two marriages as a result.

Jon spent Christmas 1982 in the Falklands. The chief at the bomb dump ordered meat from a local butcher for a Christmas barbecue, and also organised for a bunch of military nurses to come up from the Port Stanley hospital to add a splash of colour to the proceedings. It was certainly different, and very memorable.

CONFLICTS AND TERRORISM

On Christmas Day evening, the drink really started to flow and people began to lose their self-control. In particular, there was a well-known bomb dump sergeant. As the evening went on he became more and more drunk, and then he disappeared and no one saw him for a considerable time. Jon and his pals were sitting in their tent, drinking and chatting, when suddenly the sergeant walked back in. Or staggered back in, to be more accurate. He was so drunk he could barely speak. In his hands he had a Marvel milk tin – but it was no ordinary Marvel milk tin. During his absence he'd been outside on the nearby demolitions pile, which was full of missiles, 30 mm shells, hand grenades ... all kinds of ammunition that was waiting to be disposed of. He'd been snapping heads off missiles and pouring the HE powder into the Marvel milk tin. He'd then got a length of safety fuze, drilled a hole in the tin and put the safety fuze in. Finally, he'd put masking tape around the tin and written 'Bomb' on it. To be fair, he did have a plan. His plan was to light the fuze and throw the bomb onto the beach, which was out of bounds due to unexploded mines. The sergeant fully expected his bomb to set off a trail of unexploded mines and clear a safe path to the sea so that he could pop in for a paddle. Thankfully, this plan never came to fruition. The sergeant was successfully disarmed, and safely put to bed. This poor sergeant was somewhat incident-

Jon Eaton in the Falklands.

prone. On another occasion he was lying in a sleeping bag, and an inebriated colleague used the bag as a urinal, with the sergeant still in it.

As well as Christmas, Jon was also in the Falklands for Remembrance Sunday 1982, a big event which included a morning parade through Port Stanley. During the parade itself, it was wet and windy – fairly typical Falklands weather. But by the time Jon and his colleagues headed back to the bomb dump it had become positively spring-like, with sunshine and wispy clouds. Since it was a Sunday, and not a normal working day, Jon decided this might be a good time to put into practice a plan he'd been hatching.

At the bomb dump, much of the work, including the maintenance of the Skyflash missiles, had to be done outdoors, and this could only be done when the weather was behaving itself. Wouldn't it be nicer and more productive to have some covered facilities to work in? During his daily runs Jon had noticed a large pile of 4x4 timber and stacks of corrugated steel sheets at the side of the road. So on this Sunday he wandered up the road and found a Royal Engineer near the pile of timber and steel. Jon asked him what was going on with the pile. 'Why do you want to know?' was the response. Jon told him he needed some 4x4 timber and tin to build an office that he and his team could work out of. They would cut some joints, put a roof on, maybe add windows if there was some 4x4 timber ... 'What are you going to give me in return?', asked the RE. Fortunately, Jon had anticipated such a question. After agreeing to hand over a few cans of beer he'd secreted in his cabin on the *Rangatira*, and arrange for the RE to push the button to set off a controlled explosion on Mount Longdon (because who wouldn't want to be responsible for setting off a big bang), the deal was settled. With the help of the REs, Jon returned with the timber and steel, as well as a box full of handy tools, and Jon and one of his colleagues got to work. By the end of Remembrance Sunday the wooden frame had been completed, held in place with quick-drying cement. Over the next few days the roof went on, and a window was fitted. The flooring was made from old sheets that had previously been used on the airfield runway. The result was an ad hoc office that was sheltered and windproof.

Jon returned to the Falklands in 1984–85, and discovered that the office that he'd helped to build had been lifted up and moved to the bomb dumb, where it had been attached to the existing entry office and converted into a locker room with a toilet in it.

On another occasion Jon was happily minding his own business when his flight sergeant got called into the MT hangar to take an emergency call. He reappeared, shouted 'Get into the wagon!' to Jon, and immediately told him to get the EOD bag out. At the time Jon had no idea what an EOD bag was, but of course he did as he was told. The Land Rover shot off, straight over the runway and into the supply section, where the FS picked up some metal probes. An area of the beach was cordoned off, and where the wind had blown the sand away, the tail of a cluster bomb was sticking out. The idea was to touch the probe against the tail, metal to metal, and work out whether the bomb was still live. But as they prepared to do the touch test, someone nearby said 'Is that another one? And isn't that another one just over there?' It turned out that there were rather a lot of suspicious-looking devices, in an area that had supposedly been cleared. The flight sergeant was in his element: 'I'll show you what to do on this first one Jon. Watch me closely, and then you can do the next one.' Hardly the words you want to hear when you've never dealt with an unexploded device before. So Jon watched and listened. The first device turned out to be safe, so then it was Jon's turn. After a suitable amount of probing and scraping, his device was also deemed to be safe – just a tail with no bomb beneath it. Jon's sigh of relief turned out to be premature. For the third device, the FS called Jon over. After a bit more scraping, he said to Jon: 'This is what it feels like. Have a go.' Rather reluctantly Jon took over. As he was about to poke the device, he heard the sound of footsteps rapidly running away. Happily, there was no explosion, and Jon certainly learnt from the experience.

Sometimes events that took place in a conflict zone had unexpected repercussions long after the conflict had finished, and the servicemen had returned to their UK camps.

Towards the end of Jon's Falklands posting, in late 1982 after the conflict had ended, one of his colleagues, who was a keen exponent of clay pigeon shooting, managed to arrange for the Public Service Institute (PSI) to ship over shotguns, clays, cartridges and traps. It took a while for everything to arrive, but eventually it did, and on a Friday evening after work several members of the team headed down to the bomb dump, which was at Surf Bay. At the time, quite a lot of unused kit was stored in 12x12 tents at Surf Bay, with many of the armaments outside under tarpaulins. These included 1,000-pounders and cluster bomb units (CBUs), which were subsequently banned following the intervention of Princess Diana. The CBUs were stored in metal cages, hermetically sealed, before being covered by tarpaulin.

Jon and his pals headed down to the bottom end of the bomb dump, set up the clay pigeons, and started firing them out towards the sea. Of course, it's always windy in the Falklands, so the clays would blow everywhere. And when they were hit they would break up, and the fragments would be blown back inland where they would settle in various places – including all over the CBUs and the 1,000-pounders. Jon was able to attend several Friday night sessions before heading back to the UK in early April 1983.

Following completion of his fitters course he was posted to Kinloss, somewhere he hadn't worked at before. He was met at Forres, the nearest railway station, by the sergeant from the Kinloss bomb dump. Jon was a little surprised at the personal greeting, but it turned out that the sergeant was there primarily to pick up the QAS inspector, who was at Kinloss to do his annual inspection. QAS inspectors were well known for doing an extremely thorough job – they would check the explosives, check how stock was managed, and look at the book-keeping to ensure that all of the figures added up. And if things weren't tickety-boo, they would issue red cards and blacklists.

After arriving at Kinloss, Jon was shown around the base, after which he and his guide headed over to the tea bar for a brew. At this point the sergeant and QAS inspector walked in. During the chit-chat that followed, the QAS inspector was asked where he'd been working. He answered that he'd headed over to the Falklands in January for its first QAS inspection since the conflict. He added that his plan had been to stay for a week, but he'd ended up being there for more than two. He hadn't been impressed: 'It was a f***ing nightmare. There's stuff down there you would not believe. They've got these tents, and they're that worn. There are great big holes in them. The guys are doing the best they can, but I'll tell you, some things just horrified me. And you won't believe this. Somebody – and we couldn't find out who – has been shooting clay pigeons over the top of cluster bomb units!'

Jon tried to play it cool, but unfortunately his ears gave him away – they turned bright red, something his pals were quick to point out. Jon confessed that 'I might have known someone who was there at the time.'

Later in the week Jon did come clean with the QAS inspector and told him the full story. Rather than being angry or upset, the inspector was pleased to hear that the shooting had not been over the CBUs, but that it was the Falklands wind that was primarily to blame for the fragments of clay all over the tarpaulin. Over the coming years, Jon and the inspector became good friends, and met up on several occasions.

In all, Jon had three trips to the Falklands: from October 1982 to April 1983, from November 1984 to March 1985, and from June to September 2005. For the first two postings he was based in Port Stanley; for the third, he was at Mount Pleasant airfield, which had been built subsequent to the conflict in 1985. Jon's final day with the RAF was at Mount Pleasant. He returned to the UK as an ex-Armourer.

CONFLICTS AND TERRORISM

Cold War: 1947–91

The ideological differences between East and West came to the fore at the end of the Second World War and soon emerged as the Cold War. Displaced populations, housing and food shortages, and the effects of spending the last six years in the misery of war meant social change on a massive scale. In many ways it was an opportunity to rebuild and do things differently. Technological advances made during the war continued, and the space race began.

One of the most significant and frightening developments was that of atomic weapons. The devastation unleashed on Hiroshima and Nagasaki made the world sit up and take notice. The arms race (a desire to develop bigger and better weapons than your enemy) continued. The major world powers saw it as their duty to develop nuclear weapons, which are even more powerful and destructive than the original atomic bombs, as a way of protecting their shores, and the concept of Mutually Assured Destruction (MAD, one of the most apt acronyms ever) was born. The knowledge that your enemy had the same destructive capability as you, and that you could both launch within minutes of each other, leading to complete destruction of both countries, meant that there was no point. MAD only works if all parties have the capability so that no one country can hold sway over another.

For Armourers, the Cold War meant their skills were in high demand. Aircraft were kept on QRA at many bases around the globe, especially RAF Germany, which was seen as the front line. There was a constant demand for bombs, guns and missiles for either QRA or, more commonly, practice flights over the ranges. The large number of squadrons and operational camps meant more ejection seats, small arms and other associated Armourer equipment.

Although the Cold War was never an active conflict, troops from the Warsaw Pact countries were, nevertheless, perceived as 'the enemy'. Yet there were situations in which NATO and Warsaw Pact military forces would have to co-exist, albeit in an awkward and uneasy manner. A classic example was Germany, prior to the fall of the Berlin Wall in 1989. In order to drive from West Germany to West Berlin, you had to use a designated and very restricted route, referred to as the East German corridor. Your journey was timed, and if you were late you could get into big trouble. There was also a military train that NATO troops could use. Jon Eaton recalls the experience of taking the train to Berlin:

> When the train crossed the border you would pull up into this station where you'd be given a briefing. There were British

military guards on the train, and there was an officer in charge. He would have to disembark, and present all of the documentation to the East German or Russian guards; it was like a ceremony. While this was going on you would sit in your seat – you weren't allowed to leave your compartment – and watch what was going on. There was a shop at the station, and in the shop window you could see signs for Western goods such as Levi's and Coca-Cola. Occasionally someone would walk in through the shop door, and there was nothing there. It was all smoke and mirrors. On the other side of the train was another track, and there often would be Russian guards walking up and down outside the train. They would always carry rucksacks, and the British troops would throw them jeans and porn mags, which they'd stuff into their rucksacks. It all helped to smooth the way.

Many years later, after Jon had left the RAF and was working for a German company, Diehl, he met a colleague who had served in the East German air force. They got on very well, chatting about their past experiences, and it was revealing to find out how the servicemen from the other side had shared so many of the same emotions – including fear of what the other side was going to do next.

Podge Middleton had a very similar experience when he was working for BAE Systems. A new team member flew over for a meeting, and, as with Jon's colleague, it turned out that he had served in the East German air force as an engineer on MiG-29s. He talked of 'being terrified of Tornados coming and dropping bombs – we thought that we would have to launch a whole squadron of MiGs to shoot down a single Tornado.' Neither side actually wanted a war, but for those on the ground the threat was always there.

1990s: Gulf War

In August 1990 Iraq invaded Kuwait and within two days had control of the country. The Kuwait Royal family were forced to flee, and the world watched to see what would happen next. The UN decided to deploy a coalition of military forces called Operation Desert Shield, which ran from August 1990 to January 1991. Tony was working on the line at Kinloss in August 1990:

CONFLICTS AND TERRORISM

I had been on gate guard doing my two-week stint. I had just finished my last night, so on my way home popped into the section to get my mail and grab a brew. The line office was busier than normal. One of the snecs on shift said they were busy putting a couple of teams of Armourers together to go to the Gulf, and my name was on the list. I asked where we were going, but no one was saying; I just had to get myself ready to deploy. I was told that I needed to get a load of jabs and pick up some kit, and then come back to the section for midday, by which time more would be known.

Off I went, grabbed some breakfast, and popped in to see my wife, Lesleyanne, who was at work in the Coding Cell in Engineering Records; she was a Data Analyst. I told her I was going away and didn't know where, exactly when, or when I would be back. We agreed to meet up later when we might know more. She was more likely to hear the details than me because Eng Records was near the Station Ops offices. I went to the med centre where they turned me into a pin cushion, then on to stores. They passed a load of KD gear my way, and some lightweight combat clothing and webbing. I was back in the section by 11 a.m. and started trying to put the webbing together – that wasted a bit of time. I was then told to go to the RAF Regiment section, so off I went. I was issued with some brand-new canisters for my respirator, brand-new NBC gear all shrink-wrapped, three injector pens with atropine, and some tablets to take if the Iraqis used chemical weapons. Clearly things were getting serious!

By this time the others who were going had all arrived at the section, so we started putting together the tools we needed. There was still a lot of uncertainty about where we were going and what exactly we would be doing, so basically we packed everything required to load SAR kit, torpedoes, Harpoon and Sidewinder missiles, and chaff. We were done by about 1 p.m. because there were loads of people helping us. Once we had everything sorted, those of us who were going were called into a room where we were told the rough plan. The Nimrods were leaving later that night, and as well as the crew we were taking an advance party. We were following the next day on a Herc which was coming up from Lyneham, so we had to be in for about 9 a.m. That was it. Still no idea of exactly where we were going, but chances were it was somewhere warm.

Lesleyanne and I had a lovely evening, and in the morning we got up as normal and walked the dogs. We had two labs and one was just a puppy, so she was going to have fun while I was away. I went into work with her for 8 a.m. because it was easier, then we said goodbye and I walked over to the Armourers' hangar. Then it was hurry up and wait.

The Herc arrived mid-morning and they got all the stuff loaded. We were actually getting ready to board when they discovered the Herc was U/S, so we all got off and waited for a bit. Turns out it had a buggered mainwheel, so they needed to fly another one up from Lyneham. We got told to get lost and be back on camp for 8 p.m., ready to go. I phoned Lesleyanne and told her. She couldn't leave work so we agreed to have tea together and then she would drop me at work. It was mid-morning and those of us assigned for the mission had nothing to do, so we went to the pub. There was a pub called the Stables which was run by an ex-Armourer, so we went there. It was just outside the wire and near the end of the runway. We spent a pleasurable afternoon drinking beer and playing pool; we were all very relaxed. Lesleyanne picked me and my mate Rav up and took us home, where she cooked us a meal of spag bol. We ate the meal then she took us to work for 8 p.m. The Herc wasn't quite fixed, so we had a bit more waiting. My shift was working that night and one of the lads opened a bottle of vodka to toast us on our way. Then the call to board came and off we went.

Flying on a Herc is great. We were in the freight bay so once airborne you can get up and move around, find yourself somewhere comfy to sit, and while away the flight. A few of us went down the back by the ramp and played cards. Someone got out a bottle of whiskey and that was us sorted; we played cards until Cyprus, where we landed for breakfast. A quick refuel and a meal in the mess, then we were back on board. Not long after leaving Cyprus we flew over the Pyramids and down the Red Sea. By the time we landed it was dark and we had been on the go for nearly twenty-four hours.

We filed off the back of the aircraft, which had parked up near the Nimrods. A flight sergeant from the Kinloss advance party came over and said, 'Welcome to Oman lads. We're staying in the Muscat Intercontinental Hotel in Seeb.' He threw us several bunches of car keys and we were told to grab our gear and get to the hotel. A couple of the folk had been to Oman before, so they grabbed the keys and we piled into the cars. There were about fifteen of us and we had two big Toyota Landcruisers, top of the range cars with aircon and all the gear. It was about a twenty-minute drive to the hotel along some of the biggest and neatest roads I had ever seen – massive multi-lane carriageways.

We arrived at the hotel and piled out of the trucks. We were all dressed in combat gear and had our webbing and Kevlar helmets, so were all set for war. To say the hotel was posh was a massive understatement. Everything was marble and polished chrome, and there were immaculately dressed staff everywhere holding doors open, smiling, and generally making us feel very welcome. A few porters came up with trolleys and started piling our gear onto them. It was odd seeing those hotel trolleys all piled with webbing and camouflage gear. A few of us were just staring around at all the bling; it was a lot to take in. Then we started working out who was going to share rooms. The first lad approached the reception desk and gave his name. The receptionist smiled, checked his passport and gave him a key. It turned out we were each getting our own room. My room turned out to be massive. It had a queen-size bed and large-screen TV, and the biggest bathroom I had ever seen. It had a bath, walk-in shower, toilet, double sink and bidet. Next to the toilet, mounted on the wall, was a telephone. It is hard to describe just what I felt but I came to love that room and I cannot begin to tell you how many calls were made from that phone. Being able to organise your social engagements with your muckers while performing ablutions is the height of decadent luxury, and we all took every advantage of the situation. It can be mildly off-putting at first to receive a call while sitting on the throne, but one can get used to anything.

It turns out that Tony's deployment to Oman wasn't all toilet-based telephone calls. The Nimrods had been deployed in a reconnaissance role. Their job was to patrol the Persian Gulf and Gulf of Oman looking for hostile activity and shipping that was breaking the blockade imposed on Iraq. One of the biggest fears was that Saddam Hussein would also try to invade Saudi Arabia. Iraq borders both Kuwait and Saudi, and the precious oilfields in Saudi are a stone's throw away from invasion.

THE RAF'S ARMOURERS

Initially there were three Nimrods based in Oman and patrols were constant, worked in conjunction with the other coalition forces. To keep the aircraft flying there were enough groundcrew to split into two shifts on a twenty-four-on, twenty-four-off shift pattern. All aircraft trades worked together in what's known as a composite servicing model, which involves splitting the work based on trade, competency and demand. Bigger jobs such as an engine change would see all the engineers muck in to get the job done.

The airport at Seeb was well equipped, so getting equipment and ground support such as fuel and other services was not an issue. The UK forces had their own area on one side of the runway, and the US forces, who sent the most troops and equipment, were based on the other side because they needed more room. The biggest issue to overcome was the heat. Temperatures could reach 50°C, with an average of around 35°C in August. That heat was reflected back from the concrete, so working during the day could be difficult. Tony recalls an incident that occurred on a particularly hot day:

> One of the aircraft needed a radar change. The radar was in the nose cone, and to get access you had to go up into the wheel well and climb inside the cone to remove the clips. I volunteered because all the fairies were busy doing other stuff and I had nothing to do. It was the middle of the day. Normally we would have left it until the night, but the aircraft was needed so we didn't have a choice. I climbed inside and started removing the clips, but after about five minutes I had to climb back out. The nose cone was made of fibreglass, and it was so hot that the sweat was running off me. I was wearing denims which felt like they were melting. You couldn't do the normal shorts and no top because the Omanis didn't like it. But needs must. I decided that the denims had to come off, so I stripped to my pants and climbed back inside.
>
> The job was difficult because it was dark, so you had to hold a torch between your teeth. Also, the angle of the nose cone meant you were constantly slipping down towards the exit of the wheel well. Add to that the flipping great radar dish you had to work around and you get an idea of how tricky it was. Each clip had to be undone using a spanner and screwdriver (I think) and because I was sweating so much they kept slipping out of my hands. Never mind, I got there in the end. Once I had undone all the clips I got out of the wheel well and went

off to get help to remove the nose cone. I wasn't a big lad then, maybe 11 stone dripping wet, but I reckon I lost about a stone just doing that job. The radar techs were ready to remove the radar so we took the cone off and started undoing all the clips and connectors holding the radar in place. Someone brought two crates over. They were big, maybe 6ft^3. You took the wooden sides off and inside was the cradle to hold the radar while in transit; they were delicate and expensive, so you needed to take care of them.

We opened one and wheeled it in place to lower the U/S radar into. It was now mid-afternoon and the temperature was still climbing, but never mind, nearly done. We wheeled the U/S radar out of the way and opened up the next crate holding the new radar. The lad taking off the first side swore. 'What's wrong?', asked the snec in charge. 'It's f***ing empty!', came the reply. It turned out that an empty crate had been shipped out by mistake. Never mind, it was back to the office and put a call in to Kinloss – a new one would be on its way courtesy of a Fat Albert (the affectionate name bestowed on the Hercules by those who love them) from Lyneham, and should be with us in twenty-four hours. So one empty crate, one U/S Nimrod, and one thinner airman. At least I wasn't going to be around the next day to refit the nose cone. I was off shift so someone else would have that pleasure.

Even though they were a bit removed from the front line, the team at Seeb felt they were doing their bit. The work soon slipped into a routine, with shift changeover around midday. The ongoing shift would arrive and get the debrief of what was happening, and then it was a matter of waiting around for the aircraft on patrol to return. The unwritten rule and matter of pride for the off-going shift was don't leave any work for the oncoming shift, so there would be an aircraft ready to go with the third waiting to be tasked to a role. The standby aircraft might take off immediately the other jet returned, in which case the shift would see it off, or it might remain on standby if another nation was taking over the duty.

The Nimrod carried quite a bit of Armourer kit. There was whatever was in the bomb bay, usually a search and rescue load consisting of a life raft and two supply containers. They were there in case the aircraft got called to a vessel in trouble. The Nimrod couldn't land on the sea, but it could drop the SAR kit for people to use until help arrived. For a maritime patrol the Nimrod would use sonobuoys; these are acoustic devices that, when dropped in the ocean, emit signals that can detect vessels either on or under the sea. The crew would determine a search pattern and drop the sonobuoys and then monitor the responses. Once in the sea, a sonar echo is emitted and any returns are mapped, which gives you possible targets to monitor. The Nimrod carried a variety of different sonobuoys in racks aft of the galley. Two rotary launchers took care of deploying the sonobuoys; there was one either side of the rear access doors and they could be preloaded with up to six sonobuoys each. The Nimrod was pressurised when airborne, so the launcher had a mechanism that deployed the sonobuoy while retaining the cabin pressure. In addition, there would be the marker flares, a signal pistol and possibly something 'more lively' in the bomb bay such as Stingray torpedoes, just in case there was something that needed sinking.

It was a busy time, but there were also opportunities to relax and soak up the culture, as Tony recalls:

> Oman was an amazing trip. We were treated really well by the Omani people; they wanted us there because Saddam wasn't far away, and the UK and Oman have always had a good relationship. In fact it was the Sultan who invited the Nimrods to be based at Seeb.
>
> I had never experienced the Arabic culture before and have to say I fell in love with it immediately. The language is lovely, and I did try to learn bits. I bought a book and still have it today. The whole country is steeped in history, and we spent a good bit of our days off travelling around. I loved the desert; the sense of space and serenity is awe-inspiring, and you don't have to travel far to be totally on your own.
>
> The hotel was great, and we were close to the beach, although you had to be careful swimming in the sea because of the sea snakes. I was never a good swimmer and one lad on our shift, Janos, decided he was going to teach me properly. Apparently the high salt content in the sea around Oman makes it difficult to sink. Not for me – I went to the bottom like a stone. Janos gave it his best shot, but after a few sessions decided I was better off working on my tan well away from water.
>
> The souk was our main place to go on days off. It was amazing just wandering around the ancient streets and alleys with all the traders. It couldn't have changed much in a thousand years, and I mean that in a good way. Whatever you wanted you could buy. A lot of us bought Lacoste polo shirts because they were so cheap, around $5 each, and

they were great quality. Ten years later I still had some, and they looked like new. Gold was also a good price and a higher carat than the UK, and music ... My God, every other shop and stall sold cassette tapes. There were all the latest albums. You could buy ten cassettes for $1, and they would throw one in for free. The covers all looked similar, a blue background with a tiny picture of the album cover and very small writing on the back for the list of tracks. But they all worked fine, and I still have some now over thirty years later.

It was all very relaxed and there was never any hint of trouble. The only rule was don't go out with any drink on you. If they thought you had been drinking they would lock you up, which is fair enough. They have rules and you had to abide by them. Apart from anything else, the jails in Oman are very basic and you're treated like a proper criminal. It wasn't a dry country so you could drink in hotels, and there were some clubs, but if you did drink you got a cab to pick you up from where you had been drinking and take you to wherever you were going. Simple really, and in spite of the fact that we all liked a drink (or two), no one broke the rules, and if we thought someone might stray, we sorted them out. To be honest the locals were worse than us. The Omanis would head to hotels after their work and get absolutely steaming; it was funny to watch. We got friendly with a group of about three or four who would come to our hotel several times a week. They would rock up and buy drinks for everyone: beers, or jugs of long island iced tea. They would challenge us to play pool and over the next few hours would get more and more drunk. Their goal was always to out-drink us, but they never did. Once they'd had enough we would sort out the taxis and make sure they got away safely. In return they looked after us well, organising trips out on days off to places off the beaten track, and we had some great nights out in the posh clubs. There are a few places in the world I would love to go back to, and Oman is top of the list.

Bob Worthington-Harris volunteered to be sent to the Gulf War in December 1990. He was posted to the bomb dump in Dhahran, Saudi Arabia. Although when he arrived there wasn't a proper bomb dump; part of his job was helping to build one. The building process included spraying the sand with tar so that it didn't blow away – not the kind of problem you have to think about at UK airbases.

He remembers meeting Sir Peter de la Billière, who was Commander-in-Chief of the British Forces in the Gulf War. Sir Peter was accompanied by Prime Minister John Major, who visited Dhahran in January 1991. Bob took a photo of his own commanding officer standing next to Sir Peter, and it proved to be a useful bargaining tool. When he presented the photo to his boss, he inquired about a planned flight to Leuchars, and whether there might be a spare seat on it. The answer was yes, and two days later he was on his way home.

But Bob was back in Dhahran by the time of the infamous Scud missile attack launched by the Iraqis in February 1991. He was less than a mile from where the missile struck, killing twenty-eight US Army soldiers. A further 110 soldiers were hospitalised. It was the biggest single loss of life for the Allied forces in the whole Gulf War. When the missile struck Bob and his oppo had no idea exactly what was going on; all they knew was that something nearby had been hit – they could see flames and hear secondary explosions. Bob's immediate thought was: 'F*** it, we're doomed.' So while Bob's oppo was fully kitted out in his NBC suit within seconds of strike, Bob just put on his mask and left it at that.

Dhahran was a very volatile place at that time. Bob remembers a civvy who drove a forklift on the airbase, which was used to unload weapons from a low loader. The air raid siren would go off frequently, and Bob and his oppo would immediately don their NBC gear and head for a shelter. The forklift driver would just sit quietly in his cab, watching. What was he thinking? Why didn't he do anything?

Given the continuous perceived prospect of chemical, biological or radioactive weaponry being used by the Iraqis, NBC gear was donned on a regular basis. It didn't help that when the Allied forces used Patriot missiles to shoot down Scuds, the fuel droplets that were issued would change the colour of the NBC detector paper, suggesting that the base was continually under attack.

On one occasion, after hostilities had ceased, Bob and his fellow Armourers were at the bomb dump beside a Patriot Battery when three missiles went off. Great excitement! What were these missiles going to take out? Then, as they watched, one of the missiles did a loop-the-loop and crashed into the desert less than a mile away. It turned out that the first missile had been launched in error, and the other two were fired off in order to take it out.

CONFLICTS AND TERRORISM

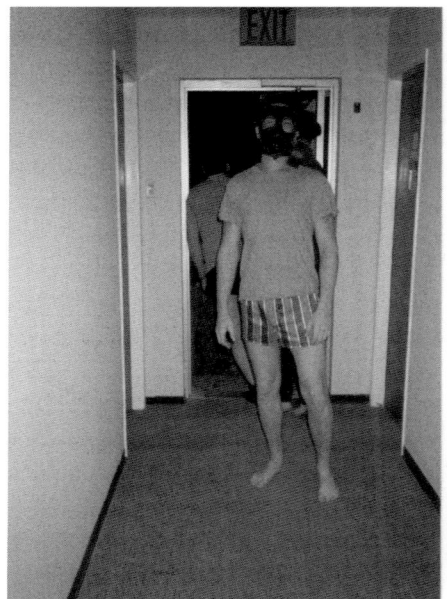 

Bob Worthington-Harris and his oppo, on the night of the Scud missile strike.

1990s: Balkans War

The RAF doesn't always deploy as an aggressor. During the Balkans War in the 1990s the RAF deployed an aircraft to fly food into Sarajevo as part of the relief aid mission co-ordinated by the United Nations. Flying in all weathers and delivering food and vital supplies up to five times a day, the supplies delivered saved countless lives. Originally based in Zagreb then moving to Ancona in Italy when Zagreb became too unstable, the aircraft flew over hostile territory risking attack from ground-to-air missiles. The crew were not armed because they were part of the peace-keeping mission, so in the event of a forced landing they had only their ability to negotiate to fall back on.

Tony recalls his time with the Hercs on Operation Cheshire:

> I did my first trip to the Balkans while the Hercs were still operating out of Zagreb. RAF Lyneham provided most of the personnel. There were six aircrew, a GE and an Armourer. There were other trades in theatre as well: a team from UK Mobile Air Movements (UKMAMs) who specialised in loading the freight onto the Herc, a supplier, RAF Police, Tactical Communications, Intelligence and others. The flying

was done by 47 Squadron SF (Special Forces) from Lyneham. These were the best crews and did all the tricky jobs in unpleasant places, so you were in good hands.

We always flew out of Lyneham on a Saturday on the transport plane with the new crew flying the plane, usually one of the standard Hercs. SF had their own aircraft specially fitted out for different ops. That aircraft would stay in theatre unless it needed to go home for repair. From Lyneham we went to Split and dropped off supplies and personnel. We might take on a few passengers who were coming home. From Split we would go to Zagreb, where the outgoing crew and engineers would be waiting for us to arrive. There was a chance to shake hands and get all the latest information, then the outgoing bods would get onto the plane we came out on and would fly home. It was a slick operation and one I did many, many times. For a while, it felt more like home than home.

During my first week in Zagreb the situation started getting very unstable. On our first night we went out to get food and came across a demonstration in the town square. There must have been about 10,000 people massed, carrying banners and shouting. Many were in uniform, and a lot were carrying weapons. Croatia was in the middle of a civil war. People were frightened and understandably so. The UN decided that we needed somewhere a little safer and easier to operate from. There had been problems getting the trucks of food to Zagreb airport, and there was a lot of tension. By the end of the week a new location had been found. Ancona Airport in Italy was about an hour's flight from Sarajevo. They could handle our aircraft and had space for us and the other nations, so we all moved across.

It was my job to fit the chaff and flare and also support the GE with whatever was needed. If there was no aircraft work, I would help UKMAMs prep the pallets of supplies or help the stacker with his stores. You did whatever you could to keep busy.

I often used to fly with the aircraft to Sarajevo in case they needed to rearm after landing. It depended on how 'busy' the locals were that day. The aircraft might do several days of flying without needing to use any flares, whereas other times they were firing every trip. Flying in and out of Sarajevo was a real experience. You got to within about fifteen minutes of the airfield, then you had to put on a flak jacket and helmet.

Most of the crew would be up front in the cockpit, apart from the loadmaster who would be in the freight bay. Once we had the fighting gear on, the GE would go to one of the para doors and I would go to the other; our job was to look out for anything coming at us – missiles, I guess. We were on comms, so you had to shout if you saw anything. To be fair, the on-board kit should have picked up anything before we did, but it helps to keep busy. I knew one GE who used to wear two flak jackets, one in the normal way and the other as a sort of nappy. I guess you can't be too careful where the family jewels are concerned. The approach was amazing. You would fly at height for as long as possible, then once the airfield was in sight the captain would point the nose of the aircraft at the ground and just go for it. At the last minute we'd level out and the wheels would touch. The Herc is an amazing aircraft; it can land on a sixpence.

Once we landed it was a matter of taxiing to the pan as quickly as possible and then getting rid of the freight. There would be a team of people and a big forklift. We would open the ramp and push the pallets out one at a time onto the forklift. Once all four were gone we would be taxiing away, closing the ramp as we went. If we had fired off all our chaff and flare, I would do a hot turnaround or reload. The aircraft would not shut down, so with engines turning I would get out of the para door with my ladder and four boxes of chaff and flare. The magazines were under each wing, four on each side. You put the ladder up, removed the empties, and slotted in the full mags, making sure you torqued up the retaining bolts. It could be done quickly, which was handy because there was the possibility of taking small arms fire. With luck the GE could help by handing up the new mags and taking the empties, but not always.

The Serbs and the Croats had positions on opposite sides of the runway and used to shoot across at each other. We were in the middle! Once the chaff and flare was sorted, it was a matter of throwing all the kit back on board and off we went. A short full-power taxi and wheels up as quickly as possible, fly down the runway, then a steep (almost vertical) climb back to height. After ten minutes or so it was time to remove the war gear and get a brew.

Not all the trips went smoothly. I remember one where we were heading back from Sarajevo. We had picked up some of

> our troops who were coming back to Italy with us for a rest. One of them had stuffed his jacket close to a bit of electronic kit and blocked the cooling fan. The first I knew about it was smoke coming from the port side. I was in the middle of the freight bay and signalled to the loadie and the GE using the fire signal (figure of eight with the arm) and pointed at the smoking kit. The loadie grabbed an extinguisher and we all headed to the offending area. I saw the coat, and the GE lifted it away. The smoke stopped pretty much instantly so disaster was averted. On another trip we were carrying barrels of raw fish and big nets of garlic. The smell was horrendous, and the freight bay reeked for weeks afterwards.
>
> It was a dangerous op. Missiles, fires and foreign food – they were all out to get you!

Operation Cheshire went on to become the longest-running airlift operation of the RAF. It was a significant achievement and ranks alongside the Berlin Airlift as an outstanding example of the power of flight; aircraft can deliver vital and lifesaving supplies in extreme conditions, giving hope to countless people.

Occasionally, the aircraft would be required to do more than just deliver food. For example, there was a trip to transport a fire engine from one location to another. This proved to be quite tricky as there wasn't a lot of room to get the fire engine in the freight bay. It was an old American-style engine and had been donated by the US. It was quite low, but the blue lights had to be removed from the top because it wouldn't go up the ramp with them fitted. Troops and military vehicles were also common delivery runs and then there was Operation Angel ...

Sally Decker, a well-known humanitarian aid worker, was rescuing injured children from hospitals in the war zone. It was just before Christmas in 1993, and there were ninety-eight injured children who needed to be evacuated to safety and provided with medical help. It was organised for the Herc to pick them up from Mostar. Tony picks up the story:

> We had done our normal four drops to Sarajevo, and after the last one, instead of flying back to Ancona, we flew on to Mostar. We were due to meet up with a convoy and fly the children and their accompanying adult back to Ancona where the UNHCR were going to arrange medical care. Once we landed, we had some time to wait as the convoy had been delayed. It was coming through one of the most dangerous parts

of the country; there was a lot of fighting, and the remnants of war were everywhere. Safe passage had been negotiated but that didn't mean that all the local militia had been informed or would adhere to the agreement.

While we were waiting we re-roled the aircraft. We started by lifting the rollers from the floor. The rollers help load and unload the large pallets of food quickly and efficiently, but they're a nuisance when not needed as you can trip over them. Once the floor was flat we started putting the seats in place, and some upright stanchions to help support stretchers. There was an Aeromed team with us – a doctor and some nurses who were going to help assess and look after the children during the trip. We all got stuck in and sorted the bay, then just had to sit and wait. It seemed like we were waiting ages – I cannot for the life of me remember how long – but eventually the convoy turned up.

The kids were brought off the buses and ambulances and we helped get them on board the aircraft. Some were walking themselves, others needed support, and a few were on stretchers. Each child had just one adult with them: a mum, dad, grandparent or someone who had been allowed to accompany them. We got them seated and settled, made sure the stretchers were secure, and got ready to leave. A lot of the kids were so little they wouldn't have been on a plane before. I don't think it was much of an adventure though. They had all lived in fear of their lives since the start of the conflict, been injured by bombs or bullets, then ripped from their homes and family to be taken to another country. Most of them were terrified because we were in uniform, and their only experience of uniform wasn't good. We had managed to get some decent rations for the trip. We had snack boxes with carton drinks, sandwiches, crisps and sweets, so handed those out quickly to help settle things down.

We fired up the engines, which on a Herc is very noisy – military transport is not known for its luxury. I was helping the GE with the start so was safety man outside. My last job was to grab the chocks and get on board through the crew door, then close up. I remember looking down the freight bay and thinking, 'Oh my God!' It was full of frightened faces, kids and adults alike. A couple of the kids were really badly hurt and had drips and oxygen fitted to them. One was so badly injured we had to fly low level all the way home because they couldn't have survived the pressure at altitude. I felt so bloody helpless. All I could do was walk around smiling and chatting to them, making silly faces and trying to tell them it was going to be OK. The drinks and snack boxes helped, but it didn't feel anywhere enough.

When we landed at Ancona, all the world and its wife were there to meet us. There were ambulances, press, VIPs; it was a f***ing circus and frightened me, never mind the kids. Everyone was running around, and nothing was organised. The kids were looking even more scared, and their adults were looking just the same. No one knew what was going on, and it was chaos. Then officials started demanding paperwork to let the kids and their parents into the country. Well, I don't know about you, but when escaping a war zone with an injured child, I may not have stopped to fill in a visa application. A few of us were getting ready to have a fight until someone stepped in and smoothed things over with the authorities. The kids were taken off to hospital and we were left to put the aircraft to bed.

I don't remember all the details of that day, but I do remember sitting in the freight bay with the rest of the crew and drinking beer. It was close to Christmas. It might even have been Christmas Eve. We had a padre with us, so we sang some carols. I don't think I have ever cried quite so much before or since. To this day I cannot recall this event without coming close to tears, and can never seem to find the words to sum up what I feel about it. It will live with me forever.

2000 onwards: Gulf conflicts

Shortly after Ade Thorne started a four-year stint in Cyprus in August 2001, the 9/11 Twin Towers attack took place. The US Air Force had an aircraft carrier just east of Cyprus, and it wasn't long before it was involved in the bombing raids that were taking place in the Gulf following the attack. Ade and one of his colleagues were asked to go over to the carrier and check out the US ordnance. The plan was that they would be taken to the carrier on a Greyhound twin-prop plane, but in the end it didn't happen because the RAF Akrotiri airbase was so congested there was no room for the Greyhound to land on the planned morning of the trip. The Americans were fine about this, and assured Ade that Akrotiri wouldn't be seeing any US aircraft.

CONFLICTS AND TERRORISM

If Ade thought that was the end of it, he soon had a rude awakening. That same evening, at around 2 a.m., he got a call from the Eng Ops Controller: 'Ade, we've got three Hornets inbound, all with weapons on board. Where can we put 'em?'

And that was how things were for the next four months, a period during which Ade never managed to get more than five or six hours sleep a night. The problem was that if the US planes, Hornets and Tomcats, couldn't positively identify a target they couldn't drop their bombs, and they wouldn't jettison the bombs into the sea because that was too expensive. If a plane was balanced, in terms of having the same number of bombs on both wings, it could return directly to the carrier, but if its load was asymmetrical, trying to land on the carrier was too dangerous. Instead, it would be diverted to Akrotiri, where Ade and his crew would remove the bombs. Logically, they could have fitted the bombs back onto the planes such that each load would be symmetrical, and they could then return to the carrier. But nothing is ever quite that simple. At the time, the government in Cyprus wasn't allowing 'offensive' aircraft to take off from the airbase, so instead the bombs had to be removed from the aircraft and stockpiled, before being returned to carrier.

At first there were no American Armourers at Akrotiri, and the RAF Armourers had never worked with Hornets and Tomcats before, but that was the nature of the job during conflicts – you just had to learn as you went along, and do whatever needed to be done. Later, American Armourers did join the RAF team, which made the work much smoother. The stockpiled bombs would be loaded onto large helicopters (Jolly Green Giants), four or five at a time, and taken back to the carrier. The helicopters weren't classified as offensive aircraft.

The process of loading the bombs onto the helicopter was far from straightforward. The helicopter would land at Akrotiri, but would never shut its engines down. Ade and his team would strap the bombs onto bomb skids, then run up the back ramp pushing the skid. As they reached the top of the ramp, the loadie would tip the ramp so that the skid would roll into the helicopter. One day, during this process, a junior officer from 47 Squadron came over and made a complaint, saying that she'd been watching them and that she thought it was 'very unsafe'. Of course, the job had to be done, so from then on they had to make sure they did it in a place that was out of her line of vision.

Bob Worthington-Harris found himself in Iraq in the early 2000s, rather against his expectations. At the time he was serving in the seat bay at Leeming. What's more, he'd just got married, and he and his wife had headed off for a dream honeymoon in Thailand. No doubt they chatted, while sitting on the beach sipping Singha Beer, about their plans for what they would do when they returned to the UK. So Bob was not best pleased to find out that, during the three-week honeymoon, one of his colleagues, someone who had actually attended the wedding, had arranged for Bob to be sent on a four-month posting to Basra to support 26 Squadron RAF Regiment – a job that this colleague had originally been assigned to do. Bob's new wife was distraught, but he had no choice, so off he went. It turned out to be an interesting trip:

> I arrived at Brize to find that I was the only RAF person on the plane to Basra. Everyone else was from the King's Regiment, and they were all Scousers. We flew to Cyprus, then we flew on to Ali Al [Salem] airbase in Kuwait – apparently the temperature in Basra was too hot for the aircraft. Eventually, we flew into Basra.
>
> I was expecting that there would be someone waiting for me, but when I started asking around no one seemed to know anything about 26 Squadron. So I got chatting with this captain from the King's, and he said: 'Come with us.' So I grabbed my gear and jumped into the bus along with all the Scousers. And to this day I have no idea where we went. It was one of those rather depressing places where you acclimatise, with massive marquee tents. I dumped my stuff, had a shower, and the next thing I heard was an announcement along the lines of: 'A Company: get your stuff, you're moving on to … wherever.' So I walked back into the circus marquee with my rolly-mat and gun, all on my tod, while everyone else moved on. And I'm thinking, 'I really don't think I should be here.' I went back to the captain, and he said, 'Leave it with me. I'll find out.'
>
> Next day I got up in full cam gear, attended the briefing, no news. Following day, civvy gear, no news. Third day, flip flops … Finally, I managed to get a lift into Basra and turned up at the main gate of the base. I saw someone and asked if they were 26 Squadron. 'Yes' was the reply. I was taken to my digs, which was basically a tent in the middle of a car park. That night I slept on the floor, not knowing about the local camel spiders and other little beasties.
>
> After getting up the next morning I was taken to see the RAF Regiment Pilot Officer, who greeted me with, 'Where the f*** have you been?' After I'd explained that I'd had a short break with the army, he informed me that they had mixed up the dates. In fact, it turned out that there had been

a complete breakdown in communications, caused in part by the fact that 26 Squadron was in the process of taking over from 63 Squadron. So although someone at 26 Squadron had arranged my initial transport, no one seemed to know that I was actually in transit. I was informed shortly afterwards by the Engineering Officer that the RAF Regiment Officer had been making lots of phone calls – first to Cyprus, checking all the hospitals and police stations, just in case I'd got pissed and ended up in a fight. Then to Leeming, asking, 'Did he get on the plane?' They even considered phoning my wife, to ask, 'Where's your husband?' Thankfully they didn't. I was not amused, and let the Eng Off know my feelings: 'Are you lot mental? I've just got back from my honeymoon, you got me sent over here, and now you've f***ing lost me!' His response was, 'Welcome to 26 Squadron.'

Apart from missing his wife, Bob actually enjoyed his time at Basra when he finally got there. It was proper, satisfying Armourer work. First, he set up the armoury, because there was absolutely nothing there. He'd met some other RAF personnel who'd been sent over from Leeming, and one of them built the weapon racks. Bob had to sort out the weapons, the paperwork, the system ... Prior to Bob's arrival, people were just throwing their guns and ammunition on the ground, and there was an incident when an incorrectly loaded gun went off, fortunately without killing anyone – it was utter chaos.

The airbase was close to the village of Shaibah, and there was a bomb dump close to the village. The dump was unusual in that there was a mosque built in the middle – it was Saddam Hussein's attempt to discourage allied forces from blowing up the dump. On one occasion Bob was sitting in the shade of his tent in the car park, when he heard a large 'boom' in the direction of the bomb dump. He looked across the runway and could see the aftermath of the explosion, and a large white cloud rising from the dump. One of the RAF patrols came back and confirmed that some local Iraqis had gone into the bomb dump with oxyacetylene torches, which they'd used to try and cut off the copper obturation bands from brass shells, with catastrophic results. As well as vaporising themselves, they'd managed to set off some CS gas canisters. The huge white cloud enveloping the village was CS gas.

Rumour had it that the Iranians were paying $10 per kilo for copper and brass on the black market, so the locals would throw ropes over the nearby power lines, connect the ropes to a tow bar, then drive off, pulling the power lines down and giving them access to the copper and brass. This led to the Allies training other local men to guard the power lines; they were supplied with AK rifles, and tents were built to provide them with accommodation. As the Regiment Armourer, it had been Bob's job to strip down and clean some twenty AKs for the guards. A few months later two of the 'guards' were arrested trying to rob a bank in Basra using the AKs Bob had provided!

2000 onwards: Afghanistan

Jane Erskine spent six months in Afghanistan, working at Kabul airport from November 2007 until April 2008. It was a challenging, but also a rewarding, experience.

One thing that not many people know about Afghanistan is that in the winter it can get cold, very cold. Temperatures of -20°C are not uncommon in Kabul. Jane remembers an incident with a Hercules following a snowstorm. The snow subsequently froze as temperatures plummeted. The jengo at the time had the not-so-smart idea of sweeping the snow off the runway, even though there was a sheet of ice underneath. Despite Jane's advice to leave it as it was, he was determined that the snow should be cleared and duly summoned a snow plough. The result was a pan that was more like a skating rink.

As the Hercules landed, Jane and her colleague went outside into the Arctic conditions, to marshal the plane into the rubber hangar. As the plane taxied towards them, Jane realised from the pilot's expression that things were not quite under control. As he tried to turn the nose wheel, the plane kept moving straight on. Happily, it stopped just in time, with no injuries or aircraft damage, but it was a close call.

Jane stayed on in Kabul over Christmas. On Christmas Day, she was told to prepare for the arrival of an additional plane from Kandahar. When it arrived and the doors opened, off stepped two elves and three Santas. The whole interior of the plane had been decorated with Christmas trees and baubles. It was a nice, festive gesture.

Of course, it wasn't all fun and games. Afghanistan was a dangerous place in the mid-2000s. There were firefights going on in the city of Kabul, and occasional incoming rockets. But it was the suicide bombers who were the biggest problem. Jane remembers the first time she experienced a suicide bomb:

> The ground shook, just like an earthquake. I stuck my head out of my little shed, and thought, 'What was that?' When the

intelligence came in, it turned out that someone had blown themselves up at the roundabout nearby. A couple of days later the ground shook again, and you knew that it was another suicide bomber. It never failed to shock, but you just had to get used to it.

Terrorism

Security has been a major consideration since the formation of the RFC, and measures such as fences, barbed wire and armed guards carrying out regular patrols help keep equipment and personnel secure. During war the threat is obvious, but are those measures needed during peacetime? The reality of service life is that you can never let your guard down because there is always someone ready to exploit any weakness. Secret or sensitive equipment, information and personnel are all critical assets that must be protected. Spying is not just something from Hollywood; it has been around since the dawn of time, and while the methods may be more sophisticated now, the aim of learning as much about your enemy as you can has always been the goal.

During training, recruits are taught about the potential threats and how to protect themselves and others. Discussing 'the job' in the pub or other public places is a big no-no. It could give an attentive listener snippets of information that, when added together, can form an accurate picture of a station and its activities. Make no mistake, our enemies know the places to target and have networks of informers actively gathering intelligence for financial gain or because of idealistic principles. All forces personnel possess an ID card that must be carried at all times and presented on demand to anyone with the authority to request it. From early in your RAF career, you are conditioned to challenge anyone you see on camp who you don't know, and to be constantly looking for suspicious activity or anything unusual: a car you don't recognise, a door left open when it shouldn't be, a bag left unattended – all *could* be perfectly innocent, but on the other hand ...

Service personnel must come to terms with the fact that they themselves are targets for terrorist acts. It may sound dramatic, but over the years there have been many attacks on personnel and their families, so ignoring the possibility could be fatal. During the 1980s the threat to personnel became so real that you were no longer allowed to travel anywhere in uniform and were encouraged to use civilian bags and suitcases when travelling. Prior to this edict, anyone serving would have been expected to travel in uniform, even when going on leave. In fact it could be an advantage because a uniform or kitbag could get you a lift, thus avoiding the cost of public transport. Service personnel who lived in their own property off camp had to wear civvies or cover their uniform when travelling to and from work and were encouraged to use different routes; a regular routine could make you a target. Tony joined up in 1987, and like many others was proud to wear the uniform. He recalls:

> It was really frustrating. We all joined up to serve our country, we worked our way through training, and to get to wear the uniform was a big deal. Something to be immensely proud of, and the biggest thing I had achieved in my life to that point. To be forced to hide away in case I became a target went against the grain, and even now annoys me. But the alternative was not worth risking so we all followed the rules. It always made me laugh though because, even without uniform, we were all easily identifiable as being in the mob: short haircuts, kitbags and a certain way of walking tall marked you out just as clearly as a uniform.

Personnel were targeted in public places and there have been numerous assassinations carried out by various terrorist groups through the decades. Perhaps one of the saddest was the murder of Corporal Maheshkumar (Mick) Islania and his six-month-old daughter, Nivruti. They were gunned down by the IRA in a petrol station near RAF Wildenrath near the Dutch border in 1989. The crime was witnessed by many people, including Smita, Mick's wife and the mother of Nivruti. She could only watch helplessly, and cradle the body of her dead daughter.

During the working week there could be long queues of traffic waiting to access stations while cars were searched and ID cards checked. Station guards had mirrors on long sticks to check under cars, and everyone doing guard shift was taught how to conduct searches of vehicles and people to look for suspicious objects.

Tactics operated by terrorists include planting bombs on vehicles without the owners' knowledge that either explode when the vehicle is opened or started, or are timed to detonate once the vehicle has arrived at its destination. Family members may be abducted, and the threat of their safety can be used to force someone to drive a vehicle full of explosives to a military or official establishment. The driver might be strapped into the vehicle, with any attempt to exit it triggering the device. They may even be followed by the terrorist with the device detonated by remote control.

CONFLICTS AND TERRORISM

Guards are trained to look for signs of people acting under duress; you have to be on constant alert because you never know when an attempt to cause havoc may be made.

Vehicle access to stations is strictly controlled, and vehicles must display a valid pass or permit that shows anyone who sees the vehicle that it is legitimate. Vehicles left parked up without a valid permit on display will be investigated, and there will be consequences for the owner. Imagine leaving your car in a public car park and forgetting to buy a ticket; you can expect the friendly traffic warden to issue a ticket the minute you lock the door and walk away. Now think of the same situation, but on an RAF camp; the minute your vehicle is spotted without its pass the guard room will be contacted and your vehicle details will be searched for on the database. If no records are found the vehicle will be treated as suspicious, a cordon will be set up around it, and bomb disposal may be called. Once they arrive on the scene they may attempt to enter the vehicle using any means appropriate to ensure that it doesn't pose a threat. Appropriate means does not include popping out to get a key cut; they may well use explosives or other damaging methods to gain entry. Returning to your vehicle at any point during this scenario is embarrassing to say the least, and your vehicle may not be in the same condition as when you left it. I wouldn't bother expecting any sympathy either; in fact the conversation may well involve you giving a senior officer a very good listening to!

During those times when the IRA was perceived as a threat, being a Northern Irishman in the RAF provided additional challenges. When Bob Worthington-Harris wanted to go home to see family or friends, six weeks' notice was required, and then when he arrived back in Northern Ireland he had to go to the Security Advice Centre (SAC) at Aldergrove airbase to check in. Of course, going to an RAF airbase immediately made him an IRA target. Later, instead of Aldergrove, Bob had to check in at Ballykinler, where there was an army base. On one occasion he arrived to find that half-an-hour earlier the army had found a 1,000lb bomb on a nearby road, set up for remote detonation when an army patrol drove by. In the end Bob decided that it was safer to keep quiet and let no one know when he was coming home.

When terrorism is seen as an active threat, incidents that might otherwise be looked upon as harmless fun can take on a more sinister guise. While Brendan Lucey was on a fitters course in 1989, there was some good-natured rivalry with the mechs. Brendan and his mates bought water pistols and would raid the mechs rooms, spraying them with water. The mechs responded by buying themselves water pistols, so that they could fire back. All good clean fun, but on one occasion things got out of hand. One of the mechs had been out at the pub and had a few too many beers. When he got back to the camp, he pulled out his water pistol at the main gate. Not a good idea. The duty guards immediately perceived him as a terrorist threat, and he was lucky that he wasn't neutralised. As a result of his action, he was severely disciplined.

Guard duty is a task that almost every serving person will have done at some point in their career. It was often viewed as a necessary evil and moaned about, but there was fun to be had too, and in Tony's case, romance:

> In 1988 the IRA were incredibly active, and the alert state was raised in every military camp around the world. All the camps were putting on extra guards and I got roped in for an extra three shifts. I was cycling up the road to start my first night shift and came up behind this WRAF in cabbage gear. She was very attractive and I unleashed my killer line: 'Are you on Gate Guard?' After several shifts together and me pursuing her for a month, we started going out together. Twelve months later we were married and are still together now.

Attacks on home and foreign soil have always been a realistic possibility. The only way to protect yourself is to make it as difficult as possible for an attack to be carried out. Acts of terror are all about fear, confusion and disruption of operations. To protect against the threat, personnel have to be employed on guard duties rather than their primary role, which is not ideal. Every time a suspicious object is reported, the action plan for dealing with it comes into force. This takes personnel away from their job and denies them the building or equipment they need until the potential threat is dealt with.

In the current political and economic climate it is not possible to maintain large numbers of serving military personnel, which means that many functions have to be outsourced to civilian agencies in an attempt to save money and release service personnel to carry out their primary role. It is an open question as to how effective this is. The reality is that there is no perfect solution; as long as a threat exists, it must be defended against.

The military have often been criticised for some of their policies on inclusion and diversity. It wasn't that long ago that any sort of same-sex relationship would have got you dismissed. The government and senior military staff thought that their policies were justifiable because anyone in such a relationship could be more vulnerable to bribery or coercion. Debt and drug offences were dealt with harshly for similar reasons. This made the military appear uncaring and out of step with society, however there are

CONFLICTS AND TERRORISM

documented occasions where people were exploited by terrorists because of these circumstances. The military has evolved, and while individuals can still get themselves into difficult situations and therefore be open to exploitation, the official policies are now more inclusive.

Over the decades the threat has never diminished; it just comes from different places, so vigilance must be maintained by every serving person. It is worth remembering that one person's terrorist is another person's freedom fighter – it is all a matter of perspective. Anyone who joins the military is making a statement. By putting on the uniform they are making a stand for democracy and freedom, and by doing so are placing themselves in the crosshairs.

Loss of Life at War and During Peacetime

The RAF is a family, and losing a family member affects everyone, especially those people at the parent station. Whilst safety is paramount and every care is taken to ensure it, there are no guarantees. The RAF has suffered losses throughout its history and each loss is felt by all. Inevitably, most lives are lost as the result of conflicts and terrorism, but training exercises and routine missions can also be potentially hazardous.

RAF Lyneham suffered tragedy on 27 May 1993, when Hercules XV193 crashed, killing all nine crew. News of the accident filtered back to the station quickly. One of the first actions carried out when a crash occurs is to seize all paperwork and records of the aircraft for further investigation. To be on camp when one of your aircraft crashes is an awful experience. The first you know that anything is wrong is when you are ordered to gather and surrender all records of that aircraft your section may have.

It so happened that Tony was away in Sarajevo when XV193 crashed. His wife, Lesleyanne, was also based at Lyneham. Tony picks up the story:

> We had got back to Ancona after the last flight to Sarajevo and the crew disappeared for debrief while me and the GE put the aircraft to bed. We got back to the hotel a little after the crew. They were sat in the bar so we went over to join them, and that's when they told us the news. It was devastating. I knew most of the crew who had died, so it was really hard to hear. The details were sketchy, but XV193 had crashed on a training flight in Scotland.
>
> What I didn't know at the time was that Lesleyanne had been at the armoury when the news broke. She had stopped off

on her way home to pick up my mail. Everyone was running around, and while she knew that an aircraft had crashed, she didn't know which one, or where. The obvious conclusion was that it was the one on active Ops in Sarajevo. She went home, and a little while later found out by watching the news that it wasn't me. We spoke on the phone that night. It was a very muted call because we were both just stunned. But the next day I was back on board with the rest of the crew flying food to Sarajevo.

This tradition of carrying on with the job harks back to the very early days of flying. The first deaths of UK airmen while on duty was on 5 July 1912.

Captain Eustace B. Loraine and his passenger, Staff Sergeant R.H.V. Wilson, were flying a Nieuport Monoplane out of Larkhill on a routine morning practice sortie. They were executing a tight turn when the aircraft fell towards the ground and crashed. Wilson was killed outright, and although Loraine was speedily transported to Bulford Hospital in a horse-drawn ambulance, he succumbed to his wounds only a few minutes after arriving there. Loraine and Wilson were the first Flying Corps personnel to die in an aircraft crash while on duty. Later in the day an order was issued that stated: 'Flying will continue this evening as usual', thus beginning a tradition.

Chapter 10

Pull Up a Sandbag

Life in the military is anything but ordinary. You often find yourself in unfamiliar situations and working with people you have never met before. There is frequent travel to foreign climes, and sometimes what awaits you at the other end can be potentially life-threatening. Anyone who joins the service develops the ability to survive, and to take whatever comes their way in their stride.

A sense of humour is one of the first attributes you have to develop – the ability to stare anything and anyone in the face and laugh is vital. Sometimes the situation is anything other than funny, and humour may seem inappropriate; other situations are so ridiculous the only thing you can do is laugh. No matter what the situation, a smile is the most effective weapon in the military arsenal.

The following stories represent some of the odd things that can happen. They don't fit neatly into any other chapter, but the fact that they happened deserves to be recorded. You may have picked up on the fact that Armourers are inherently sociable creatures. Their gatherings are renowned for hospitality and fun. A big part of that fun is the remembering and retelling of stories. The tradition of feasting, and recounting great deeds goes back to the feasting halls of old; the great and the good are gathered, the drinking horns are overflowing, and each warrior has their story to tell. The Armourers proudly continue that tradition. We remember our brethren and their epic deeds. So pull up a sandbag (take a seat) and enjoy!

Following Her Majesty

While Brian Morton was at Gaydon in the late 1950s, one of his corporals was a chap called Jack. Brian remembers Jack as being a bit of a character:

> He'd been up and down the ranks over the years: corporal – airman – airman – corporal. He must have been in the service for twenty years when I met him.

One year, during late spring, he went away and was gone for three months. Eventually he turned up and had to go and see the CO, who gave him a grilling: 'You've been AWOL for three months. What's going on? What have you been doing all this time?'

Jack replied: 'I've been with our patron.'

'What do you mean?', said the CO.

'I've been with Her Majesty. I was at Ascot, and she was there. I was at Newmarket, and she was there. I've been following her around all the racecourses.'

The CO was not impressed, and immediately told Jack that he would be docked three months' worth of pay. Jack put his hand in his pocket, pulled out a wad of notes, and said: 'I don't think I'm going to be unduly worried Sir.'

Bonfires and Fireworks

Armourers often find themselves responsible for the station fireworks display. Modern times have seen a decline, with budgets and health and safety hampering events, but there was a time when budgets were big and as long as no one died, it was a good night. The station fireworks displays in the 1980s and 1990s were awesome. The build-up to the display would involve weeks of prep, with the chosen few spending hours working out the display and spending the budget on the biggest and best fireworks available. There would also be a massive bonfire that would be weeks in the making. All sections would hoard anything that could burn and deposit it on the ever-growing heap. Tony recalls two firework-related incidents:

My first firework display at Kinloss was really spectacular. I wasn't involved in the display, but managed to get along and watch. The lads had done a marvellous job of setting everything up. We were on a big field and there were ropes around to stop people wandering into danger.

The event always started with either the station commander, his wife, or some other local dignitary starting the bonfire. The flames of the bonfire quickly lit everything up. Then it would be time for the fireworks. The display would start well with rockets and a lovely static 'Welcome' message, then it was on to the mortars.

PULL UP A SANDBAG

In the Kinloss display the first mortar shot skywards and came back down almost where it had taken off from, and landed in a massive tin of fireworks. The lads were using a big ammo container and had left the lid off. There must have been about £2,000-worth of fireworks that went off, and that was about half the display. There were armourers running everywhere, dodging missiles. Of course, the crowd loved it! A few people commented that the display only lasted about half the advertised time, but overall it was a jolly good show.

Lyneham always put on a good display, and one year we outdid ourselves in more ways than one. On the day of the display there were about six of us on the field getting things sorted. We had borrowed a 4-ton truck from MT and started by setting up the welcome board. It was about 10–15ft high, so one of the lads used the cab of the truck to stand on to drive the wooden posts in using a sledgehammer. First couple of blows were fine, but then it went wrong. He swung and missed the stake, and put the sledgehammer straight through the windscreen of the truck. Embarrassing, but nothing a trip to MT for a replacement wouldn't sort. New truck obtained and we were back in business.

The next couple of hours were busy. We got everything laid out and prepped: mortar tubes buried in the ground facing a safe direction, rows of rockets tubes set up around the area, and safe points to store all the fireworks. It was a big show, so we had about six or seven different firing points set up. The chief was a great lad and had some great ideas. He had put the display to music, so timing was key; we all had a script and would carry radios on the night.

The bonfire was built and prepped. It was massive, maybe 20ft or higher, and we had created a hollow passage into the middle where we were going to use a 'small' amount of PE and some aircraft fuel to get it going. There was a wire line running from the dais where the CO's wife was going to start the bonfire. When she pushed the button, a rocket would fly down the wire into the heart of the bonfire and we would be off.

Once the prep was done, we had a few hours before the display was due to start. We couldn't leave the field unattended, so three of the lads went off for food and the rest of us stayed behind. I went and got my dogs from the house (I only lived around the corner), and one of the others got out their golf clubs. He had just taken up the game and was keen to practise. He was hitting tee shots and doing well, and one of the others wanted a go so a ball was set up and the driver handed over. It's funny how someone who has never played golf before can hit the ball so well. The ball was struck sweetly and flew straight as an arrow for well over 100 yards, right into the side window of the 4-tonner. The window smashed into a thousand pieces. We didn't need a side window so decided to keep the truck and cough up later; we didn't want to put out MT again with a request for another truck.

The appointed hour came, and so did the crowds. We set the bang in the heart of the bonfire; we only used about a quarter of a stick of PE and a very small bottle of aircraft fuel – just to get the party started, you understand. The rocket was hung on the wire and rigged for firing, and all the fireworks were set out at their various firing points. The CO's wife set off the rocket, which flew down the wire. As soon as the rocket disappeared into the centre of the bonfire the chief fired the PE and there was an expectant hush over the crowd, then BANG – the whole bonfire was lifted about 10ft in the air in a mass of flames and sparks. When it landed it came down as a pancake. It could only have been a couple of feet high, but was spread right out and the fire was raging like an inferno. It lasted a good five minutes then died down. Meanwhile, we got on with the rest of the display, which went well. There were the usual stray rockets and mortars, which sent us running for cover at times, but otherwise it was impressive.

The tidy-up took a couple of hours. We still had the 4-tonner (complete with well-ventilated cab), we had our Land Rover, and we'd borrowed a box van from the safety equipment section. It had a wide set of steps at the back to make it easy getting in and out. One of the lads reversed it into the corner of a building; some bricks were knocked out and the metal steps were completely mangled. I reckon the chassis was bent as well but didn't say anything. So that was it for another year, three wrecked vehicles and a flat bonfire to mark the display. On the plus side, one of us found out they could play golf pretty well.

Brian Polson is another armourer with memories of Bonfire Night, albeit in days when the celebrations were slightly lower key. Back in the autumn of 1958, after more than four years at Gaydon, he was nominated to help prepare the Bonfire Night celebrations for the children of the officers at the camp. Everyone loves Bonfire Night, so building the bonfire and preparing the accompanying children's activities was great fun.

As Tony's stories illustrate, fire and armaments don't tend to go well together well, and the bonfire was built in a distant corner of the base, well away from the buildings and aircraft. Brian recalls one of the nights shortly before the big event:

> It was really foggy when a team of us headed over to the area where the bonfire was being built. It so happened that the bonfire was only a mile or so away from the village of Lighthorne, and there was a lane heading from the base into the village. I was in charge, so I said to the lads, 'Let's go down to the pub in the village. It's foggy, so no one's going to know.' So I took them all down to the pub and bought them a drink as a treat. No one was ever the wiser, and we made sure we stayed sober for Bonfire Night itself.

Under the Carpet Race

A legendary initiation ritual at the Changi base in Singapore was the 'under the carpet race', an event that occasionally took place in the sergeants' mess. The mess was very old, and on the ballroom floor was a massive and very ancient Indian carpet (probably very valuable). Events were organised to welcome new arrivals, and during the course of the evening several of the more experienced members would casually mention to the 'new boy' how much they were looking forward to tonight's race, even how disappointed they were not to get into one of the teams last time.

At the appointed time, the teams would be chosen, naturally including the now-eager new recruit, and the edge of the carpet would be lifted for the teams to race under and back. First team with all members through would be the winner. The signal was given to go, at which point the only person to actually go under the carpet would be the new boy. The rest of the members would then spend the next hour or two standing on the carpet chatting and drinking but mainly ensuring that whichever way he crawled his path was blocked. Eventually he would be allowed to emerge, now resembling a coal miner and somewhat in need of a drink, but hopefully a little wiser.

Medical Memories

Requiring urgent medical care is never fun, but it can result in lots of vivid memories – both good and bad.

Derek Binnie was 19 in 1977, and was working in the bomb dump at RAF Honington in Suffolk. One sunny afternoon, while out doing stuff to bombs, he began to feel unwell and was taken to the camp's medical centre. After being diagnosed with an appendix that was about to explode, he was taken 35 miles to the RAF Hospital in Ely and given an emergency operation.

What Derek discovered next surprised him. The post-operation ward at the RAF hospital included a mix of young, fit RAF guys and very old, and in some cases very ill, non-RAF civilians. It was an odd mix. And it provided Derek with some vivid memories, some amusing, others very moving:

> The first morning after my op, and still feeling a bit sore, I opened my eyes and saw an old guy next to me with a colostomy bag hanging from his bed. He didn't look too well. I gingerly got up and began to shuffle to the toilet. I'd got about three feet and heard a soft, 'Son … Son …' When I looked back it was my new bed-neighbour who was trying to catch my attention.
>
> 'Yes, can I help?'
>
> 'Are you going to the toilet son?'
>
> 'I'm trying to but I'm a bit sore.'
>
> 'Can you take my teeth with you and give them a clean, son?'
>
> I looked at his bedside cabinet and was met with a glass full of teeth, together with his Steradent and brush. 'Erm, Yes, OK.'
>
> Well, I thought I was in slightly better shape than him to carry out the brushing of a set of false teeth. So off I went with my glass of teeth to cross off something I'm sure might be on my wish list one day.
>
> There was also an Armourer from Honington in the ward. He was in the corner of the ward, so we could have a conversation from our beds. He was in to have an examination for kidney stones. It turned out that having an examination meant having a camera inserted into his kidney via his penis. Luckily he was out cold for the examination, but I'll always remember when he woke up after it. Very slowly, he made his

way to the loo for a wee … But I don't think I or anyone else was ready for his screams from the toilet, which I'm certain were heard throughout Ely. Nor will I ever forget his beautiful words when he returned, his face in a contorted gurn: 'IT'S LIKE PISSING F***ING GLASS!'

There was also another very old man in the bed opposite. Most mornings, during my shuffle to the loo to clean a set of false teeth, he'd try and entice me over to his bed. For the first two days I pretended I hadn't heard him, as God knows what delights were in store, but on day three I finally went over, and he proceeded to say: 'Have a look at this, son.'

He then pulled down the cover and revealed that he was almost black from his waist to the top of his legs. Not too sure what happened to the blue … he was just black.

'I've had a hernia operation, son.'

'Well, I hope you get better soon. Anyway, I can't stop – my neighbour's waiting for his teeth.'

I was in that ward for a week. One abiding memory is of the daily doctor inspection. You had to sit upright in your bed regardless of how you felt. Every patient had their rank and name taped to their bed. The whole thing was a real eye opener for me at that age.

Towards the end of my stay a part-time physio breezed in wearing a blue tracksuit. He flew in like Larry Grayson on speed. Holding his clipboard and looking at the beds, he went over to the old guy in the bed opposite, sat him up, propped him up on his pillows, bent him over, got a polystyrene cup, and started to beat his back saying, 'Come on Mr Simpson. Get as much up as you can.' This continued until the old guy was able to muster the strength to say, 'I'm not Mr Simpson.' Larry Grayson stopped in his tracks and headed off to see a nurse. It turned out the list of patients on his clipboard was wrong, and Mr Simpson (who apparently suffered from bronchitis) wasn't in that bed. The old man with the black bollocks who'd had a hernia operation was, and he was now a bit the worse for wear.

My final memory … A few beds down from Hernia Man was another poor old soul who was trying to recover from an operation. Towards the end of my stay I was half asleep in the middle of the night and heard a bump and 'clang'. A commotion then ensued as two male nurses ran in, and realised that this old guy had fallen out of his bed. Everyone else was asleep, but I was listening in. I thought I could hear them arguing, in whispers, about who should have made sure the side of the bed was up, but I might have misheard. Slowly I drifted back off to sleep.

In the morning, when I woke up, this same old guy was on the bed in a body bag. Everyone was waking up, and suddenly a team arrived to take his body away.

So, after a week recovering from an operation, I left feeling physically better but mentally traumatised.

Stop that Hearse!

Occasionally Armourers will be asked to do something that really isn't part of their job description. Garron Clark-Darby describes one such situation:

> While I was at Upavon, I had the dubious honour of taking a funeral parade for a very senior retired officer who had died of old age at his house near the base. 'You've just done your SNCO training,' said the CO. 'You must know what to do, and I'm bloody certain nobody else here does'.
>
> The idea was that the hearse would enter the base via the main gate, and the route from there to the camp chapel would be lined either side at intervals with smartly dressed young airmen who would pay their last respects by performing the drill manoeuvre 'rest on reverse arms' as the cortège passed.
>
> Over the next few days I duly taught a couple of dozen 'volunteers' the appropriate drill, and on the day of the funeral itself everything went swimmingly, right until the point where the coffin had been removed from the hearse and was being taken into the chapel. It turned out that the trestles on which the coffin was to be placed were still in the back of the hearse, so when the pallbearers entered the chapel they suddenly realised that they couldn't put the coffin down. The chief mourner was promptly sent to retrieve the trestles from the hearse. Unfortunately it had just driven off, albeit very slowly, as they tend to do. All the young airmen lining the route, and me of course, were treated to the sight of the diminutive and ancient chief mourner following the hearse at a brisk trot with the black ribbons on his top hat flowing in the wind as he repeatedly shouted 'Stop' in a hoarse whisper that was very

respectful of the funeral, but as a consequence could not be heard by the driver, who just carried on, slowly – but still slightly quicker than the chief mourner could trot.

The ensuing mirth among the troops could not be controlled or disguised, and as a consequence nobody asked me to do another parade for quite a few years.

Load Team Dining

When you're loading nuclear weapons, load teams must comprise the same group of Armourers. These are four-man teams, and only one person can be absent, for example on leave, at any one time. For all major exercises, the team works together. This helps to generate great team spirit and camaraderie.

Podge Middleton describes his team's approach to dining during an exercise:

> Before an exercise started, when we knew it was pre-planned, the guys on my load teams all coughed up 10 DM, and my wife cooked and baked for the exercise. So we'd have a roast chicken and salad, or maybe a birthday cake, which we would carry around with us for the next three days.
>
> We were working from aircraft shelters, and you were fed in the shelters with 'hotlocks', pre-prepared meals served in tins, but because we moved around so much we'd quite often miss the food turning up. So we looked after ourselves. If we missed a meal, we had one with us.
>
> Our load team decided to dress to eat. So we'd be wearing our NBC suits, and we'd go into the HAS. The HAS would have a set layout, where all the weapons would be. So as you went in through the doors, on the right-hand side would be JP233, the airfield denial weapon. That became our table. Man 4, always a junior, was responsible for looking after the food in his rucksack, and making sure I didn't forget to carry my machine gun.
>
> So we'd lay out a tablecloth. We had napkins. We had knives, forks and spoons. We had a candelabra made of ejection seat pipes. We even had little fake candles we'd put in the top. We'd put our dickie bows on. And we'd have a Prosecco bottle, or Asti as it was then, which we filled with

lemonade. So we'd go 'Pop!', and out came the glasses. And then we'd sit there, dining in, while the HAS staff looked over at us, totally gobsmacked.

Locked out of the HAS

Another of Podge's recollections is of an incident that happened to his load team in Laarbruch:

> We were on a strike-loading exercise for 15 Squadron. Strike was a nuclear weapon – a training round. The process is that once you've finished the load, the HAS is secured, you've got the bomb on the aircraft, and the aircrew turn up. They then take control of the weapon, and we leave. Once the aircrew have control of the weapon, they shouldn't leave the HAS.
>
> When you'd finished loading the aircraft, you had to move the trolley that the bomb had come in out of the HAS. Much of the time the electric pan on the clam shell doors of the HAS didn't work, so we had to move the doors by hand.
>
> So on this occasion we lifted the giant bolt on the floor, pushed the door open, pushed our trolley out, then started to close the HAS doors. As we did that, the aircrew walked out. We're saying, 'You shouldn't be out here,' then clang! And the HAS doors closed. Everybody is now outside the HAS. And the HAS is locked. Bolts on the inside. So we have a fully armed Tornado, with its practice nuke on, ready to go, and no one can get to it.
>
> Next door to the HAS is a hardened shelter that was used as a store shelter. It was my job to tell someone that we had a bit of a problem. So I got on the phone to the operations centre, onto the Armourer control, a guy called Mick. The conversation went something like this:
>
> 'We've got a bit of a problem. The aircraft's loaded, but we're all locked out.'
>
> 'Is this an inject?'
>
> 'No, this is no duff. We're locked out of the HAS.'
>
> 'Impossible!'
>
> 'It's not impossible mate. I've got the aircraft here. We're here. But we're locked out of the HAS.'
>
> 'Oh my God!'

PULL UP A SANDBAG

There's a bit more banter, backwards and forwards, ending with Mick's, 'I'll get back to you.' He hadn't a clue what to do really.

I go outside, and OC 15 Squadron had turned up. We've now got the crew, the Di staff for the taceval, and the wing commander. He was really switched on and quickly took the situation in.

Each HAS had holes in the side to put cables in for power sets. The wing commander saw there was a hole, looked around at the crew, and saw there was a guard who was as thin as a rake, and said, 'You. Remove your clothes. That's an order.' So he got down to his shreddies, we got grease off the HAS doors and greased him up, and we shoved him through this hole in the side of the HAS. And because the rules were that you always had to have two people in a HAS at any one point, the commander got the navigator to stick his head through the hole while the guard opened the HAS doors.

Armourers in Amsterdam

As will have become clear during the course of this book, Armourers and beer tend to be a potent combination. Garron Clark-Darby remembers an alcohol-inspired trip to Amsterdam:

I was looking for a way to give a treat to the bunch of twenty or so lads who worked for me on the flight line, and somebody mentioned that the Amstel Brewery in Amsterdam was quite keen on British servicemen and would happily give a free tour of the brewery and a little bit of hospitality. The trip was duly arranged for a weekend, and a coach was booked. We would arrive at the brewery late morning, spend the day in the plant, come out about teatime, find somewhere for dinner, and get the bus back to Gütersloh about 10 p.m. Perfect, but sadly it didn't quite work out like that.

We arrived at the brewery to be met by an animated and apologetic little chap who explained that they had forgotten that the entire plant was having the floor painted that weekend and thus, sorry, we could not enter. By way of apology, he proposed that we go straight to the hospitality suite where instead they would show us some educational films of the plant. Now, when a brewery offers 'hospitality' to a bunch of 20-year-old British lads, that means only one thing. The beer immediately started to flow, without any notion of measure or reserve, served by attractive Dutch-costumed 'wenches', interrupted only by occasional small nibbles and bits of bread and cheese.

By the time we left the brewery, still only about 2 p.m, all the lads were a bit more relaxed than I had intended. I managed to corner them (literally) and give a safety briefing before releasing them into Amsterdam. 'Stay together.' I said, 'Avoid prostitutes, don't get into fights, and be back here for the bus at ten.' I might as well have not bothered. One got mugged, because he was in the red light district on his own. Several duly experienced the pleasures of the ladies of the night, and several more, some of whom were married, had tattoos done. When it came time to board the bus half were still at large, and I flew around the back streets of old Amsterdam rounding them up, like herding cats. The poor old German bus driver had hopes of making a few Marks on the journey back by flogging the lads some beer, but by then they'd all had a skin full.

RAF vs US Marines

Socialising is a big part of life in the RAF and none more so than when overseas. Another important aspect is international relations and so every opportunity is taken to mingle with the locals. Tony recounts a trip to Sigonella:

The hotel was just outside the base we were operating from. It was a US naval airbase and they had all the amenities on site including bars, bowling alley, cinema, the lot; you name it and the Americans have it. That night was the Superbowl, so we went along to watch it in one of their bars. Some American marines were drinking at the bar and we all got chatting. They were well on the way to being drunk, and at some point one of them started saying we Brits couldn't hold our drink and they were better than us ... the usual. The gauntlet was thrown down: a drinking contest, one of them versus one of us. They fielded a strapping young marine, probably early 20s and very fit, hours in the gym and full of testosterone. We fielded the painter and finisher, who was a lass from Glasgow. She was only about 5ft tall. As she walked up to the table I'm sure all the spams thought they had this in the bag. They started on beer, stubby little cans of Budweiser or Coors. The first two were placed on the table. The spam grabs his and down it goes, with our lass keeping pace effortlessly. And on it went. By about twenty cans you could see the spam was struggling. There were funny little 'windy' noises every time he drank, whereas our girl was quaffing with consummate ease. She took pity on him and suggested they switched to shots. The look of relief on his face was obvious. And so they lined them up. Vodka, neat. They racked up about four glasses each and down they went, another four and down the hatch. Another four and our American cousin was looking very ill. His eyes had glazed over, and his mates were having to jolly him along with encouragement. That and hold him up. By the next round he was done. He slid off his chair on to the floor and stayed there. Our lady politely finished her drinks and, not wanting to waste anything, drank his as well. One-nil the Brits. The rest of the marines were in awe and we didn't buy another drink all night.

The Akrotiri Arrows

During his time at the Akrotiri airbase in Cyprus, Ade Thorne was a keen darts player. A team of Armourers, including Ade, decided to enter a local darts league. The fact that the Gulf War was in full swing at the time wasn't going to stop them throwing their arrows.

Ade remembers one particular match, in a pub in Limassol, during which the senior member of the Armourers' team had to take a phone call from Aki Ops. It turned out that a plane had taken off, but when it had reached a certain height and the air pressure decreased some items in the hold, which had not been properly packed, started flying around. This caused a considerable amount of noise. Not knowing what was going on, the pilot put the plane into a dive and called for an immediate return to base. Ade and his boss leapt into a car and headed back to Akrotiri. They met the plane taxiing in, identified the problem, sorted it out, and then headed back to the pub in Limassol in time for the doubles.

The darts league continued throughout the Gulf War, and the Armourers' team didn't miss a match. They even managed to finish second in the league one year.

The AOC visits Ancona

Operation Cheshire in Ancona was a high-profile operation and ran from 1992 to 1995. This meant there was a constant stream of visitors throughout its duration. Everyone wanted to drop in and say hello, to boost the morale of those working on the op. Ancona was also used as a drop-off and pick-up point for people heading out to or back from theatre. They could hop on the Herc at Sarajevo and come back to Ancona, and then get a flight or take advantage of the local amenities for a bit of R&R.

The press loved coming to say hello, and the BBC reporter Kate Adie dropped in several times. Prime Minister John Major visited with his entourage and stopped long enough to drink Guinness with the personnel and say hello. It should be noted that 47 Squadron had a long and very amicable association with Guinness and often carried a barrel with them for just such an occasion. Visits of high-profile people were strictly managed, and the detachment commander would keep a wary eye on everyone and everything to make sure all was as it should be. An Air Officer Commanding (a very senior RAF person) decided to drop in on a tour of all the camps and squadrons involved in the operation, and Ancona was going to be the last stop on his way home. Tony recalls the AOC's visit:

> The AOC was on board a Herc doing the round robin of all the camps, and they stopped off at Ancona last. One of the lads decided to give the AOC a bit of a special welcome, so persuaded someone to drive the Land Rover around the pan towing him on a palletiser. He had managed to get an RAF flag from somewhere, so was proudly waving this flag around on the end of a long wooden pole. It looked really impressive, but it didn't go down well with the detachment commander. To be fair, having someone being towed around a busy pan by a dodgy Land Rover, while standing on a palletiser, had disaster written all over it. The lads were guiding the Herc into its parking slot so the det commander could speak to them, but you could see he was fuming. We stopped the aircraft and opened the crew door at the front. The AOC walked down the steps and shook hands with the det commander then said: 'Thanks, it's the best welcome I have ever had. I get fed up with the spit and polish and everything looking perfect!' I think everyone breathed a sigh of relief at that, so nothing more was said.

Rest and Relaxation in Bahrain

Ade Thorne remembers an R&R trip to Bahrain, while he was on a four-month posting to Ali Al Salem airbase in Kuwait. Conditions in Kuwait were pretty rudimentary, with two men sharing single rooms and toilet facilities that involved holes in the ground. Food was basic rations, and entertainment involved watching videos in a tent. So the five-day R&R trip to Bahrain was something to relish:

> The Americans flew us down in a Herc. We were picked up by the minibus and driven to the Intercontinental hotel. We walked into reception and were greeted by these Taiwanese girls with not a lot of clothes on. They were holding trays of cocktails, which they gave us as we were checking in. We then walked through to the bar and there was John Smith's on tap – OK, so it's not the greatest beer ever, but when it's free it's a lot better than nothing. So with your beer in your hand, you looked out of the window, and down by the pool there were lots of stewardesses from British Airways, Virgin, and Qantas, all sunbathing topless. I thought I'd died and gone to heaven. We got talking to the stewards and stewardesses, and they invited us to block parties in the evenings – all we had to do was bring some beer. Honestly, I cried when I had to board the Herc five days later to fly us back to Kuwait.

Never Sleep in the Party Room

Sometimes you have to learn the rules the hard way. Tony recalls one such lesson, during a short trip to Sigonella:

> Our fourth and final night (not bad given we were only meant to be away one night) was a real blast. We'd had a great day out touring round all the sites and soaking up the culture, and ended up with a slap-up meal in Catania. When we got to the hotel there was a party going on. Whenever the RAF go away anywhere they always have enough rooms for everyone plus one. The spare room can be used for parties, which saves anyone having to stay up just because the party is in their room. We went to the party and carried on drinking. The party

room was always well stocked with booze, so there were all sorts getting drunk.

The next morning I woke up in my bed without any memory of the party or getting back to the room. I had this uncomfortable feeling that all was not quite right, but couldn't put my finger on it. As my eyes started to focus I saw a Bic razor on my bedside table. Bit odd because I didn't own a Bic ... Moment of panic, lift bedsheets, all in order, relax. I got up, showered and dressed; we were flying home that day so one must look one's best. All was good with the world and breakfast was on the cards. I arrived in the hotel restaurant ready for the feast. A couple of the others were down already and it's fair to say that we were all afflicted by that common tropical disease called red eye. However, my condition was worse in that I had mislaid an eyebrow. Just one, the one that normally sat above my left eye, and I hadn't even noticed until someone dropped it into conversation. Turns out I had fallen asleep in the party room, a cardinal offence, and my punishment was to have an eyebrow shaved off. Not a problem and it could have been worse. I have seen half-and-half shaving, heads to toes, so an eyebrow was nothing. Until I remembered that when we got back I was due to travel home with my fiancée to meet her parents for the first time. Oh well, these things happen down route!

Propwash Sailing

Operations can sometimes be boring. War is 5 per cent chaos and 95 per cent boredom, and boredom leads to the troops creating their own amusement. Tony recalls his time on Operation Cheshire:

I didn't always fly with the Herc to Sarajevo. There were other jobs I needed to do such as prepping the chaff and flares or even sorting things out for the GE. If I wasn't flying I would see the aircraft away, then get on with whatever else I needed to do. Each Herc would reverse out of its bay onto the taxiway, so I used to watch the engine start, remove the power cable and watch them back. To reverse, the Hercs change the pitch on the propellors so that the engines push the aircraft back; it's a neat system. If you are in front you get a bit of prop wash, but it's not too bad.

The aircrew were a great bunch. I had done countless trips with them and there was always banter. On this particular day,

PULL UP A SANDBAG

the captain decided to have some fun with me. He applied more power during the reverse to try and blow me over. I managed to stay on my feet, but I could see them all laughing. It got me thinking ... all that power and energy from the prop wash had potential.

While they were away, I scavenged some bits and bobs. I had an idea that, if it worked, would give us all a laugh. The key item was a pallet truck, the sort they use in warehouses to move the pallets around. It's two long blades with a wheel on each tip of the blades and a set of dolly wheels at the other end. You slide the blades under the pallet and lift it off the floor using the hydraulic system fitted, you pump the handle (which is also used to steer the palletiser) which jacks up the blades and pallet, then you move the pallet to wherever you need. So palletiser, check. Next was a mast and spar. I found a long broom handle, maybe 6ft long, and some lengths of wood. One length of wood was secured to the handle of the palletiser, so it was vertical. The broom handle was secured across the upright. Next were the sails. I used four nylon drop zone markers; they are rectangular high-visibility sheets, which I secured to the mast and taped together so there weren't any gaps between. I reckon I had about 16ft^2 of sail. The idea was to park the palletiser in front of the aircraft with the sail at the front and use the prop wash to propel me forward. I would stand on the blades and steer it using the handle.

I didn't say anything to the crew. Only one person knew what was happening, and that was the supplier. The aircraft came back, and we got it ready for its next trip; there was about an hour between trips. The crew got on board, and me and the supplier helped get them ready. Once the engines were turning I got the palletiser out and parked it in front of the aircraft. The captain signalled that he was ready to reverse, and by now all the crew were staring out of the windows and cupola bubble (a clear Perspex dome) on the top of the Herc. I was wearing a flying suit and jacket and flying gloves, and sporting a pair of Ray-Ban Aviator sunglasses so I looked the part. I faced the aircraft and gave a smart salute. I then did an about turn and mounted the palletiser. I had one hand on the steering handle and one on the crossbar where it crossed the mast. The captain applied the power and nothing happened for a few seconds, then the sails (and the legs of my flying suit) filled with air – but still no movement.

The engine note increased as the captain applied more power, and all of a sudden I was off. I shot across the pan, crossed an access road and straight up a concrete ramp into one of the big supply warehouses. The palletiser slowed so I turned it round and descended the ramp, using gravity to take me back to where I started. I was surprised to see that the Herc was still there.

After a few minutes they moved off to take the food to Sarajevo. When they returned a couple of hours later, they all came piling off the aircraft and surrounded me. Apparently, they had all been laughing so hard they couldn't control the aircraft. The captain was in tears, so they had to stop while they composed themselves. One member of the crew had fallen off his perch on the edge of the bunk because he was laughing so much.

Of course, they wanted a repeat performance, so I obliged. This time all the people on the op came out to see the mad Armourer, and we put on a proper show. I was marched to my aircraft and there was a formal ceremony. This time the captain applied more power from the off and I shot across the pan and up the ramp like a scalded cat. I had so much momentum that I flew straight across the warehouse this time and went out the other side and off one of the loading ramps. It was a 6ft drop onto tarmac. I survived, but the palletiser didn't.

The next day I made the Mk2 version using an old three-wheeled commode. It had twin front wheels, sort of pram-sized, and one smaller wheel at the back. The sail and mast were the same arrangement, but I had to rig up a way of steering the thing using some rope. The effects weren't as amazing as the Mk1, but there was definitely more comedy and some of the crashes were spectacular. It all turned into a bit of a sideshow, and whenever I donned my flying gear people would come and watch. Someone even took photos of one of the later attempts using the commode.

Golf Tales

Although Jon Eaton wasn't a regular golfer himself, he met some very talented players during his time as an Armourer – perhaps unsurprising given that his first posting was to Leuchars near St Andrews, the home of golf.

Later, when Jon was working at Kinloss, one of his colleagues was a very talented young golfer named Hamish, whose father was a greenkeeper at a prestigious golf club. Being a competitive player, Hamish always liked to have the latest equipment, so when Ping brought out their new i2 clubs he decided he wanted a set. Jon describes what happened next:

> Hamish ordered a set of i2 clubs, which required going down to London for a fitting. At the time he had a brand-new, Mark 2, racing bronze-green Golf GTI car. So he got into his car and drove down from Kinloss, on the Moray Firth, to London. And on the way down he got three speeding tickets. A sheepish Hamish admitted that, as a result, they were the most expensive golf clubs he'd ever bought. He also talked of selling his new car and buying a pushbike instead, because one more ticket and he'd lose his driving licence.

The reputation of St Andrews had its benefits. While Jon was at Leuchars he acquired some money as a result of a life insurance policy, purchased by his grandfather when Jon was born, maturing. Jon used the money to pay the deposit on a little cottage in the village of Ceres, around 8 miles from the Old Course at St Andrews. He moved in with one of his colleagues from Leuchars, and when he was posted to Kinloss a second airman moved in. The rental they paid covered the mortgage. However, when he was stationed at Kinloss Jon decided that it would be better to sell the cottage. He takes up the story:

> One weekend I drove down from Kinloss and went into an estate agency in St Andrews. I told them I was planning to sell a cottage in Ceres, and they said that they had some clients who might be interested. I'd paid around £32,000 for the cottage, and after seeing the property and taking some photos the estate agents valued it at £54,000. Three days later I had a call from a girl at the estate agents saying, 'Would you accept an offer of £74,000?' The purchaser was an American who was coming over for the British Open at St Andrews the following year; he had been sent the photos and decided that this was where he wanted to stay, and offered £74,000 on the spot.

The Roermond Earthquake

There is one day and time that Derek Binnie won't forget – 4 a.m. on 13 April 1992. The location was the SSA (nuclear bomb storage site) at Brüggen, and the incident that is etched in Derek's memory was 'the Roermond Earthquake'.

Derek was an Armourer sergeant working on the 'buckets of sunshine' at the time, and when an earthquake of 5.3 magnitude struck at precisely 3.20 a.m. he was at home in Roermond in the Netherlands. Unfortunately, he was part of the SSA duty crew, so when the quake struck he was immediately called in to 'check the weapons are OK and not damaged inside the buildings'. So, after leaving his shaken wife Denise and their kids at home, he set off the few miles to Brüggen. Derek describes what happened next:

> When I arrived at approximately 4 a.m. it was like Blackpool outside the SSA. There were lots of vehicles, lots of people and lots of lights. When I went into the site I had to wait for my police building escort before we could enter the first building. When he arrived, I could tell right away he was badly shaken. When I asked him what was wrong, he said that he'd been up inside the lookout tower when the quake struck, and that it had been swaying. I had to phone up to SSA police control to ask for another policeman as this one was broken! He clearly needed time to recover from the shock.

St Mawgan SPERM

While Bob Worthington-Harris was working in the bomb dump at St Mawgan, one of his colleagues, Steve, started informally publishing a comic called Southern Peninsula Explosive Regional Magazine – better known as SPERM. On one occasion he posted a picture of a very well-endowed man, on which he superimposed the head of one of the flight sergeants. This didn't go down well, despite Steve's assertion that it was actually a very flattering representation.

On another occasion, Steve spilled the beans on a rather imaginative set-up at the bomb dump. A number of boxes of 114 tail units were being stored there, and the boxes had been arranged so that they looked, to the untrained eye, like a solid block of boxes. In reality the outer boxes were concealing an open area inside with deck chairs and sun loungers. As a result, the dumpies on duty would be able to recline and top up their sun tans when they were manning the dump. All of which was great, until SPERM magazine published an incriminating photo, after which the sunbathing area was quickly cleared away.

SPERM closed down when Steve was posted to another base. Bob did meet up with him again many years later, at which point Steve was an instructor. No doubt the inventive skills he had displayed in earlier years were great assets in his later work.

PULL UP A SANDBAG

Luxury London Trip

Sometimes it was the occasional unexpected treats that made you appreciate life in the RAF. Brendan Lucey recalls a trip to London from Leeming in the late 1980s, where he was working on the flight line helping to set up squadrons:

> It was a Thursday, and one of the senior officers asked, 'Is anyone planning to go to London for the weekend?' It so happened that I was planning to go down, by train, so I said 'yes'. 'Well, we can fly you down,' he replied.
>
> It was a Bank Holiday weekend, and it turned out that there was an air vice-marshal who was going up to Scotland for fishing. He was catching the Queen's Flight jet to Leeming, then getting a helicopter ride from Leeming to where he was staying in Scotland. His plane would then be flying back to London, and there were spare seats on board.
>
> This was an executive jet, HS125. Lovely plane. Very comfortable. I'd never been in anything like it before. The thing was, I was planning to go clubbing in London that night, and by the time I'd get home I would need to dump my bags and head straight out again. So I decided to dress up in my clubbing clothes. There I was, dressed up really trendy, alongside a rigger who was hung over from the night before, looking a bit the worse for wear. The steward on the plane who was taking the IDs walked over to me and said, 'Hello Sir!' He clearly though I was someone important. His face fell when he saw my ID! But it didn't matter. We still got the cucumber sandwiches during the flight, and I even got to the club on time.
>
> Better still, some guy gave me a free train ticket back to Leeming – for some reason he couldn't use it – so the whole weekend's travel cost me absolutely nothing.

Oil Rig Injuries

Anyone out there been airlifted off an oil rig in the North Sea? Bob Worthington-Harris has, and it was a memorable experience:

> When I was at Lossiemouth in 1993, there was something in SROs about looking for volunteers for an oil rig exercise. The exercise scenario: heavy thick fog was surrounding an oil rig

and a ship accidently runs into it, cutting the domestic site where the workers sleep from the oil platform by severing the gangway.

Before we set off for Beatrice (the name of the oil field), we had to practise being airlifted by 202 Squadron search and rescue Sea Kings. Once that was done we headed off for the oil ring in the Sea King. On arrival we were briefed fully that it was a scenario similar to the Piper Alpha disaster, and that the purpose was not only to provide experience for our SAR but also Raigmore Hospital in Inverness. We were to be injured oil rig workers and would be casevac'd (casualty evacuation) to Raigmore for treatment.

Having to sleep on an oil rig is like sleeping on a boat – it rocks and rolls. I joined the Royal Air Force not the Royal Navy, so didn't enjoy the experience. The following morning after breakfast we were made to look like casualties – fake blood, bones sticking out, and laid out all around the rig. Then the alarm went off to signal the emergency. Not long after, crews of engineers began searching for the wounded and treated the wounds. I had a compound fracture of my tibia with loads of fake blood pooled inside it. When the rescuers raised my leg to immobilise it, the blood poured out, adding realism to the exercise. Once I was treated and laid on a stretcher, I was taken to the helipad and loaded onto the Sea King with several other wounded personnel. We flew directly to Inverness, where the hospital staff processed us quickly into a triage before removing our wounds and cleaning us up.

The results of the exercise were never passed on to us, but I was informed that they were passed to Number 10. It was another exciting thing to have done, and not the kind of thing you would get the opportunity to do as a civvy.

Chapter 11

Life as an Ex-Armourer

There comes a time for every Armourer when you have to move on; a time when you swap life in the RAF for a future on civvy street. For those who signed up in the days of National Service, life in the RAF might have lasted a mere two years. For others, it can be more than thirty. Deciding to leave the RAF is as big a decision as the one to join; although for some there is no decision at all because their time is up, or they have a medical issue that forces them to leave.

Every Armourer we spoke to has pride in their service and the jobs they did. The range of experience is massive and covers many decades. The aircraft may have changed, and the technology certainly has. Processes are different, but the people have remained constant; their attitude and ethos have never wavered.

One question has sprung up from the writing of this book: How is it that Armourers can recognise each other anywhere in the world, and within moments of meeting will be comfortable in each other's company? It is highly likely that beer will be involved, and stories shared. What is special about this trade? The answer may lie in the nature of the work. From the moment you say 'yes' to being an Armourer, you commit yourself to working in a dangerous environment – one in which your personal safety relies as much on your oppo as yourself. This requires Armourers to get to know each other quickly and establish trust. The job needs to be done, but the holy grail is celebrating its successful completion in the bar afterwards, and ideally with all the people you started out with.

There is talk of the Armament trade being amalgamated with other aircraft trades. The Fleet Air Arm has been using this approach in its squadrons for years. You join as an aircraft engineer and learn all aspects of every trade. You may specialise, but the expectation is that you can do everything. This does raise concerns because working with explosives is not to be taken lightly. It takes countless hours of training and years of experience to be competent, and above all safe. Some air forces around the world chose to move to the combined technician model, notably the

THE RAF'S ARMOURERS

Royal Australian Air Force and the Royal Canadian Air Force. However, it's worth mentioning that they later decided to revert to separate trades. The Armourers continue to thrive!

So how does it feel on the day that you hand in your ID card, and walk away? It seemed that for all those we talked to, it was a hugely significant and often very emotional moment. One person said it felt like you were 'giving up a massive part of yourself'.

That old adage, 'Once an Armourer, always an Armourer', seems weirdly appropriate. You may have left the RAF and your colleagues behind, but in your head you will remain an Armourer for the rest of your life. And generally, the future for ex-Armourers turns out to be pretty good.

For many RAF Armourers, reunions and online groups are a big part of their lives, providing the opportunity to relive old times and chat about former colleagues – both the good ones, and the not-so-good ones (more commonly referred to as 'arseholes').

Many former Armourers also enjoy reliving old experiences. For Brian Polson, a return to RAF Gaydon provided him with an opportunity to drive around the former airfield in a Land Rover; in 1978 the airfield had been acquired by British Leyland, and later became the headquarters of Jaguar Land Rover. The main runway had been converted into a test track.

More recently, to celebrate his eightieth birthday, his wife paid for Brian to have a flight in a Spitfire, complete with a loop-the-loop, a truly memorable experience for a former RAF man.

No doubt we've all seen homeless people in shop doorways and wondered whether they might be ex-service personnel. The Royal British Legion reckons that 3 to 6 per cent of those sleeping rough were formerly in the armed forces. There is no denying that some Armourers end up in really testing circumstances when they leave; much is down to individual experiences and the support people have received.

However, what does make a difference is that Armourers have a trade and formally recognised qualifications. The mechanical and electrical engineering skills are transferrable to civvy street either in the aircraft industry or beyond, in industries such as plant machinery and construction. Qualifications such as HGV or PCV can open doors into industry, and many Armourers will have service training in leadership, health and safety, and project management. In addition to their service and trade training, personnel are entitled to an annual education allowance, which can be spent on any course that helps in learning new skills and gaining qualifications. As Armourers reach the end of their service there is a resettlement program which means you can get career help and attend courses to help you make the move to civvy street.

LIFE AS AN EX-ARMOURER

But equally importantly, Armourers have the kinds of interpersonal skills that are particularly desirable for potential employers. They're used to working as part of a team, but they are also excellent when it comes to taking responsibility. They are used to dealing with urgent tasks, and when asked to do a task, they will complete it efficiently and safely. All of this was part of the job description, and it stays with you for the rest of your life.

It was interesting to see the range of job roles of the ex-Armourers we spoke to. Unsurprisingly, some had switched to similar jobs involving non-military aircraft. Others had switched direction completely. In Tony's case, he joined IBM as a technical writer, but within a couple of years was working as a manager, with a number of employees reporting to him.

As Tony recalls, the decision to leave the RAF wasn't taken lightly:

> When I joined in '87 I honestly wanted to do twenty-two years or more and could reasonably expect to reach sergeant or C/T provided I did my job and worked hard. This would have given me twenty-two years' worth of experience and memories, and a decent pension from when I left. In short, my life was sorted. However, the end of the Cold War meant that things changed. The review of the armed forces in the '90s led to redundancies and massive uncertainty. Lesleyanne left in 1995, and that was when I decided that, at the end of my twelve years, I should leave as well.
>
> I have always been one to take the initiative and not wait around for things to happen, so I decided to use my annual education allowance. Initially I took GCSE Maths because I failed Maths at school, and I thought the certificate would be useful. I then went on to study for a C&G in Technical Authoring. That was after reading an article in the Forces Resettlement Bulletin; it sounded like a job with prospects. By the time I finished those, I had a year left. So I signed up for an HNC in Business Information Technology. The world was going computer mad so I thought I should join the bandwagon. The technical authoring and HNC got me through the door at IBM and I never looked back.
>
> My big worry was how was I going to fit in. Service life gives you a perspective and sense of humour that many don't understand. But within a few days at IBM I realised I was going to be OK. The people there were great, and because I just got on with things, I fitted in perfectly. The sense of humour was OK too. Sure, I had to censor myself a bit, but at the end of the day we're all human and prefer a laugh to get us through the day.

Whilst my sixteen years at IBM was enjoyable and gave me some excellent experience, I always felt life had more to offer. In 2015 I took redundancy and, with no particular plan, set up my own business. My only rule: to be open-minded. Try anything but if it doesn't work, walk away. Driving, training, tutoring and assessing have formed the core of my business but a chance meeting led to perhaps the most unusual and off-the-wall opportunity.

I am an advanced riding tutor for RoSPA and back in 2016 I was asked to mentor a student preparing for their next bike test. Tim and I hit it off straight away. It turned out that Tim has his own production company and he invited me to help him on a job filming the Southampton half-marathon. My role was to help him build the jib, a tripod with long arms onto which you can mount a camera. It's used for all manner of different shots, and being mobile makes it an invaluable piece of kit on set. It's the chance to wield a spanner and get all technical, making sure the kit is built properly. It's quite complicated and involves loads of components including lots of electrickery. Admittedly nothing is going to go bang, but as we all know, technology can be fickle. Live broadcast brings a certain pressure; there is only ever one chance to get 'that shot', so in many ways it is the perfect job for an ex-Armourer. It has led to me being on set at various events such as Royal Ascot, the Derby, BBC Radio Newsbeat, BBC Radio 5, Newsnight, The Victoria Derbyshire Show, the 2019 election in the BBC newsroom, and in the quadrangle of Windsor Castle for the funeral of Her Majesty Queen Elizabeth II. As an ex-servicemen, to be a part of the funeral was both humbling and the proudest moment of my professional life. Way back in 1987 I took an oath to serve HM and here I was, able to pay my final respects as the coffin passed within a few feet. I wore my medals, my veteran's badge and my Armourers pin with pride in this final act of service.

There is no doubt that my time in the RAF had a massive influence on me; it gave me confidence, skills, and a wife and a sense of belonging, of being part of something bigger than just my own world.

And what of the other Armourers we spoke to? What did they end up doing after handing in their ID cards?

LIFE AS AN EX-ARMOURER

After his National Service, **Bill Lanfear** worked at Westlands in Weston-super-Mare, building helicopters – so after two years of arming aircraft, he switched to building them, albeit a very different type of flying machine.

Brian Polson left the RAF in 1959 and spent most of his working life in the construction industry. He feels that there are parallels between military life and the work he did outside. People tended to move around within the construction industry rather than leaving it altogether, just as they do in the armed forces. So it was important to treat people with respect, because you never knew whether you'd come across them again – and if you did, you didn't want to start on the wrong note.

Bill Morton served nine years, leaving in 1969. Like many Armourers, he soon found a job that enabled him to use the skills he'd developed in the RAF, working on Lightnings in Saudi Arabia. He liked the Middle East, and later worked in both Saudi and Oman as a Munitions Inspector. Between jobs he decided to go to Rhodesia for six-month holiday and ended up working in a casino near Victoria Falls. There he met his future wife, who was twenty-two years his junior. They moved to South Africa, where they got married and started a family. By now Bill was running a swimming pool company. But towards the end of the apartheid era, they moved to the UK. After returning to the UK Bill settled in Oxford, where he became a bulldog – that's an Oxford University policeman, in case you didn't know. He also invigilated for exams at the university, and worked at the university Estates Directorate. Unsurprisingly, he became a fan of Colin Dexter's Morse stories, and remains so to this day.

Derek Binnie served twenty-nine years in the RAF, leaving as a Chief Tech at RAF Leuchars in 2004 and becoming a Health and Safety Officer in Arbroath in a food production company. So, in his own words, 'I went from missiles to meatballs!' He was also sent by his company, on a weekly basis, to help set up Health and Safety at food recycler ReFood's plant in Widnes until 2016, when he decided to retire at 58 to look after his 9-month-old grandson. Persuaded to carry on at Arbroath part-time, he did that until the plant closed in December 2018. At this point he retired, aged 60. Since then he's discovered that he actually has a buried talent for photo editing and currently participates in that hobby, posting much of his work on Twitter @binzoboy. As Derek says, 'It's a hobby that buys my wine.' Married to Denise since October 1978, they both now enjoy early retirement.

Mike Steel served in the RAF for twenty-two years. At the end of the first Gulf War, after working as Chief Tech on the 15 Squadron Tornados, he returned to RAF Wittering in Cambridgeshire, where he was demobbed. Initially he got a job as a technical writer for a local company, but decided to look overseas for work. Job offers included a uniformed role with the Omani Air Force, but instead he ended up in Abu Dhabi working in special technical services. This proved to be the start of a new life that lasted twenty-seven years. During that time, Mike got divorced and met, then married, Anna, a Russian doctor. In 2004 Anna was offered a job working for the Dubai Health Authority, so the two upped sticks and moved to Dubai. Mike found a job in real estate, which was a booming industry in those days. Always on the look-out for opportunities to return to a life working with aircraft, Mike was offered a job in Nigeria to start up the new airline Ark Air. When this task was completed, he returned to Dubai to enjoy semi-retirement while waiting for his wife's contract to end. In December 2019, Anna finally retired and together they left the Emirates and moved to Northern Cyprus, where they enjoyed socialising with new friends, walking in the stunning scenery, and keeping up with all of Mike's old air force pals. He loved socialising, rugby and the Hash House Harries (a drinking club with a running problem).

In September 2022, shortly after we finished working on the first manuscript of this book, Mike died after a short illness.

Ade Thorne left the RAF in 2015 after serving thirty-seven and a half years, leaving as a warrant officer from his last post as a project officer for air cannon ammunition. Moving in with his partner **Jane Erskine**, they settled into deepest, darkest Somerset. Jane had left three years earlier, in 2012, and went to work part-time in Asda at Taunton, eventually becoming their head fishmonger. In 2015 she left Asda and took a job in the local surgery as a dispenser – so she went from counting bombs and bullets to counting pills and potions; the ingredients might be different, but the process is exactly the same. As for Ade, with a reasonable pension he just wanted a part-time job to keep himself active, so he trained to be a coach driver. His complete career swing therefore took him from bombs to buses. After a few years he became a qualified driving instructor and assessor approved by DVSA. He continues this role today, instructing either in the classroom or out on the roads. Ade and Jane are season ticket holders at Southampton FC – well, somebody has to be. This sees them travelling all around the country most weekends throughout the season, always meeting up with old friends and colleagues for a social.

Garron Clark-Darby had the rank of sergeant when he handed in his ID card in 1988 after seventeen years' service. After a couple of office jobs, he discovered that he had a talent for contractual matters so trained to become a legal adviser and went to work for a well-known German car company. Later, he also qualified as a certified data protection officer (DPO) and subsequently became senior legal adviser and DPO for a German telecommunications company. He was there for almost twenty years but retired, a little bit early, in 2021. He is now assistant curator at the

LIFE AS AN EX-ARMOURER

Trenchard Museum and also provides ordnance advice and guidance to the local historic aviation trust. Additionally, he has recently been asked to join the council of RAF Halton Apprentices Association in the heritage role, so he's continuing to keep himself busy.

Podge Middleton was serving at RAF Marham when he had a major back operation in 2001, following which he decided to leave the RAF. He'd served twenty-six years and left as a Chief Tech. In 2002 he joined BAE Systems at Warton, initially working on the Typhoon project before moving onto familiar ground in Tornado Customer Support. Working with Tornados involved regular visits to RAF stations, which meant that he kept in contact with many of his old comrades – one of the positive aspects of staying in the aircraft business. Bizarrely, in his early days in Tornado support he dealt with an issue that he'd raised himself eighteen months earlier! Podge continued to work with Tornados until they went out of service with the RAF in 2019, at which point he took early retirement.

Bob Worthington-Harris left the RAF after twenty-two years in 2011. He moved with his wife Heidi and two children to a small village near Alton Towers in the Staffordshire moorlands. He retrained as a gas and oil domestic heating engineer, starting his own company. The business goes from strength to strength due to the experiences Bob gained in the RAF, and the motivation to succeed and provide for his family. Bob and Heidi have also turned their hand to trying to be property developers. There's only so much Sarah Beeny, along with Phil and Kirsty, you can watch before you think, 'It can't be that hard.' Look out for *Tenants from Hell* or maybe *House in the Country*, depending on how it pans out. He has on occasion played cricket for his local old boys' team, but prefers to view the game from the pavilion as there is less chance of pulling something other than a pint.

Brendan Lucey left after seven years of service and moved to the Middle East for five years, during which time he worked on the Tornado aircraft weapons system. He returned to the UK to continue working in the defence industry, getting involved with various weapons integration programmes and extending into communications and air defence. During this time, Brendan gained an honours degree in Engineering (2:1), which helped him to move across from systems integration and into the safety engineering discipline within the defence industry. He is married and living 'somewhere in England', and is currently preoccupied with home improvements and funding offspring through university.

For most RAF Armourers, leaving the RAF doesn't mean leaving the memories behind. When the memories involve friendships, camaraderie, practical jokes, and late nights in the NAAFI bar, that's a good thing. But not all memories are happy ones. Some memories are deeply disturbing.

THE RAF'S ARMOURERS

Post-traumatic stress disorder (PTSD), mental illness caused by exposure to traumatic events, can affect anyone, even Armourers who coped perfectly well at the time.

The experiences of **Martin Turner** encapsulate the kind of events that can lead to PTSD:

> During Gulf War 2, I was in Brize Norton. 'Nothing to do with us,' I thought. But what not many people knew was that Brize Norton, like other RAF bases in the UK, was fighting wars from a distance.
>
> One day I was called to the boss's office, and he said, 'I'm going to train you up on this.' It was a Geiger counter. I thought, 'What's all this about?' He promptly went on leave.
>
> At the time they'd changed the gymnasium at Brize Norton into a mortuary – the secondary purpose of a gymnasium on any camp. There was air-conditioning to keep the place cool, and they would carry out all the post-mortems on the returning bodies of British servicemen who'd been killed. One of my jobs was to check the bodies before the post-mortem, using my Geiger counter to check whether they'd been contaminated with depleted uranium, because the US and NATO forces were using depleted uranium in their weapons.
>
> We'd go to the gym, and I remember I used to put Vaseline on my nose because the smell was appalling. The first time I went in, on a steel table in front of me was a black lad. His body was perfect, but I could see an entry wound where a bullet had entered his body. I stared at him for four or five seconds – it was my first experience of a body in the mortuary – then I turned to the right. There were a couple of staff there. They were civilians, police forensics and surgeons. They were in the middle of their autopsy, and weighing body parts on a set of scales. That didn't bother me at the time. They were doing their job – checking that the way in which the individual had been killed was lawful, I guess.
>
> They stopped, and led me over to a table to do my checks for depleted uranium on a new arrival. There was a body bag, but it wasn't human shaped. It was more folded up. They opened it up, and all I could see there was an arm with a tattoo. What disturbs me the most to this day is that I can't remember what the tattoo was, but I know it was a tattoo. That's the bit that sticks with me, and I see it in my dreams. I did my Geiger

counter bit on what was left of the body – a few homogenised bits of flesh and bone. Then they took me to a bench, and there was nothing on it but paper towel and ten to twelve small pieces of bone. They told me that a tank had been hit, and after the munition entered the tank its occupants were pretty much vaporised, and these bones were all that was left of those who had been inside.

We were offered counselling by the padre and I encouraged my guys to go and some did. I did not because I thought I was OK. How wrong I was.

I still struggle to recount these experiences, and every time I do I go cold, I get clammy, and the hairs on my arms stand up. But I feel I have to do it in order to get over it; it's therapy.

Martin's departure from the RAF was very different from others we talked to. In his own words:

I was medically discharged from the RAF in 2004. To say this was disappointing would be an understatement. It's OK when you know in yourself that you are broken, but when the medical staff at RAF Henlow, during the process of a medical board, tell you officially that you are broken – well, quite frankly that f***s you up.

I made a clean cut from the RAF and isolated myself from all aspects of it. Big mistake. From 2004 to 2009 I spent time in hospital for weeks at a time, and recovering for months at a time. Both physically and mentally I was not in a good place; the 'PTSD-related symptoms' were getting the better of me. I wanted to work, but the physical and psychological barriers to the commitment that I have always given were too great. I think my second mistake was concentrating too much on my medical condition and the things I couldn't do, instead of the things I could do. The things I could do were, however, hampered by the strong medication I was on.

Because of my limitations, I have led a life of volunteering so that I won't let anyone down if I am incapacitated. To that end, I joined the Armourers Branch at its inauguration in 2015 and have put my organisational skills 100 per cent into helping support other Armourers ever since. I am proud of what I have done, and it was important to me for my sanity that I had the opportunity to use the skills that the RAF gave me. It is also important to say, if it wasn't for the commitment and support of my wife and boys, I don't know if I would have been here today. Later on, the re-engagement with my rugby and Armourer families cannot be underestimated, as them just being there was therapy in itself. I wear my bulletproof mask every day. However, I am here. Sometimes I struggle, but I am here and hopefully doing the right thing.

As Martin mentioned, in 2015 the Armourers formed an RAF Association Branch. The position of welfare officer was available, and based on his own PTSD experience he knew there and then that he had to do something to help, and took on the role. He spent four years as welfare officer and went on to become Chairman of the Royal Air Forces Association (RAFA) Armourers Branch 1366. He takes a very active role in the branch, and is universally liked and respected within the Armourers community.

The RAF Association is a charity that was formed in 1929, and in the intervening years it has provided comprehensive support across the RAF community. Its stated aim is to ensure that no member of the RAF community should ever be left without the help and support they need. This help is provided in a number of ways. Here are a few examples:

- For veterans, there are several retirement complexes around the UK, and support for those suffering from dementia.
- For those with financial or mental health issues, the RAFA helpline can be contacted on 0800 018 2361. The helpline deals with more than 40,000 enquiries a year, and practical support is provided when needed by trained volunteers and association staff.
- For those who are still actively serving in the RAF, subsidised childcare is provided for over 400 children of service personnel.

The Armourers Branch, which is registered as a separate charity, provides support that is more specifically targeted at those who served as RAF Armourers. This doesn't apply only to Armourers who are paid-up members of the branch; it applies to anyone in what is known as 'the Armourer family'. The branch members are conspicuously generous with their contributions, with thousands of pounds raised each year to provide the means for the branch to function. Here are some examples of the support provided within the Armourer family:

- A standard bearer attends the funerals of former Armourers. This is very important to the Armourer family. Wreaths are also provided

LIFE AS AN EX-ARMOURER

by the branch. Most families greatly appreciate the attendance of the standard bearer, and the feedback is warm and heartfelt. The RAF Armourers are a family, so when one of their number dies it is entirely appropriate that the Armourer family is represented by the standard at the funeral. It is a sign of respect and represents Armourers who could not attend. The Armourers Branch has a main standard bearer, but funerals take place all over the UK, so there is a team of deputy standard bearers who can attend when needed. The only problem is that RAF branches are only allowed to have a single standard, so when it needs to be passed on to one of the deputies in another part of the country this involves either a meeting halfway, or popping it in the post – apparently this works pretty well.

- Welfare is provided for any Armourers with health, financial or mental problems; welfare is provided not just for the Armourers themselves, but also their spouses, civil partners and dependents. In some cases, after chatting with the Armourers Branch Honorary Welfare Officer (HWO), follow-ups are carried out, in the main by the RAFA welfare team in the local area of the individual in need. Often people are reluctant to contact the HWO, the association, or anyone for that matter. They have feelings of guilt and think that they don't deserve the help that is offered. The reality is that anyone might need help, as Martin discovered, and it is great to know that this help is available.
- On a festive note, Christmas boxes are put together for all RAF Armourer personnel who are on operations over the Christmas period. These boxes are then sent out all around the globe.

As Chairman of 1366, Martin is very aware that Armourers are not 'bulletproof' and when confronted by circumstances beyond their control he stressed that they should take that courageous first step and ask for help – help that was not so readily available when he was suffering in the early 2000s. Every welfare contact is totally confidential, and when the branch cannot solve the problem its chairman and committee will probably know someone who can.

As has been mentioned many times throughout this book, the Armourers community is a family – a large, occasionally dysfunctional family, but a family nevertheless. Its members have trained hard, worked hard, and played hard. So it's pleasing to think that when they're no longer active Armourers, they remain part of the family, and the camaraderie and support continues until the day they die.

Chapter 12

Ade Thorne's Falklands Diary

Generally, overseas deployments in war zones are planned. You get told where you're going, and when, and you can plan for the trip. But not always. Sometimes, external events dictate your first overseas deployment.

Ade Thorne had joined the RAF in 1978, as a weapons mechanic. He was 17 when he signed up. His first three years were spent in the UK, learning the trade. But all that changed in 1982. What follows is Ade's own diary, together with photos taken at the time.

Mid-April 1982

I was working as part of an EOD team up at Otterburn ranges when we got the call to return to Wittering ASAP. There I was informed that I would be part of a team travelling south to the Falkland Islands, to which I replied, 'Where's that?' Eight thousand miles south by boat was the answer. I was not impressed. I get sick going to the Isle of Wight.

The Otterburn team.

Otterburn range.

ADE THORNE'S FALKLANDS DIARY

We had two weeks to get the kit together, including 1 x 4-tonner complete with eight tons of gear including gallons of Racasan (toilet flush) and 2 x LWB Land Rovers with trailers. A team of eleven was assembled:

Flt Lt Al Swan ('the boss')
Wo Dave Trafford
Flt Sgt Doc Knights
Chief Tech Hank Hankinson
Chief Tech Mick Sidwell
Sgt Pete Herrington
Jnr Tech Ade Thorne
SAC Ken Soppett-Moss
SAC Paul Grace
SAC Dave Fields
SAC Tony Moreton

The Squadron brief was to be part of 1 (F) squadron support. We were to form five two-man teams to clear all areas of land required to operate the Harriers on portable operating strips once the ground was secure.

30 April

We said goodbye to our families and headed towards Marchwood military docks on Southampton water to board the RFA *Sir Bedivere*. Unfortunately, there was a fuss about the vessel having two Bofors guns at the front,

Dockside at Marchwood.

uncovered, so it couldn't be classified as a merchant vessel for transit. As a result, we were ordered off, left all our vehicles and kit on board, and got a coach back to Wittering.

During the following week a BL755 cluster bomblet exploded during a standard clearance at West Freugh range in Scotland. It unfortunately killed Sergeant Ginge Rutter and LAC Boothroyd and injured two others. RIP both. The first two RAF EOD deaths since 1956. It was a trial drop of the munition, a task which we were to face hundreds of times in the forthcoming weeks.

7 May

We travelled to Brize Norton and caught a VC10 to Ascension Island via Dakar in Senegal. On arrival we were billeted in Two Boats village. It was on the equator, yet it was pissing down. Here I remember supping Pina Coladas in a swimming pool, thinking, 'This is a lovely war'. Was I in for a rude awakening in the weeks to come.

Next morning at breakfast there was a sign outside the tent which read, 'Whoever has nicked the 21 x 1,000lb bombs can they please return them to the ESA by midday and nothing will be said.' Later, of course, we found out that this was the Vulcan Black Buck missions. [The Black Buck operations were a series of long-range bomber missions launched from the UK to the Falkland Islands during the Argentinian occupation. At the time they were the longest-range bombing raids ever recorded.]

10 May

RFA *Sir Bedivere* sailed into Ascension. We managed to get aboard an RM Gemini and go out to the RFA. At this point we had to climb up the rope ladder dropped over the side. It was quite scary watching my 50-year-old WO attempt to pull his way up, surrounded by hammerhead sharks which were circling our boat. We then set sail every night to avoid the Argentinian submarine threat, and also to dump waste and make fresh water. We had four times as many people on board than we should have.

Showers were something else. We got called forward by room to the showers. We went in, four at time, and stood in the showers. A navy guy shouts, 'Water on, armpit armpit, bollocks, arse out', then as we stepped back to apply soap another four moved into the showers. We applied soap to the four areas then swapped back over. This time we had double 'Armpit armpit bollocks arse out'.

ADE THORNE'S FALKLANDS DIARY

14 May

We set sail south. As we were RAF, we were employed as enemy aircraft watchers up on the bridge, doing one hour on, four off. One night during my shift, when I knew we were close to the islands, I had been following a really bright, white light silhouetting the hills of the Falklands. It was so dark; I really couldn't see a hand in front of my face. Eventually I plucked up the courage to shout out, 'Red *(because I was on the port side)* 110 plus 60'. The officer on watch came out saying, 'What's up?', to which I replied, 'Bright light sir, been following us for a while now, moving around a bit.' 'That's the planet Venus you stupid c***. If you look through the binoculars you can see another planet and the distance between the two doesn't move. That's how you know it's a planet. The movement is us rolling about.' It was so dark I couldn't even see the binoculars two feet in front of me, and thankfully it was so dark he couldn't see how red-faced I was.

For the next few days, we just sailed around and around. The lifeboat station drills were horrendous; we wouldn't have stood a chance if we were to go in. We had to link arms and crawl out onto the cloisters deck where the water was washing over us, knee-deep at least. Frightening.

23 May

I was on bridge watch again. Suddenly a light flashed across my face from about 100 yards away. Turns out this was HMS *Ardent* escorting us into San Carlos Water. Some watcher I am. I didn't even see or hear her.

As daylight broke, what a sight – SS *Canberra*, naval and other civilian vessels everywhere, helicopters buzzing all over the place. As I stood on the deck taking pictures, a marine on a Mexeflote said, 'You won't be doing that at 2 p.m., mate. Argies come at 2.' He wasn't wrong. I could have set my watch by it.

Suddenly all hell broke loose – metal tins being banged, ships horns being blasted, lots of small arms fire, then a massive whoosh as a missile fired by one of the warships cracks past us. Our brief was to go back to our bunk and lie down, pushing mattresses against the bulkhead. On the way down I saw some Argentinian Mirages, I think, go flashing past. They were so low. I remember thinking, 'brave bastards', because they were just met by a wall of tracers, missiles from the ships, etc., and they kept coming. If we didn't get them, then the Harriers or Rapier batteries had a good go as they left. Once I got back to my bunk the rest were there already, with Dave Fields playing his guitar and singing loudly to the tune of 'Let me take you through the streets of London'. Lots of nervous energy being released. The running commentary from the bridge was absolutely brilliant, because you have no idea what is going on above decks and it's bloody frightening, I can tell you. We had a couple of bombs hit us but luckily they didn't explode. One bounced through the crane on the front, skipped off the water and into HMS *Sir Galahad*. We were attributed to a kill of a Mirage, but we also put a volley from a GPMG through the wardroom of HMS *Fearless*.

Above: San Carlos Water.

Left: Hiding in our bunks.

ADE THORNE'S FALKLANDS DIARY

The night before HMS *Antelope* had exploded, unfortunately killing one of the RE guys trying to defuse a bomb. He was on Flight Lieutenant Swan's and FS Doc Knight's EOD course. So, it was getting very close to home now, as the reality was sinking in.

Mirage attack.

HMS *Antelope*.

24 May

It was decided that we should move ashore, both us and the Navy Fleet Clearance Dive team. All of our explosives were too much of a target if we stayed on board any longer. So, at 2 a.m. we moved the vehicles out of the back of the RFA and onto a Mexeflote. A few minutes later we arrived at Ajax Bay. Our 4-tonner got off okay, but unfortunately our first Land Rover jack-knifed as it drove off because the acute angle of the ramp and the beach was too sharp. So, we had to sledgehammer off the towing hook. From then on, the 4-tonner had to tow the trailer. I swear WO Dave Trafford waded ashore carrying his demob suitcase above his head as if he was looking for a hotel!

It was so dark, and we could only move the vehicles inshore a few hundred metres because that's when the road stopped. We slept in the vehicles for the rest of the night. In the morning we moved into the old sheep refrigeration factory, which became known as 'the Red and Green life machine', and looked for somewhere to settle down.

There were some hooligans from Poole or Hereford that were moving on and who obviously saw that we were 'naïve crab fats', as they called us, looking lost. So they gave up their corner so we could set up our camp beds. The RSM from 45 Commando appeared outside, and wasn't impressed as he looked around. 'Oh for f***'s sake, the bloody Air Force has arrived. F***

The RSM's favourite Land Rovers.

ADE THORNE'S FALKLANDS DIARY

Storage boxes next to a med centre.

me, only they would bring a 4-tonner decked in white Arctic camouflage and two Land Rovers with bright red wings and f***ing blue lights on top. Get them covered up now.' For the next few hours, we made a mud paste to cover up all the bright colours so we weren't such a target.

We watched on as pretty boy Dave Fields got his towel and wash bag out and went to find the shower block. On turning a corner, he saw this bloke stood stark naked in a washing-up bowl full of the dregs from what looked like a coffee boiler above. He looked at Dave and asked what he was after. When Dave told him, he replied, 'Son, when you have been on shore for five days you can join the queue for a wash in this bowl. But when you do, some advice: Do your teeth first and your arse last.' I believe that man turned out to be Lieutenant Commander Rick Jolly, the top surgeon.

Over the next few days, we sat in a scrape outside watching teeny weeny airways [Army Air Corps] doing their thing. Getting ready for the daily action of the air raids which never failed to appear on time. With no EOD action we doubled up as stretcher bearers as the helicopters came in. We went out to a few ships that had UXBs on and helped identify them, but it was mainly the navy boys that defused and dumped the bombs over the side. They did a great job there. Once we had a great hot shower while we were out on the RFA *Sir Lancelot*. It was like a ghost ship because it was evacuated while a UXB was being dealt with.

Of course, we all went down with Galtieri's Revenge at some point. The s**t tent was just a 12 x 12 with a large trench dug inside it. You

The RAF EOD team, just off the ships.

went in four at a time, hung onto the makeshift scaffolding pipe, dropped your trousers and leant back over the trench to do your business. It was obviously not the time to stop and chat. The rat pack toilet paper was like shiny paper too. Absolute nightmare.

On one of my many trips, as I pulled by trousers up, I saw my knife fly out of my top pocket and in slow motion do a couple of spins before going headlong down into the trench. It wouldn't have been so bad but it didn't even land in my own poo. I had to retrieve it because I only had the one knife.

Another time when an air raid sounded, the helicopter went to ground on full power and blew the tent away. There was our Warrant Officer and Mick, plus another couple, all bare-arsed hanging over the trench, God, how we laughed!

We also managed to start saving water in any way we could find. We washed our socks and underwear daily and then hung them on a piece of string tied around our abdomen so they dried against the warmth of your skin.

We were starting to enjoy experimenting with the rat packs, but the Royal Marines had set up a field kitchen, which was a welcome alternative, and we got two hot meals a day. We were starting to get into the flow of things now. But May 27th changed all that.

27 May

We were queueing up for tea like we always did. Tonight, it was babies' heads, mash spud and peas. The format was that after you got this course, you then rejoined the queue, eating away, so by the time you got back to the serving point you got your pudding. Tonight was rice pudding. Then rejoin the queue again to get your cup of tea, which also helped clean out your mess tin.

The building we were housed in was the Field Hospital, but it had been decided not to paint a Red Cross on the top because of the close vicinity of all our supplies and ammunition, which were being offloaded every day.

ADE THORNE'S FALKLANDS DIARY

This particular night the RSM came out and ordered everybody to go back to their individual pit spaces and only come back to the kitchen when they were ready for next course. So, we did.

Back in our room we all were munching away when the air raid sirens started going, banging of metal tins etc. I thought, 'Blimey, they're late tonight'. We thought it was probably another high-level attack from a Canberra bomber as had happened a few nights earlier. Next thing small-arms fire opened up, and there was an almighty bang, a loss of air, and a rush of wind whistled past us. All the lights went out, the air was full of dust, and various people were shouting and screaming. Scrambling around for my tin lid and rifle I tried to crawl towards the door in pitch darkness, struggling to breathe because of the dust. I can remember the smell of explosives. I love that smell. 'Get up, get down!' was being shouted. Obviously lots of confusion. I felt down my left leg and it was very wet, warm and sticky, but I could feel no pain, so I thought I had to keep going. Eventually we were all outside in a huddle. Looking to the back of the building there was a large fire where the Marines galley was. It was not a good scene; 26 men were injured and were being treated for some bad blast injuries, and unfortunately five men lost their lives in that attack.

In the half-light I looked at my leg and I was relieved to see that the cause of the wetness was Mick Sidwell's rice pudding. At that point there was another almighty bang and we all dived for cover. A Sea King was lifting a double stack of ammo to go to the front line at the time of the air raid, so he just cut the rope. Somehow this stack had now ignited, and as it grew hotter the ammunition started to cook off. Suddenly we have mortars, rounds, 66mm rockets whizzing all over the place. While this was going on Al Swan came up and said it was two Skyhawks. One dropped its stick of four down on the shoreline and the navy were dealing with them. For our four, we had one bomb go off, one had gone right though the building and was up on the hill unexploded, and the other two were lodged inside the building. One was in the metalwork which ran inside the wall; the other was in the roof.

For the next two hours, alongside the navy lads, we carried sandbag after sandbag up from the beach to try and put a block between the bombs and the operating theatres, which were still 100 per cent functioning. Somebody found some old railway sleepers which we managed to put up under the now bulging ceiling and this seemed to do the trick. Al and Dave Fields climbed up into the roof to try and identify the bombs. They were French with what they believed were impact fuzes which had malfunctioned, probably because they were dropped so low and so fast that the retard didn't have time to function correctly. This fact was reported on the BBC

World Service, much to our disgust, a few days later. Just in case the fuzes were time-delayed, ideally Al wanted the hospital emptied, which of course it couldn't be. So, on the critical times, every hour, the non-critical staff moved out and we moved in to get a hot brew and also reassure the medical staff that all was fine. That continued throughout the night. Al, and Doc I think, climbed up the hill to find our fourth UXB and detonated it, which lit up the night sky and alarmed a few people who hadn't been told what was happening.

The next day the ammunition stack had cooled down enough for us to start clearing up the area, which was an important helicopter pad, both for outgoing stores and incoming casualties from Goose Green. So, in teams of four, we picked up stretchers and gingerly walked up and down picking up anything we could find, such as ammo boxes with all the heads of rounds poking through the sides, grenades, rockets and mortars which had been

Post air raid at Ajax.

Bomb damage.

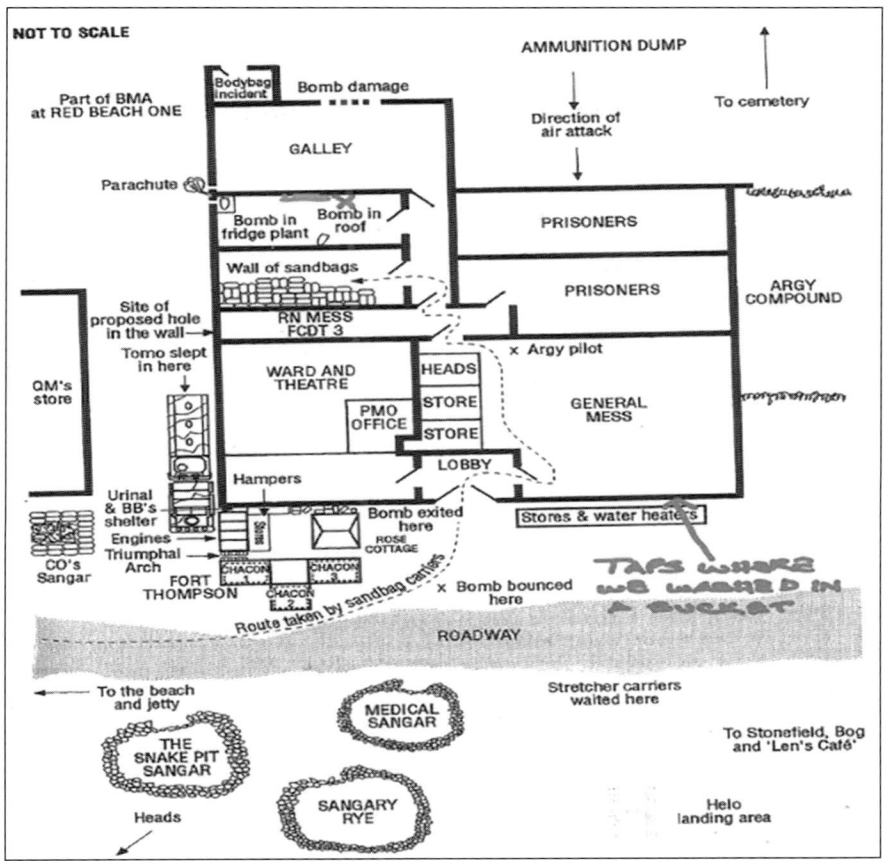

Site plan. Ade's team was located in the room that says 'Wall of sandbags'. Prisoners were not there at this time.

propelled out but not gone off. A similar job in peace time would never have been done like that, but time was of the essence so needs must. I have to say it was a bit arse-tightening to start with, but there was so much to do we just got on and did it. I remember a marine coming up and saying, 'Fair play dude, that was nonchalant but cool.' If only he knew ...

It was at this time, roughly, that my mum back home received a letter from the station commander at RAF Wittering saying that because we obviously had no means of communication, he could put her mind at ease. Her little boy was doing fine and was aboard the SS *Atlantic Conveyor* bobbing around in the South Atlantic. Now I'd never even seen the thing, let alone been on it. I guess at some point the 1 Squadron support lads must have been. Then on the midday news came the story that the SS *Atlantic*

Conveyor had been hit by an Exocet missile and had sunk. Apparently, it took numerous phone calls to EOD Ops before she finally believed that I wasn't onboard and that I was somewhere on the islands.

Goose Green was now in the hands of the Paras, but at some cost. Helicopter after helicopter brought in many casualties, and then the bodies. Sat in our room, a medic come through and asked for anybody who was blood type A Positive to come forward. I knew I was A Pos, but I thought, 'No way. I might need all my blood.' Anyway, 10 minutes or so later he came in again and said, 'Come on fellas. People are dying in here.' I just looked at my dog tags and put my hand up. I was absolutely bricking it. I went through the makeshift door, guys laid out with all the medical teams around them. Total respect for all of them. Anyway, they got me to lay down, checked my dog tags, put a needle in, and I watched my blood disappear off behind a screen. I tried to make light of it and asked the Medic for a cup of tea, a biscuit and a kiss, to which he said, 'Lippy on or off flyboy?' with a wink. Next day I can remember all the Paras that had been killed during the taking of Goose Green being carried to a large mass grave on a hillock overlooking the sheds, and us all gathering up there for a small service. It was in total silence apart from the sound of the helicopters continuing to and fro between the ships and bridge heads. We also witnessed a Mirage being taken out by a Rapier missile. Finally, when the burial was over, we helped to construct a POW compound for the expected 1,500 Argies from Goose Green.

Early June

Now it was our turn to move on to Goose Green. We were told to get everything we could carry and wait for the Chinook. When it came it touched down but never really eased up on the power. Trying to walk up the back ramp carrying locators, shovels, explosive kits, personal bags etc. was bloody hard work. Likewise coming out again; once you got hit by the blast from the engines off you went on your arse, sliding across the ground.

When we arrived, we managed to get set up in the old schoolhouse. As the prisoners were moved back to Ajax, we moved up onto the airfield to sort out the mess left behind. The grass strip was littered with helmets, rifles, and fighting kit. We just moved them all into similar piles. Lots of different agencies then picked up what they wanted to take.

Pucara aircraft littered the skyline. We weren't sure if they were booby trapped, so a decision was made to pull out all the ejection seats. This was taken after an earlier explosion had killed an Argentinian who had been

ADE THORNE'S FALKLANDS DIARY

Above left: Goose Green airfield – wheeling and dealing.

Above right: Pucara with seats pulled.

tasked with moving boxes of ammunition by the sheep-shearing sheds. Unfortunately, as an ammunition box exploded, he was trapped in a fierce fireball and subsequently died. We obviously didn't know if the box was booby trapped or just unstable. Coupled with things like rocket launchers strapped onto the kiddies' slide, 1,000lb bombs wired up on the shoreline like mines, and numerous other weird and wonderful items, the decision to pull the seats was made. We removed all seat pins, tied a rope around the handle, and ran away, bravely pulling the rope. They should have been zero-zero seats, but I reckon only a third worked correctly.

After we had completed that job, we moved onto the napalm clearance. There were loads of tanks on the airfield, but we were summoned to a couple of people's sheds/outhouses where there were lots of containers with a weeping liquid crusted around the lids and another set of liquid containers. Not nice stuff. We commandeered a tractor with a sledge and extremely carefully lifted all these items onto the sledge and transported them up to the airfield where we started constructing a large bonfire.

Next, we were asked to clean up the Argie rifles. The FN was similar to our SLR except that it had an automatic function. In the evenings we would take half a dozen and strip them down, clean and oil them. The test firing was the best. By now we had all swapped our ammo for tracer. No such thing as 4-bit – our mags were full of the stuff. We used to throw a coke can into the water, let it float out a bit, then shoot away. One night, with some army officer looking on, I fired just one shot and sunk the can from about 30yds. I just said, 'There you go. No need to zero this one.' He took it off my hands quick. I didn't tell him that it was pot luck, and that I was aiming for the other can. I always fail the annual 25m range shoot. News soon got around that we had successfully reconned these rifles, and next day up on the airfield a Lynx landed and the crewman asked if he could have some to strap in the doorway. Of course, the answer was 'what are you going to give us in return?' A selection of porn mags was good enough for a couple of FNs with ammo throw in. Following that was a Sea King, I think from one of the carriers, which again took a few rifles in exchange for Tony Moreton's 18th birthday cake, freshly made by their cooks.

After we had cleared and tidied up the airfield, the sheep sheds, and the properties in and around Goose Green, we set about clearing up the cluster bomblets which were strewn all over the place. For every CBU dropped, on average fourteen bomblets did not explode for whatever reason. There were some still inside CBUs that were either jettisoned or that belonged to a Harrier that had piled in. Al Swan took us to one side and reminded us of Ginge, and told us not to take risks and that it had to be done manually. So we basically reverted to how we always used to do it – we formed a FOD plod line and slowly advanced forward. As we found a bomblet, we checked as best we could to see if it was an A or B body. If A, we marked it and moved on. If B (fingers crossed) we picked it up and ripped off the coronet and spring stuff at the front, so it just left a plain bomblet to put in our pockets, and then we moved on. Over 600 bomblets were recovered this way between Goose and Darwin. These were placed on top of the napalm and other items, linked with det-cord, ready for the big blow.

Our final task at Goose Green was to check over thousands of Argentinian 105mm rounds to see if they looked serviceable. They did, and were airlifted up onto the front line for future use.

We were at Goose Green for about two weeks, I think. The juniors did a day each as housemaid. Whilst everybody went out, we stayed back and cleaned up the house. Tried to do some dhobi for everyone and hung it out to dry. Breakfast was fried bacon grill. Lunch was always soup or stew and rat-pack biscuits, or something like that. But the evening meal was brill. The night before, in the early hours, we would sneak out into the allotments and dig up some spuds, carrots, and maybe a cabbage to go with the lamb that we had found hanging in a nearby deserted property. We also went out and shot some geese – we ate well that night.

Goose Green school house – feeling good.

The boss and Doc went over to Darwin following

a report of a 1,000lb bomb, but they forgot to take any tools with them. That's where the story about a man defusing a bomb with sticks comes in. They got two small sticks to remove the detonator and CE pellets. The number of minefields littered everywhere was a nightmare, but again we did not have time to do anything about them apart from mark them as best we could and move on.

It was now time to ignite the bonfire. That was a bit tense because Al lit it with safety fuze, and as he did so a Sea King appeared with a big rubber portable fuel bag tethered underneath. I remember him running up the track waving his hands to get the helicopter to veer off, which thankfully it did. A few minutes later the bonfire ignited – about 300m wide and at least a quarter of a mile high were the estimates. It certainly was a massive fireball with all that napalm.

One day the air raid sirens sounded and we thought the Argies were conducting a counterattack. We all legged it back into the centre of Goose. It turned out to be a false alarm for us, but not for the poor buggers up the coast at Bluff Cove, as the Argies attacked the two RFAs that were unloading.

Whilst at Goose we heard on the BBC World Service that the end was near, and the final battles were commencing. So we packed up our kit ready to go. Then we heard that the white flag was flying over Stanley so we broke out the King Teds and waited for a Chinook to take us back to Ajax.

The Chinook duly arrived, and we ferried all the kit aboard, bit by bit. Then I felt a tap on my shoulder. It was the loadie pointing at my weapon, which was slung over my shoulder. But it was the wrong way up; it should have been barrel down. In my haste to turn it round I caught the bottom of my magazine catch which sprung off and covered the whole back ramp in rounds of ammunition. Another harder smack of the head followed, and as we lifted off all I could see was lots of Gurkhas picking up my rounds. That flight back to Ajax was scary. We were all sat on the floor huddled up around the kit, no glass in the windows, back ramp open – it was as noisy as hell. I could see through the cockpit window underneath the pilot's legs, and how we never went in I will never know. Best and worst roller coaster ride I've ever had.

15 June

Now back at Ajax. It still housed the hospital, but there were hundreds, if not thousands, of POWs. There were a load inside, and I can't remember if it was Dave or Tony who got the job of sitting in the doorway with a GPMG

POWs at Ajax.

in case any of them moved. They all had P&O passenger level cards around their necks. A for officer, C for conscript etc. I remember one guy had a really strong American accent. As I was coming back up one of the passageways, I bumped into an old mate from my home town. He was a chef with 16 Field Hospital Paras, and was on the RFA *Sir Galahad*, which had been bombed. He only had what he was stood up in, so I gave him my trainers. Dunno why I had them in my bag still, but I did.

The next few days we got lifts by teeny weeny airways across to San Carlos and Port San Carlos, Kelly's Garden etc., for various small jobs. Each area was designated a colour, so you just held up that colour and the pilot either said 'yes' or 'no' to climbing on board. The boss and the WO flew ahead to sort things out, and we then boarded the MV *Elk* the next morning, complete with vehicles, and set sail for the capital.

18 June

Stanley was a complete and utter mess. The Argies had totally trashed everything, and they had crapped everywhere too. The boss met us at the quayside, and he had managed to secure rooms in two houses for us to stay. The one I stayed in belonged to Romeu and Hilary Pauloni, whose son was in the RAF stationed at Kinloss. The other five stayed up the road with Chick and Walter Felton. Our hosts obviously provided us with shelter, but had no rations or running water. So, our first job was to cordon off the Falkland Islands company warehouses on the quayside to search for possible IEDs, whilst loading the landies with bags of flour, sugar, tea, spam and anything else we could blag. That, coupled with bags of peat to light the fires and get some hot water. They put an RFA on the dockside and we had to go down and remove all our clothes and jump into this big bath, basically a square of pallets draped in a tarpaulin filled with water, wash off, then get out and move to another one which was a lot cleaner. From there we all got issued a new set of DPMs. The old gear went for burning.

ADE THORNE'S FALKLANDS DIARY

We checked over the warehouses and a few shipping containers down by the Governor's house for booby traps. One thing I noticed was the amount of officer ration packs, with cigarettes, whisky etc., whilst the poor conscripts on the mountains got bugger all. Mind you, their boots were much better than ours. There were crude traps everywhere. The boss picked up a coke can and a grenade fell out of the bottom; luckily it was only a smoke grenade. Leaving Stanley to the Royal Engineers, our job now was to concentrate on the airfield. They needed the runway and operating surfaces clear to get the first Hercules in and establish an airbridge.

At first the airfield was full of POWs, but they quickly got moved on. The Vulcan might only have got one and a half bombs on the runway, but it

Pucara at Stanley airfield.

Munitions strewn around.

Above: Stanley airfield.

Left: The first Hercules to land.

made one hell of a mess everywhere else. There were about twenty aircraft of different types, some of which we needed to pull the ejection seats out of as they looked like they had been tampered with. The ground was littered with UXBs, fired shells and empty cases, rocket pods, missiles. You name it, it was there. There were British, American, French and Israeli-made weapons. It took nearly four days of hard graft to clear the stuff away to the edges of the operating surfaces to allow them to bring in the Hercules.

30 June

After the boss nabbed a crew seat back on the Herc to the UK, we continued the clean-up for another ten days before finally leaving the Island on June 30th on the RFA *Sir Geraint*, straight into a force 14 hurricane. It was four days before I even got out of my pit. Fourteen days sailing back to Ascension seemed a lifetime. One night, sat up on deck when the paras were celebrating Para Day, 4th July I think it was, I suddenly got hit on the head. Thinking it was one of them I turned around. Dave put his lighter on to reveal a flying fish flapping around on the deck. Suddenly another one, then another. In a flash the Chinese cooks were up and smacking the fish and putting them in a bucket.

At Ascension Island we were ferried ashore by a Wessex, and then a good old 'gozome bird', the VC10 to take us to Brize Norton. All the way back from the Falklands there were daily Tannoys about the spoils of war, and that an amnesty was in place. Loads of stuff was dumped overboard as a result, but not mine. I fully expected to catch the bus back to Wittering to collect my car and then drive home. Bearing in mind that we had no correspondence from the UK in nearly three months, we didn't know what was going on at home. In the arrivals hall at 5 a.m., while we waited for our bags and the so-called thorough search, this RAF policeman just said, 'Job well done boys. Enjoy your time off and go meet your families.' Little did we know, but Al had got everybody's families there. I had twenty-eight family members in total. It was pretty emotional and overwhelming, for sure.

From there we went to my auntie's in Swindon for some good old bacon butties and a cup of tea. More importantly, a sit-down toilet with a flushing mechanism that doesn't rip your guts out if you don't move away quick enough, like there was on that bloody boat. At home, all the neighbours were out in force. The house was fully decorated with Union Jacks and RAF flags. It was really, really very humbling. Although to be honest I was knackered, and just wanted to go to sleep. Plus, all my good clothes were at Wittering. I was pretty grumpy.

Two days into my leave we were ordered back to camp so we could attend the memorial service at St Paul's Cathedral. Then in October we marched through London on the victory parade. As is tradition, the RAF, being the junior service, were at the back behind the Household Cavalry. I didn't care though cos I was able to trample loads of horse manure into the red carpet in the Guildhall.

In the seven short weeks that we were on island, we were shot at, bombed and rocketed, but we all survived – well, apart from Doc, who got frostbite in his big toe. We had cleared 900 UXBs/bomblets, hundreds of plastic mines, tens of thousands of rounds of ammunition and a few tons of napalm.

Welcome home at Brize Norton.

The neighbours come round.

The Thorne family (Ade is second from the right).

All eleven of us got some form of award, starting at the top with Al receiving the Queen's Gallantry Medal, and Ken and I receiving the Queen's Commendation for Brave Conduct. There was a Mention in Dispatches for Doc, and task force Commanders' Commendations for the others. I will never know why Ken and I were singled out to get the QCBC. They said

Medal presentation.

that all five juniors were put forward, but it would undermine the value if we all got it. Load of bollocks. I got it because I was the only J/T, and Ken because he's got a double-barrelled surname. Seven times we got the bloody thing presented by various bigwigs.

Postscript: 2007

In 2007, as a Flight Sergeant I returned to the Falkland Islands as an FS Arms Engineer. I took time out to find Romeu and Hilary's daughter, and we

Romeu and Hilary with Ade.

arranged to meet her parents in the old house I stayed at in 1982. I presented them with a plaque on behalf of 5131 BD Squadron as a thank-you for looking after us back then. Once word got out who I was, I quickly became a tour guide showing people Ajax Bay, Goose Green and San Carlos. At least it got me out of that boring blooming office.

Left and below: Ajax Bay galley area.

The red and green life machine.

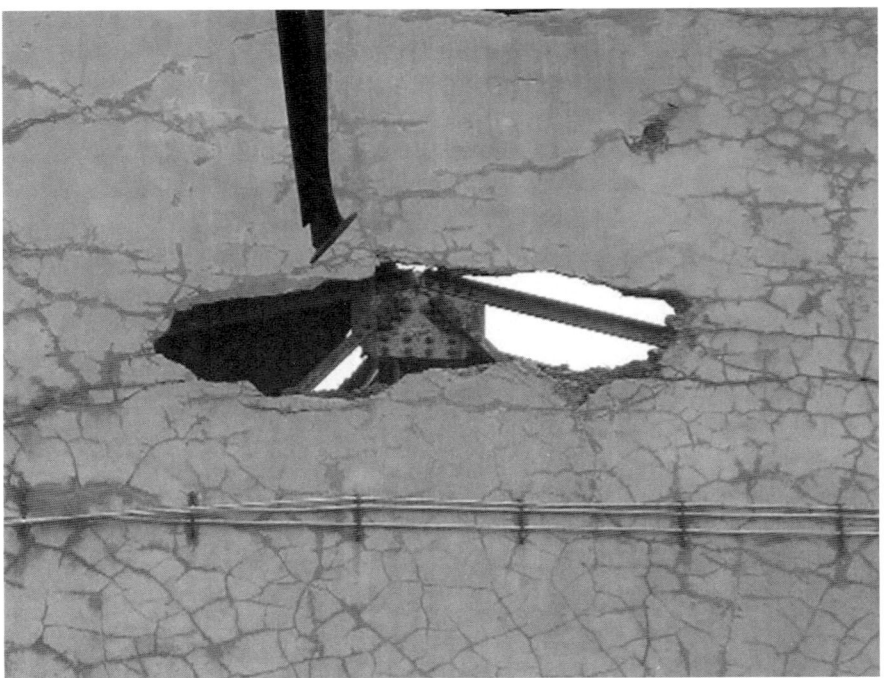

Bomb hole.

Outside Goose Green school house.

Ajax Bay refrigeration plant.

ROYAL AIR FORCE ARMAMENT SUPPORT UNIT
EXPLOSIVE ORDNANCE DISPOSAL UNIT
ROYAL AIR FORCE WITTERING PETERBOROUGH CAMBS PE8 6HB
TELEPONE STAMFORD (STD 0780) 4501 (GPTN 835) ext 5830

PLEASE REPLY TO OFFICER COMMANDING
EXPLOSIVE ORDNANCE DISPOSAL UNIT
YOUR REFERENCE
OUR REFERENCE
DATE

FALKLANDS CITATION

L8171807 Junior Technician Thorne A

Junior Technician Thorne formed part of the RAF Bomb Disposal Team that deployed to the Falklands during the recent conflict.

FOLLOWING AN AIR ATTACK ON 27 MAY 1982, THERE WERE 31 CASUALTIES AT THE AJAX BAY HOSPITAL. DESPITE THE POSSIBILITY OF FURTHER ATTACK JT THORNE DISPLAYED COMMENDABLE COURAGE IN HELPING WITH THE REMOVAL TO SAFETY OF THE WOUNDED

IN THE POST ATTACK BOMB DISPOSAL OPERATIONS, UTTERLY REGARDLESS OF HIS OWN PERSONAL SAFETY, HE ASSISTED HIS SUPERIORS IN THE REMOVAL OF OVER 200 ITEMS OF HIGHLY DANGEROUS UNEXPLODED ORDNANCE.

AT GOOSE GREEN SETTLEMENT HE CONTINUED TO AID HIS SUPERIORS IN SUCCESSFULLY DEALING WITH A VARIETY OF VERY DANGEROUS BOMB DISPOSAL TASKS. THESE INCLUDED THE REMOVAL OF DANGEROUS WEEPING NAPALM CONTAINERS, HIGHLY UNSTABLE EXPLOSIVES AND MANY RANGES OF POTENTIALLY LETHAL ORDNANCE WITH WHICH HE WAS QUITE UNFAMILIAR. ALL THESE TASKS WERE CARRIED OUT AT CONSIDERABLE PERSONAL RISK, WITH COURAGE AND COMPLETE DEVOTION TO DUTY, OFTEN IN THE MOST EXTREME WEATHER CONDITIONS OF BELOW FREEZING TEMPERATURES AND DRIVING SNOW AND RAIN.

THROUGHOUT THE OPERATIONS, DESPITE SHORTAGES OF FOOD AND WATER AND LIVING IN THE MOST UNHYGENIC CONDITIONS, HE MAINTAINED A CHEERFUL AND UNCOMPLAINING ATTITUDE. BY HIS ACTION HE SET A MAGNIFICENT EXAMPLE TO OTHER MEMBERS OF THE SERVICES IN THE HIGHEST TRADITIONS OF THE ROYAL AIR FORCE.

FOR HIS GREAT BRAVERY AND COURAGE, HIS UNSTINTING SUPPORT AND UNCOMPLAINING FORTITUDE UNDER EXTREME CONDITIONS OF ACTIVE SERVICE, HE WAS AWARDED A QUEENS COMMENDATION FOR BRAVE CONDUCT.

Citation letter.

THE RAF'S ARMOURERS

Peaceful bomb alley today.

Medals – South Atlantic Medal with Rosette and Oakleaf
  GSM – Air Ops IRAQ
  Queen's Golden Jubilee
  Queen's Diamond Jubilee
  Long Service and Good Conduct with Bar (30 years' service)

Pucara seat pins and picture – an original painting of bomb disposal operations, 1982.

How to Talk Like an Armourer: A Glossary of Trade Terms

Introduction

Why on earth do you need an introduction to a glossary? Well, the RAF Armourers have a language all of their own, and a lot of it don't make any logical sense until it is explained, and sometimes it still don't make sense. If you think it's hard work trying to understand everything, just try serving for a day, then you'd know how difficult it is. Thank heavens for the glossary!

AC – Aircraftman, the rank you attain on joining the RAF. You hold this rank as you undertake basic training at Halton and initial trade training.

Admin – A ubiquitous term typically used to describe anything boring or mundane, possibly associated with paperwork. May also be used as a euphemism for something less boring but which one didn't want to shout about. For example:

> Chief: 'Airman, where are you going with that crate of wobbly?'
> Airman: 'Oh, hello Chief, I'm just off to do some admin.'

AF – After flight servicing. Tasks completed on an aircraft after it has been flying. Examples include checking for faults, topping up fluids, making sure everything the aircraft set out with is still attached, and anything it was meant to leave somewhere (i.e. bombs) were actually left. It's sort of like tucking up your aircraft for the night after a busy day.

AGSE – Armament ground support equipment. Let's face it, saying 'armament ground support equipment' each time is knackering, so this little acronym, pronounced as "aggsy", saves so much energy. AGSE refers to

HOW TO TALK LIKE AN ARMOURER

any bit of kit used by Armourers in support of fitting weapons to aircraft. Trolleys, jacks, forklifts, hoists and loaders fall into this category.

AOC – Air Officer Commanding. Think very, very important person with a senior air rank such as air vice-marshal. An AOC has a massive amount of responsibility and will spend a lot of time touring and inspecting their domain. RAF stations and squadrons will be forewarned of a visit and usually given ample time to paint all the kerb stones white and the grass green because, as we all know, shabby kerbs and brown grass does not win wars! As a result, all AOCs are convinced the whole world smells of fresh paint.

AP – Air publication. The military runs on paperwork (actual or virtual) and the RAF is no exception. APs cover many subjects; their main focus as far as Armourers are concerned is aircraft and explosives, but they also cover a variety of other subjects including bodily functions.

APC – Armament practice camp. An area where aircrew can practise using their aircraft's weapons. The whole point of having an air force is being able to tackle threats whenever and wherever they appear. To be able to meet operational requirements the aircrew must be familiar with their aircraft and associated systems, including the weapons. Every squadron needs to practise using their weapons, either by using the ranges around the UK or, because the weather is pretty naff in this country, going somewhere more temperate where you are guaranteed being able to fly every day. Regular locations included Cyprus and Belize, although scaling back of the armed forces has reduced this significantly. Without weapons it is just another airline, and without practice you are not ready to deal with the threat!

Appo – A shortened form for apprentice. A long time ago, in a different world (well, it seems like it) potential RAF engineers could join on an apprenticeship scheme. They would enlist, do their basic training, then head off to their Armourer training, which would last up to three years. Once qualified, the appos had an industry-recognised qualification and a larger pay packet than an LAC or SAC Armourer. The apprenticeship scheme fell out of favour in the industry despite it producing highly skilled engineers – a shame really because engineering skills are vital and there is no short cut to gaining them.

Babies' heads – A gastronomic delight created by military caterers, and undoubtedly the mainstay of the fighting force. It can loosely be described as a steak and kidney pudding with suet dumplings. When served correctly, the dumplings peer expectantly from the stew looking remarkably like the heads of babies, hence the name 'babies' heads'.

Bear – This refers to the Tupolev Tu-95, a Soviet military aircraft that first saw service in 1956 and is still in operation today. In fact, its expected end of service is 2040. Employed in various roles such as maritime reconnaissance (spying) and as a strategic bomber, it is a four-engine turboprop aircraft with contra-rotating propellors, which makes it one of the loudest aircraft. And we thought we used old kit!

Beer call – A beer call is a ritual gathering of the section at the end of a busy week or shift. Most sections hold a beer call on a Friday afternoon, possibly involving an early stack. It is an opportunity to dissect the week in a friendly and constructive manner. Misdemeanours, cock-ups, excitement and highlights of the week will be recounted. A beer call is usually followed by a trip to the NAAFI bar and then a saunter into the nearest town, village or city.

BF – Before-flight servicing. A before-flight servicing is carried out just prior to the aircraft flying to make sure it has everything it needs – fuel, oxygen, tyre pressures, oils, weapons, parking permits, toll cards, etc. – and is fit for the role.

BFA – Blank firing adapter. This neat little device is fitted to small arms for training or exercise purposes. The more realistic the training the more effective it is, so training involving weapons is best when you can run around the countryside shooting your weapon and not shouting 'Bang!'. (This method is also used, however, because it's cheaper than firing rounds.) The personnel will be issued their weapons, magazines and a quantity of blank rounds. A blank round is filled with an explosive charge but does not have a bullet; the end where the bullet would be is crimped over. Even though a blank round doesn't have a bullet, powder residue, gas and wadding can still be ejected from the muzzle, so a BFA is fitted to disperse this. BFAs are painted yellow and are very easy to see, so in the heat of the exercise, the training staff can make sure everyone has one fitted. BFAs must be securely fitted otherwise they become a yellow projectile, which kind of defeats the purpose. They are fitted by the Armourers in the armoury before the weapon is issued, as Armourers have the prerequisite gorilla-like grip (and tools) to ensure proper fitment.

Bivvy – Back in the mists of time, the person who invented the MFT decided that all trainees must make a bivvy. This is a temporary shelter to

HOW TO TALK LIKE AN ARMOURER

keep you warm and dry. Part of the instructions for joining the RAF in the 1980s included a kit list, and on that list was bungees x 4. Their purpose was a mystery until you got to MFT, whereupon you were issued with a green poncho and two trees. You had to construct a bivvy using the trees, the poncho and the bungees, then sleep under it for a night. The real purpose of the bivvy was to provide amusement for the rock apes in charge of the MFT. These days the kit list will not include bungees; it will have been replaced by bell x 1 so you can ring for someone to come and tuck you in at night.

Bomb dump – See ESA.

Bucket of sunshine – An endearing term for a nuclear weapon.

Bundu – A word inherited from South Africa and used to describe any area of wilderness or desolation. Over the years us Brits have mis-pronounced it (who'd have thought!) and it is often pronounced 'bondu', which means something else entirely and could be interpreted as a derogatory term.

Cabbage (as in 'dressed like a cabbage') – This phrase describes the act of wearing disruptive pattern material (DPM) clothing; that's camouflage to you and me.

Cannon – A much-used word that over time has come to mean a large-calibre (a bore larger than one inch) weapon. A cannon is usually capable of rapid fire, for example the 27mm Mauser fitted to Tornado aircraft. The end result of being hit by multiple rounds from a cannon is generally accepted to ruin one's day (and aircraft).

Carrier – A general term for a piece of equipment that is used to suspend a bomb, missile or similar from an aircraft. If it works properly, the item it is holding is released when the pilot wants it to be released. May also be called role equipment.

CBLS or **ceebly** – Carrier bomb light stores. This allows up to four lightweight or practice bombs to be loaded to one weapons station on an aircraft, thereby increasing the capacity for training purposes. The RAF ethos is constant training so that when it kicks off everyone can deploy rapidly and be operational instantly. Aircrew need to be ready to use the weapons their aircraft can carry, so regular practice allows them to become familiar with flight characteristics and delivering the weapons to the target accurately. Dropping live 1,000lb bombs is expensive and noisy; a 3kg practice bomb is a lot cheaper and more environmentally friendly.

CBU – Cluster bomb unit (BL755). An area denial weapon. Now banned thanks to Princess Diana.

Chaff – Finely cut strips of tin foil designed to confuse radar guidance systems on a missile. When your aircraft is being tracked by a missile determined to ruin your day, firing chaff into its path can confuse the guidance system and cause the missile to miss you. Assuming of course that the missile is using radar guidance and not heat-seeking. See "Flare" for another option to live!

Character building – A general term for describing anything brutal, painful, abusive or hurtful. What doesn't kill you …

Charge – The word 'charge' has many uses in the military. The obvious one is 'Charge!', accompanied by the waving of bayonets or swords. The RAF don't do that; that is for the army. 'Charge' could also be used to refer to something that holds a charge or pressure, such as an oxygen bottle, but its main use revolves around military discipline. Anyone who has been caught doing something wrong could be 'charged' with their offence under Queen's (or King's) Regulations or military law. The seriousness of the offence will determine how the charge is processed, and by whom. Offences in training are common and are usually dealt with by the training staff, most likely the OC and SNCO, and may result in jankers, stoppage of privileges such as a weekend pass, or a small fine. More serious offences attract the attention of senior officers and could be heard by a court martial. The outcome of a court martial could see the defendant locked up in a military prison or dismissed from the service. Any charge and subsequent hearing will involve a lot of marching around, and the defendant will not be wearing their hat – very inconvenient on a cold day! By not wearing their hat, the defendant is identified as being under suspicion of committing an offence and is not entitled to wear their service badge until their case has been heard and decided.

CIO – Careers Information Office. Where life-changing and life-making decisions are made.

Crated – If someone is judged to be guilty of 'criminal activity', for example, talking shop in the bar, appearing in public wearing uniform to impress the ladies, being late for wheels, etc., the offender may be crated. That is to say, they would have to buy a crate of beer and donate it to the tea bar as recompense for their crime. Judgement would be swift and merciless with no opportunity to offer a defence. See also 'Slabbed'.

C/T – Chief technician. See 'Snec'.

DAC – Dangerous air cargo. This is freight carried on a transport plane, such as a Hercules or VC10, that is determined to be dangerous. Explosives, fuel, batteries, and the SAS are all examples of DAC. An aircraft carrying DAC will be required to park away from other aircraft or habitation in case something really nasty happens.

DE – Direct entrant. Describes someone who joins the trade on the promise of rapid promotion provided they survive an extended term in training. You bypass the ranks of LAC and SAC on completing your trade training and are unleashed to the RAF as a JT with the further incentive of being promoted to corporal quickly. Promises were not always fulfilled for a variety of reasons. The term DE can also be used as an insult because, as we all know, DEs have bypassed the important rites of passage of actually working for a living as an SAC.

Deployment – Being sent away to work, usually somewhere dangerous like Afghanistan or Iraq, but not always.

Det – Detachment. A period of time spent away from home that usually involves hard work and slightly harder drinking. Your det might be in a sun-soaked faraway location such as Deci or Arizona, or it might be somewhere less glamorous such as Machrihanish or St Athan. Either way, they were always good fun.

Det cord – Detonation cord. Det cord is used in bomb disposal as a means of initiating explosions and cutting through things. It comes on a roll and looks like washing line. You unroll your required length and cut off what you need. It is initiated by a detonator and can be a lot of fun to play with.

Dhobi – This phrase refers to laundry, specifically dirty laundry. 'I'm just off to do my dhobi' means that the washing of dirty clothes is about to take place. Dhobi is a phrase picked up by troops serving overseas in places like India. Dhobi translates as laundry man in Urdu.

Di staff – Direction staff. They assess the operational capability of a squadron or station to perform its role. Di staff may be local, brought in from other stations, or from other NATO countries depending on the level of the exercise. Generally, they are best avoided at all costs because they have the power to 'inject' little scenarios into an exercise to test the response. They might stop an airman and tell him he has come across an injured person and needs to practise first aid (a suitably 'injured' person will be provided), or walk into the Operations Room and announce that the camp has been bombed.

Discips – Disciplinary staff. A breed of people recruited especially for their ability to be arseholes in any situation. They join as General Duties and are promoted to SAC, whereupon they scuttle around as guardroom staff under the direction of the SWO. If they paint enough kerbs and count enough blankets, they are encouraged to develop their shouting and marching skills. If they can shout loud enough and march far enough, they may be promoted to corporal and sent to a training camp to guide and nurture (i.e. torment) new recruits or old sweats who had returned for more training.

Dispersal – Part of the airfield away from the main site where aircraft could be parked. Mainly used during operations or exercises, the idea was that if attacked, the damage would be limited to one aircraft away from key installations.

DPM – Disruptive pattern material or camouflage clothing and known as multi-terrain pattern (MTP) since 2010 (is it too much to pick a name and stick with it?). There was a time, not so very long ago, when the military went off to fight wearing bright red jackets and very shiny buttons. The Boer War was around the time military chiefs realised this strategy was fundamentally flawed because our troops were very easy to spot and therefore to kill. The first step was introducing khaki clothing. This worked okay, so the next evolution was clothing that breaks up the outline of the wearer by using different colours in an irregular pattern. Camouflage, or 'camo' as it's more commonly referred to, has become quite fashionable, and is available in a variety of patterns and colours. Pink and black is the latest trend. One hesitates to consider where this allows the wearer to 'blend in'.

Dumpy – Someone who works in a bomb dump.

Early stack – Leave work or finish the shift before the scheduled end. Whether you work regular daytime hours or shifts, your scheduled finish

HOW TO TALK LIKE AN ARMOURER

time is always a target to be beaten. A good and respected shift boss always looks to get people away if the work is done. Phrases such as 'The job's a good un, time to knock off', 'That's all folks', or 'Why are you still here?' are guaranteed to get a positive and rapid response.

EOD – Explosive ordnance disposal. The ubiquitous term for getting rid of unwanted explosives including UXBs. Found a UXB? Who you gonna call? Not Ghostbusters, that would be stupid. Call 999 and ask for them to send an EOD team – although these days you would end up with an army EOD team rather than one from the RAF.

EOFE cart – Electrically operated fire extinguisher cartridge. An explosive cartridge that, when initiated, breaks a seal in the aircraft fire extinguisher system to release the extinguishant and put out a fire (hopefully!).

ERU – Ejector release unit. Used to secure bombs or other disposable stores to an aircraft, giving the pilot the option to release them when the time comes. Also, HDERU – heavy duty ejector release unit, for really big bombs, and LDERU – light duty ejector release unit, for nice little ones. An ERU uses an electrically fired explosive cartridge to force the store away from the aircraft by powering a piston or pistons that exert force on the store. Once the store is away from the aircraft, gravity takes over. There is also an electro-magnetic release unit (EMRU) that uses magnets to release the store. No force is applied on the store to push it away from the aircraft; instead, the slipstream and gravity ensure safe release or separation from the aircraft. As weapons and aircraft develop, so do the ways of ensuring safe separation and targeting. We have come a long way from simply dropping the bomb over the side of the cockpit.

ESA – Explosive Storage Area (AKA bomb dump). A place designed specifically for the safe storage, preparation and maintenance of explosives. Personnel who were employed there were affectionally known as dumpies.

Expendable stores – Weapons fitted to an aircraft that are not intended to be returned to the bomb dump.

Fairy – A fairy is someone who is qualified to work on aircraft electrical systems or avionics. Your typical aircraft has miles of wiring, from thick bundles of cables down to tiny individual wires running to some vital components. Next time you want to blow your mind, check out an aircraft wiring diagram; it's like the London Tube map on acid. Engines are easy. If they misbehave, a hammer usually sorts them out. Airframes can be tamed with speed tape. In contrast, electronics requires magic spells and potions, hence the term 'fairy'.

FFE – Free from explosives. This is a phrase used to describe something that is much safer to work on than the alternative. Some jobs require a declaration to be signed. For example, returning empty ammunition boxes required the dumpy to sign the MoD form 6485 FFE and place it in the box. Linen labels are stuck on the outside of the box, and it is sealed with lockwire and a tag. When the box is opened at its destination, one can reasonably expect it not to contain anything explosive. Sometimes one is disappointed.

Fish – Torpedoes. Initially coined by the navy, the phrase is used because a torpedo 'swims' under water. At least, that's the logical reason, but you can never be sure with the navy.

Fitters course – This course offers an SAC the opportunity to advance to Technician. The course is awarded on merit to an SAC who has consistently demonstrated aptitude in the trade and the RAF, and is therefore worthy of promotion. It takes and builds on all the skills taught during the mechs course.

Flare – Flares have many uses, often as markers or position indications. They burn brightly with intense heat, and the flames can often be seen for some distance. In the world of aircraft defence, the flare can be fired to fool a missile into thinking it has found a target. The heat from the flare imitates the heat from an aircraft exhaust so the missile picks up this heat signature instead of the aircraft and explodes harmlessly well away from the aircraft. This assumes of course that the missile is using heat-seeking not radar guidance. See "Chaff" for another option to live!

FOD – Foreign object damage. Jet engines, and aircraft generally, are highly sophisticated and frighteningly delicate pieces of kit. A stray screw or bolt, when ingested by a jet engine, can cause catastrophic failure. The blades of the rotors, or 'fans', can become chipped and break away, which leads to further destruction and can possibly bring the aircraft down. Not a good outcome. FOD refers to any item that could damage an aircraft: stones, lumps of soil, screws, bolts, tools, watches, pens and cigarettes are just a few of the items that can be termed FOD.

HOW TO TALK LIKE AN ARMOURER

FOD plod – The act of patrolling the dispersal, taxiway or runway to look for FOD. Regular checks are carried out to look for items that could be sucked up by the jet intake. Usually, a shift would be tasked to carry out a FOD plod. They would form a line and walk the area, picking up anything they find along the way.

FS – Flight sergeant. See 'Snec'.

FTJ – Final test job. This is work carried out in the workshop to complete the hacking and bashing phase of trade training on either a mechs or fitters course. It involves filing all six faces of a mild steel block square by hand to fine tolerances. It also involves cutting, filing, riveting and attaching an alloy plate to the steel block. Further tasks included drilling holes, and tapping and dying threads, and on a fitters course you have the added bonus of wiring up a circuit, including soldering, forming connections and looming. The standard is high and people have been reduced to tears; let's leave it there because I'm getting emotional.

Gash job – This is an unimportant, trivial or undemanding task, but one that still needs doing. Collecting mail from the post room, organising the section air publications library, sweeping the hangar, and tidying up the tool store could all be deemed gash jobs. The phrase can also be used to describe a job that doesn't meet the usual high standard of quality required when working on aircraft. For example, 'Airman, you made a gash job of that. Do it again!'

GDT – Ground defence training. GDT is undertaken on a regular basis to ensure that all personnel are able to carry out some basic but important tasks. It covers NBC drills including how to put on your respirator correctly, weapons handling, responsibilities for those doing guard duties (stop and search procedures), first aid, fire safety, and tactics for attacking or defending yourself from attack. Training is carried out annually by the RAF Regiment and, once completed, you are issued with your green card (RAF Form 7192, Certificate of Weapon Qualification). In the interests of keeping current, GDT is now known as MOD1, but it does still happen.

GE – Ground engineer. An engineer who works on the ground, as opposed to a flight engineer who is part of the aircrew. Hercules planes have GEs who fly down-route with the aircraft; their role is to take care of all the engineering jobs when the aircraft lands. The GEs are all experienced snecs who have worked on the Hercs for some time. They undergo specialised training that covers all trades, not just their own, and they can self-certify work for the purposes of the aircraft log.

Gimpy – An affectionate term for the GPMG.

Gizzit – An item of interest acquired by an Armourer on their travels. Ideally the item is unique or precious in some way, possibly even aesthetically pleasing. Examples include weapons (deactivated), munitions (inert), flags (always popular, especially from squadrons or visiting aircraft or crew), street signs (travel boasting), drinking vessels, sharp implements (bayonets, knives, pens, etc.) and the old favourite, signs from other camps or sections or possibly something to do with traffic management (the old standby!). Always displayed with pride and protected with the lives of everyone in the section. Imagination is the only limit.

Gozome bird – Pronounced with an emphasis on the last e. This is the plane taking you home after a detachment, deployment or trip. Somehow the phrase 'my flight home' does not carry the same importance. Best not to miss it; awkward questions will follow.

GPMG – The general-purpose machine gun, or 'gimpy'. The gimpy has been in service around the world since the 1950s. It can fire around 1,000 7.62 calibre rounds per minute so is an effective light machine gun, and it has a range of 3,500m. You are much better being behind this little beauty. In front of it can be quite scary.

GSE – Ground support equipment. This term describes a wide variety of kit used in the job but not specifically Armourers' kit. Houchins, ladders, lifting tackle, steps and gantries are a few examples that fall under this banner. Many stations have a GSE bay or section, and its job is to maintain the plethora of kit.

Hacking and bashing – An affectionate term for the workshop phase of either the mechs or fitters course. It refers to the recruits' somewhat clumsy attempts at filing, drilling and shaping of metal.

Hangar pilot – This term refers to someone who is playing around with the controls of an aircraft when they should be doing something else. Aircraft are extremely shiny and attractive objects, and many young children dream of becoming pilots, flashing around the sky defending their country from the enemy, like Biggles and Worrals whom Captain W.E. Johns immortalised in so many books. I would suspect that many of us who are lucky enough to work on aircraft will, at some point, sit in the cockpit and allow our imagination to wander. All of this is fine until you remember that sitting in a real aircraft playing with the controls could cause a serious 'Oh s***!' moment. Moving the joystick to evade an imaginary enemy bearing down on our tail will move the control surfaces for real and could trap the fingers of the rigger checking the aileron. Flipping the safety cover from the fire button and pushing the tit (the service way of describing a button) could have disastrous consequences. 'Hold on!' I hear you say, 'what about all those safety devices that stop these things from happening?' Good point and well made; however, wherever people and machinery mix there is a chance that things will go wrong. Over the decades there have been many examples of people answering some very awkward questions about why they thought pushing the button was a good idea and how they plan on paying for the damage!

HAS – Hardened aircraft shelter. HASs are concrete structures built around the airfield and designed to protect aircraft during air raids. Depending on the aircraft, a HAS can hold one or two jets, and it is a relatively safe place to prepare the jets for operational duties.

Hide – Pretty much what it says. During the Cold War, squadrons would deploy on exercise to simulate war with the Russians. A favourite place for hides was the forests in Germany. A deployment would see the squadron pack up all their gear and go and live in the woods for days, or even weeks. The idea was to stay concealed, so hides would be built, usually by stringing up camouflage netting from a tree or from posts in the ground.

Hotlocks – Meals prepared by the cooks either in the mess or field kitchen, then delivered to the front-line sections in containers designed to keep the contents hot. Mainly stews and sometimes with dumplings, affectionately known as babies' heads. The meal was high in everything and designed to keep you going.

Houchin – A ground power unit used to generate electricity to provide DC power for an aircraft when the aircraft is on the ground. Houchins can be static or movable. Some are self-propelled, and others can be towed. They can be diesel, mains or battery powered.

IED/IEED – Improvised explosive device/improvised electrical explosive device. IEDs are home-made, usually by terrorists, and flipping dangerous.

They are designed to create fear as much as they are to cause damage and harm. It is remarkably easy to make a bomb. The big trick is making it safe so that it doesn't blow up before it is supposed to.

Inject – A problem of indeterminate size introduced into an exercise to test responses.

ISO containers – Metal shipping containers that are used around the world. Designed to be loaded at source then transported by road, rail or water easily by simply transferring them from the various modes of transport using cranes or forklifts. They also make great bases from which to operate once you arrive at your chosen war.

Jankers – Punishment for some heinous crime such as marching out of step on parade, growing facial hair, walking on the grass/parade ground, etc. This crime is normally committed during training and the perpetrator is generally oblivious to the fact that they have committed the crime until the SWO or appointed minion apprehends them amidst lots of shouting. Punishments include, but are not limited to: parading at the guardroom for inspection throughout the day (early morning, lunch, tea and evening); carrying out menial tasks during your free time such as working in the kitchens peeling potatoes; sweeping up areas around the camp; litter picking; painting, etc. The duration of your jankers varies depending on the severity of the crime. Anywhere between one and four days is common. Everyone who joins the RAF as an 'other rank' ends up doing jankers at some point.

Jengo – Junior engineering officer. On graduating from Cranwell, and whatever course they were studying, newly qualified engineering officers would arrive at their first posting all bright-eyed and bushy-tailed, dreaming of their careers and everything they will achieve. Those with sense took stock of their situation and listened to the wise old snecs and followed their guidance. Those who didn't caused chaos with their ground-breaking and revolutionary ideas that were going to change the world and cement their places in the RAF history books. Most came into line reasonably quickly without losing face, but the more determined could expect derision and a label that could follow them for the rest of their career.

JNCO – Junior non-commissioned officer. Someone who has attained the dizzy heights of corporal. One of the hardest-working ranks in the RAF engineering trade. They are qualified to sign off work and expected to do it as well.

HOW TO TALK LIKE AN ARMOURER

Jolly – A very light-hearted way of describing a journey, normally a flight but not limited to. For example:

> Tom: 'I say old boy, what are your plans today?'
> Dick: 'Well the CO has planned a little jolly for us to the range.'
> Harry: 'Spiffing, can I come along?'
> Dick: 'No Harry, we are flying there in the crates and you can't fly!'

JP – Jet Provost. The Jet Provost was a training aircraft used by the RAF from 1955 until 1993. It was the first jet budding young pilots would get to grips with and also budding young Armourers. They were used in Armourer training on the airfield at Cosford to give you experience of flight servicing and aircraft handling (marshalling and start up/shut down). A great little plane.

JP233 – This weapon contained area denial and runway cratering weapons. It was designed to deny access or use of an area. The JP233 is no longer in service.

JT – Junior technician. An SAC with an ego. Either joined as an AC, fought their way up to SAC, then got offered a fitters course. Or joined as a DE and therefore is slightly self-important.

KD – Khaki drill uniform. Issued for travelling somewhere hot and desert-like. The uniform is lightweight and made from either cotton (nice) or man-made material (horrible). It is designed to look smart and keep the wearer cool. It consists of long- and short-sleeved shirts, long trousers and shorts, short and long (knee-length) socks, and desert boots (if you were lucky and stores had any). In the 1950s and before you might also have been issued with a pith helmet. They stopped issuing those because of connections to the Empire that we were trying desperately to forget. The last sentence is made up, but it sounds believable!

Kipper fleet – A beautiful phrase to describe those aircraft employed on maritime patrol duties. It refers to the fact that the aircraft spend most of their time flying over the oggin, either employed on search and rescue or, especially during the Cold War, looking for suspicious vessels. The Russians were known to use fishing trawlers as spy craft, monitoring the movements of the Royal Navy and RAF.

LAC – Leading aircraftman. On completing basic and trade training, you are sent to your first camp sporting two propellor blades on your rank badge.

Landie – The shortened form of Land Rover, that most British of all transport.

Line – Line, working on the. 'Line' is used to describe working on aircraft that are involved in flying duties (operations or training). Typical jobs would be arming, rearming, downloading, role changing, refuelling and performing basic flight safety checks (oils, pressures etc.). Sometimes referred to as 'first line'.

Liney – All the trades that work on the line are often referred to as 'lineys'. Of course, Armourers are the best; the others are just 'pan trash'.

Loadie – Loadmaster. An aircrew trade responsible for the load carried by an aircraft. Jobs include working out the weight distribution, security, manifest and making the tea/coffee on flights for the rest of the crew. Typically found on transport aircraft such as the Hercules or C-17.

LWB – Long-wheelbase Land Rover, as opposed to SWB; good guess – short-wheelbase Land Rover.

Machine gun – A weapon that is designed to fire continuously when the trigger is pulled. They are autoloading, use full-powered rounds, and can sustain heavy rates of fire that really upset the people on the other end. The GPMG is the best-known example used by the British military. Not to be confused with a sub-machine gun, which fires smaller rounds and only one round per trigger press.

MASS – Master armament safety switch. This little device, often referred to as the MASS key, is all that stands between the Armourer working safely on an aircraft and something very nasty happening. All aircraft systems need power, including the armament systems. The MASS provides a break in the system between the power supply and all the wiggly wires that lead to the nasty stuff. The switch must always be in the 'safe' position unless the aircraft is being readied for combat or the system is being checked. One of the first safety checks on an aircraft with weapons systems is that the switch is in the safe position and that any physical key is removed and in the control of the responsible Armourer (probably an oxymoron). No work will be carried out on the system until it is definitely safe.

Maxival – The maxival (maximum evaluation) is a no-notice callout announced by the station siren and Tannoy system. As with the minival,

HOW TO TALK LIKE AN ARMOURER

personnel have to be at their war role within the specified time carrying twenty-four hours' kit. Personnel can expect to be at work for at least twenty-four hours, but more likely forty-eight to seventy-two hours. The maxival would involve the whole station and squadrons housed there, and would be evaluated by personnel from the station and Command. The intelligence would report some sort of hostile activity, usually in a different country or miles away from your location, but as the exercise developed, the threat would increase and you would rapidly find yourself 'at war'. It would start slowly, but the Armourers would be rushed off their feet prepping bombs, rockets, guns and missiles, ready to load the planes. The Armourers would be arming the planes as fast as the dumpies could deliver the gear. Then Command would change their mind so it would be bombs off and re-role, probably several times. There would be interesting little diversions such as a mortar attack or IED planted by a terrorist. Coaches full of people would mysteriously crash to test the first aid response. Things would degenerate rapidly, and it wouldn't be long before the station was getting bombed by hostile aircraft. They'd start with HE, then progress to chemical weapons, so before long you were in full NBC gear running around like a lunatic. The end was always the same – a full-on nuclear strike that saw every plane on the station armed and launched into the sky. 'Endex, endex, endex' would announce cessation of hostilities, at which point everyone would go home apart from the Armourers, who still had to disarm all the planes, put all the bombs and guns away, and get the aircraft ready for their nine-to-five jobs. First in last out, that's the Armourers.

Mechs course – Mechanics course. This is the initial trade training for a recruit once they have completed their basic training. The course involves all the core skills of being an Armourer, including how to dodge discips, drink copiously and belt out a tune in any situation. It also involves filing metal blocks, falling asleep during lectures on paperwork, and getting to play with dummy (safe) Armourers' toys.

Mess – A word used to describe the dining facilities and, in some cases, socialising and living quarters. From the old French word *mes*, meaning portion of food. There will be several messes on the camp to cater for the different ranks. For example, the officers' mess looks after all the officers on camp. It is the most prestigious and will offer high levels of service, possibly even table service and food cooked to order. There may well be accommodation attached, and it will offer events such as the Battle of Britain Ball (black tie) and other entertainment. The sergeants', or SNCOs', mess offers similar functions. The junior ranks mess is more likely to just offer food and is more akin to a cafeteria in that you queue for your food and then find a table. The size of the camp and number of personnel determines the level of service provided. In some ways the different messes are an extension of the class system; this may sound archaic, but it does mean you can relax in familiar company without worrying too much about upsetting someone more senior than you. There is a strict non-fraternisation or invitation-only policy, meaning that an officer cannot walk into the SNCOs' or junior ranks' mess without first being invited.

MFT – Military field test/training. During basic training, trainees reach a point where they must demonstrate their ability to work as a team under battle conditions. Full military kit (see 'Cabbage') would be worn, and rifles would be carried, along with full NBC gear. During the exercise you practise first aid, armed patrols, attacking and defending a position, and how to eat from a military field kitchen. At Swinderby in the 1970s, 1980s and 1990s, trainees would be bussed to RAF North Luffenham to spend three days under battle conditions living in tents and bivouacs (see 'Bivvy'). It must be stressed that this in no way prepares you for life in the real RAF; subjects such as which cutlery to use first (outside in or inside out), how to order room service, polite conversation and hotel etiquette are completely ignored. Interestingly, while researching the book we found out that MFT does still happen, although it may be called something different. It is good to know standards are being maintained.

Minival – A minival, or mini evaluation, is a no-notice station or squadron exercise to test operational capability. The start of the exercise is announced by the sounding of the station siren and announcements over the Tannoy system. On hearing the siren and Tannoy, all personnel are required to get to their war role as quickly as possible carrying twenty-four hours' kit. Time limits were set for personnel to be at their station: thirty minutes for personnel living on camp and one hour for those living off camp. A minival might be called just to test the response times of the station, or it might be aimed at a specific squadron or section. They generally didn't last long, often around eight hours or less, but were often called several times a year. Performance would be monitored by the Station Execs or their designated deputies, and rigorous feedback would be given to highlight areas that needed work.

MT – Mechanical transport. Every RAF base will likely have an MT section that controls all the transport on the camp. From cars to trucks and all points in between. In the heady days of the war and up to the late 1990s there would be a host of RAF MT drivers and maintenance staff. These days the

HOW TO TALK LIKE AN ARMOURER

RAF leases a lot of vehicles and employs more civilians to manage their transport needs. Times change!

NAAFI bop – The Navy Army Air Force Institute are responsible for running shops and bars on camp. Back in the day, they would hold a weekly disco, or 'bop'. The NAAFI bop was a Mecca for all the hip young things to strut their stuff. Some remote camps would bus in the locals to help with fraternisation. This is unlikely to happen now.

NATO potato – This refers to a very keen individual. Someone who has fully embraced service life and takes every opportunity to dress in their cabbage gear. They will also know the answer to every military-related question, ever! Don't get me wrong, joining the RAF is a life choice, but there are limits; no one likes a smart arse.

NBC gear – Nuclear, biological and chemical resistant clothing. During the Cold War it was olive or drab green on the outside and had a charcoal lining. These days it is more likely to be camouflage. The suit comes in two parts: over-trousers and over-jacket or smock. The idea is that, when bad things happen (ideally just before), you stop what you are doing, bring out your vacuum-packed suit and quickly pull it over whatever else you are wearing (removing your webbing first, of course). The trousers have string braces to hold them up, which you have to cross over the shoulders then tie around the waist (there is a specific method for everything in the military to avoid anyone having to think). Once the trousers are on you then pull the smock over your head. Suit fitted, it's now time to don the rubber over-boots; one size fits all – just make sure you do up the laces properly. Respirator next, then pull up the hood of the smock, securing it in place with the drawstring. Finally, you pop on the inner and outer gloves. The suit is designed to repel anything the enemy can deploy, and unless you are too close to a nuclear explosion it certainly stops everything, including air. This kit is often worn for several days at a time during exercise and deployment. Within minutes you are sweating like a marathon runner in the desert. When the time comes to remove it, you will be black from head to foot thanks to the charcoal lining.

No duff – A phrase used when describing a real problem to someone; often used when the 'problem' is a little far-fetched, for example:

> Podge: 'Sir, we are locked out of the HAS.'
> OC Ops: 'Is this an inject, Podge?'
> Podge: 'No duff sir, no duff!'

OC Arm – Officer Commanding Armament (or Armourers). A thankless job that requires shoulders made of Teflon.

OC Med – Officer Commanding Medical Section. The medical section and associated staff performed the vital function of issuing Brufen tablets for any known malady, from headaches to missing limbs.

OC Ops – Officer Commanding Operations. A commissioned officer responsible for the day-to-day organisation of the squadron or station flying programme. It is generally their fault that Armourers spend hours loading an aircraft for a specific role only to be told when they have just finished to re-role the aircraft for a different mission.

OCU – Operational conversion unit. Each aircraft type has an OCU to train aircrew on the specifics of that aircraft and the different roles that aircraft can perform. Aircrew will be posted to the OCU prior to being posted to a squadron or station.

Oggin – A term for the sea or ocean, commonly used by people working on the kipper fleet.

OJT – On the job training. A classic strategy employed to save money on training.

Oppo – A phrase to refer to your mate, friend or colleague, either at work or undertaking some R&R. You could always use the term 'mate' but that would be too easy, and you'd miss out on the opportunity to use a different phrase instead.

Ops – Operations. A ubiquitous term for anything official. Sometimes it really was official.

Over-sign – All work is carried out by a tradesman and must be over-signed by a supervisor. The tradesman can be any rank, but the supervisor must be an NCO. The signatures are confirmation that the work has been carried out in accordance with the appropriate AP. The job sheets are stored and can be used in evidence should something go wrong. You have been warned!

Pan – Term used to describe the concrete bays used to park aircraft.

HOW TO TALK LIKE AN ARMOURER

Pan trash – Anyone who works on an aircraft line, especially those who aren't Armourers.

PE – Plastic explosive. PE comes in sticks wrapped in a greaseproof-type wrapper. It is very safe to handle and malleable. When warmed up it can be shaped and moulded to suit whatever job it was required for. It becomes dangerous when you introduce a means of initiating it, typically with a detonator.

Pigstick – An evocative name to describe an article of EOD equipment. A pigstick is a hollow metal tube fitted with an explosive cartridge at one end which, when initiated, propels a jet of water at high velocity to "cut" through the outer casing of an IED and disrupt the electrical circuit without detonating (hopefully) the device. In polite company you may prefer to use its official name which is "disruptor", lest you cause the raising of eyebrows and delicate souls to swoon.

Plumber – A term used within the RAF to refer to Armourers. It is believed to derive from the Armourers' role in maintaining gun turrets on heavy bombers and other turret-equipped aircraft. These turrets were hydraulically and electrically powered and contained pipework, just the kinds of things that plumbers would get stuck into.

POL – Petrol, oil, lubricants. The term POL refers to any fluids or substances that may cause fire or some other hazard such as burning or irritation of the skin. Paint, cleaning fluids, glue etc., all fall into the POL category. Sections who use POL have a metal store or locker away from the buildings into which all these items are stored. This prevents many a nasty accident.

PTI – Physical training instructor. Fitness is an important aspect of being in the military and initial training will involve meeting lots of PTIs. The collective noun for PTIs is 'bastards', purely based on what they put you through in their exercise sessions, fondly known as 'beastings'. During the 1980s and 1990s the PTI trade training camp was RAF Cosford, so any Armourer passing through on their mechs or fitters course was certain to meet some very shiny and enthusiastic trainee PTIs.

Q – Qualifications in the RAF are referred to as Qs. An Armourer can amass a large variety of Qs throughout their career. All jobs require some form of training; some training will be local, but for the more specialised equipment or jobs training is undertaken at other military or civilian locations. You can be locally Q'd, that is, certified as competent to carry out a task at your current posting, or the Q may be transferrable. For example, an Armourer might have had a local Q to load a Harpoon missile onto a Nimrod – a useful qualification if you worked on Nimrods, but not so much on a squadron of Tornados. A small arms Q is transferrable to any station or location, so this Q enables you to work on small arms anywhere.

QRA – Quick Reaction Alert. The RAF maintains aircraft in QRA in anticipation of any situation they may be needed for; for example, search and rescue, and intercept of unknown/unauthorised aircraft in UK airspace. The phrase was coined during the Cold War where the V bomber force was on constant operational readiness as a reactive force, replacing the term 'scramble' from the Battle of Britain. Essentially, QRA and scramble are the same thing – get the aircraft in the air as quickly as possible because something bad is happening.

R&R – Rest and relaxation. Armourers work really hard loading and prepping the bombs, loading the aircraft and counting the bullets, so at the end of a busy shift a bit of R&R restores the balance.

Rat pack – Short for ration pack. Rations are issued for a variety of reasons, often during exercise or deployment to the field, and contain everything the person needs to survive for a period of time. For example, a twenty-four-hour rat pack contains all the calories needed to live on for twenty-four hours. Contents vary, but staples include stews and fruit puddings, butter, jam, and biscuits that are so hard you can use them to build a shelter. Some rat packs even include toilet paper, because war can be scary.

Rigger – A rigger is someone qualified to work on airframes. The term harks back to the early days of the RFC when aircraft were wooden frames and struts held rigid by rigging wire. Riggers often wear gloves because otherwise their knuckles drag on the ground.

Rock apes – An affectionate term for members of the RAF Regiment. Known for their intelligence, they are the military arm of the RAF and responsible for, among other things, marching and shouting.

Role equipment – This is equipment fitted to an aircraft to allow it to carry specific weapons. For example, CBLS is a piece of role equipment designed to enable the aircraft to fly with practice bombs fitted.

HOW TO TALK LIKE AN ARMOURER

Round – A round is the complete or intact unit of ammunition. It comprises the case, propellant, primer and projectile. It can also be used as a subtle prompt to indicate who should be buying the drinks. For example, at an Armourers' gathering in the NAAFI it is not uncommon to hear parlance such as, 'My throat is as dry as a camel's hoof after a trek across the Sahara so come on, whose round is it?'

RSP – Render safe procedure. UXBs, IEDs and IEEDs need to be made safe, and because each bomb is different, military EOD specialists developed numerous RSPs that can be followed and that will lead to the bomb being made safe. Nothing is ever as simple as it sounds, so following an RSP didn't always guarantee success, but it does greatly improve the chances. Variables such as bomb impact, weather, terrain and the person who made the IED mean the EOD operator has to remain alert and flexible.

SAC – Senior aircraftman. The rank achieved after joining, surviving basic and trade training, and being in your first posting long enough to blag your way through TATs.

Safe heading lines – These are lines painted on the pan or dispersal that direct the way an aircraft should point when it is armed. Think of your typical fast jet loaded with Sidewinder missiles and 27mm Mauser cannon. If something untoward were to happen, you don't want a Sidewinder flying off toward the NAAFI. You point it in the direction where it can do the least harm – the officers' mess, perhaps.

Safe separation – It is not easy to drop a bomb from an aircraft flying at Mach 1. Have you ever stuck your arm out of your car window while travelling at speed? Your arm can be forced backwards and possibly into the side of the car. This is the problem faced when releasing stores. You need the store to be clear of the aircraft and not affected by its slipstream, and it must not remain attached by a wire or electrical lead. That would be disastrous. Another important factor to consider is when to finally arm the weapon, that is, to put it in a state where it explodes either on impact or at a pre-designated time. Until that time you need the weapon to be as safe as possible. Can you imagine a finally armed bomb slapping around underneath the wing of a fast jet? Safe separation is achieved by using ERUs to force the store away from the aircraft. Final arming can be achieved by using snatch cables to withdraw a safety pin, timers or veins on fuzes that only start when the bomb is in free fall and/or electrical leads (LEFAs) to make the final connection. The same phrase is used to describe the process of ejecting aircrew from a fast jet using ejection seats. You need to propel the crew away from the aircraft at speed to prevent them being hit by the tailplane or other sticky-out bits.

Sangar – A concrete or sandbag construction that was used as cover by an airman when on guard duty. It might be just a sandbag wall, a concrete pipe or something more substantial. Generally, the inside of sangars were colder than being out in the open, and they never had any amenities.

SAR – Search and rescue. Until recently, the RAF played a vital role in SAR, operating helicopters and using its maritime patrol aircraft to search and co-ordinate rescue operations. The kipper fleet played a vital part in SAR, and when the Royal Yacht *Britannia* was in commission, an aircraft would be on dedicated standby, or following the yacht whenever it was at sea. The responsibility for SAR now lies with other civilian agencies, although the military can still be called upon to assist in certain situations.

Scaly – Scaly refers to a married service person who is therefore fettered by love and responsibility. Any issue are referred to as scaly brats.

Seat-stick-interface problem – This beautiful phrase is a polite way of pointing out the idiocy of the aircrew. When a jet returns to base the aircrew debrief the ground crew on snags. Sometimes the snag is genuine, for example a blown tyre on landing. But sometimes the aircrew get carried away. For example, 'Friction locks cause throttle levers to stick'. Even if you don't know anything about engineering or aircraft, it's obvious that the entire point of a friction lock is to cause friction or 'stickiness'. This is a classic example of a seat-stick-interface problem.

Sgt – Sergeant. For a description, see 'Snec'.

Singly – This word refers to an unmarried service person. Unfettered by love, they are free to roam at will and do as they please. Time off usually includes 'scaly bashing', which is essentially inviting oneself to a married colleague's house and eating their food and drinking their beer. When the fridge is empty, the singly can move on to the next unsuspecting household. The plural is singlies.

Slabbed – See 'crated'. Instead of buying a crate of beer the guilty person has to buy a slab (twenty-four cans on a cardboard tray surrounded by shrink-wrapped plastic). If you are now considering the difference between the two, you need to be crated and slabbed at the same time.

HOW TO TALK LIKE AN ARMOURER

Smeg – To destroy or blow up, using explosives. For example, 'We smegged those old .303 rounds with a blob of PE and some det cord.'

Snag – A snag is a problem with an aircraft that could prevent it flying or limit its operational capability. When aircraft fly they develop faults that need to be investigated when they return to base. The investigation work is known as snagging. Some problems, like a loose or missing bolt, are easily fixed. Others take some working out, like an intermittent electrical fault. On return to base the aircrew will debrief the ground crew on any problems, using the F700 Aircraft log to raise a problem (done online these days). The ground crew investigate and note findings and the resolution in the log. That way there is a complete audit trail of snags. A lot of snags are found to be seat-stick-interface problems.

Snec – Senior non-commissioned officer (SNCO), someone holding the rank of sergeant (SGT), chief technician (CT) or flight sergeant (FS). Requirements for the role included the ability to drink vast quantities of anything without falling over, shoulders made of Teflon, and being adept at dodging work of any kind.

Sooty – A sooty is someone qualified to work on aircraft engines. They are easily identified because they are generally covered in more soot than Dick Van Dyke on the set of Mary Poppins.

Spams – Americans. During the war, Britain depended on the US for lots of things, including food. We started importing large quantities of specially processed American meat, or spam for short. From that point on American troops (and civilians) became known as spams.

SROs – Station or Squadron routine orders. Military life is governed by rules that are published and disseminated to the personnel. Back in the day, they were pinned to noticeboards in every section, and everyone had to read them on a regular basis to make sure they always had the most up-to-date information. Nowadays they probably use an app!

SSA – Supplementary Storage Area. A safe place to store your buckets of sunshine.

Stores – A multi-use word, 'stores' could refer to weapons fitted to aircraft, or somewhere equipment is stored.

SWO – Station warrant officer; GOD.

Taceval – A station, squadron or command exercise on a massive scale. A tactical evaluation (taceval) involves everyone on camp and lasts for at least three full days, testing every capability to its limit. Tacevals are evaluated by specialist staff from Command, and the evaluation would often involve NATO evaluators and observers, so you really didn't want to mess it up. As with a maxival, there would be trouble kicking off somewhere that would escalate and lead to a full-on war with Russia. As Armourers, you can expect to be on duty round the clock, grabbing sleep when you can and availing yourself of the hotlocks meals. Sensible sections would have their own stock or 'rations' to supplement the ones provided. The Di staff have unrestricted access to everywhere on camp and can pop up at the most inopportune moments to 'inject' interesting and challenging little tasks to test an individual, section or squadron. Detailed reports are written, and woe betide the station or squadron that fails any element. Otherwise it's a case of minivals and maxivals until the situation is rectified or the problem is posted.

TAT – Trade Ability Test. Something an LAC must pass in order to be promoted to SAC.

Tea bar – The most important area of any squadron or section. This is where Armourers gather at tea break or after work (when the hangar doors are shut) to partake of refreshments. During working hours the refreshments could grace any temperance hall: tea, coffee (or a blend of both) are available, and also a variety of life-sustaining snacks. Anything from crisps, chocolates, sweets and, in the case of flying stations that provide food rations for their aircraft (Kinloss and Lyneham spring to mind as two that did), a selection of aircraft meals. Armourers are known for their love of sports, and many are lean athletic gods in peak physical condition. To maintain this status, you will find games such as darts, cards and Uckers readily available. There may even be a TV and VCR/DVD/BlueRay/Xbox or even Netflix. The tea bar is funded by its members through a weekly collection of subs. After working hours, beers may well be available. The tea bar is decorated in abstract and entertaining ways depending on the available skills and resources. Hand-painted murals, photos, beer mats, deactivated (who checked the AK-47 on the wall?) weapons are examples, but imagination knows no bounds. There will always be a plentiful supply of gizzits.

The hangar doors are shut – A phrase used to remind someone to stop talking about work because drinking is now taking place.

HOW TO TALK LIKE AN ARMOURER

Threshold – A term used to describe the limits of a runway during normal take-off and landing. The threshold is marked at each end of a runway by wide black-and-white stripes known as the 'piano keys' or 'keyboard'.

TM – Trade manager. The TM will be an SNCO and have a lot of experience in their respective trade. Most commonly found working in offices, they are responsible for advising on all aspects of their trade such as manpower requirements for stations, skills, promotions and recruitment needs. All the RAF trades have a TM; there may even be more than one.

TR – Turn round service. This is a small service carried out on an aircraft between sorties or missions. It is a basic refuel, rearm and 'make sure it is fit to fly again'. Associated terms are OTR (Operational TR), OTR load and QTR (Quick TR). There is an element of pride in being able to see your aircraft in and get it ready to fly again in a short time. Fast jets may only take ten to fifteen minutes to be readied.

U/S – A short way of saying 'unserviceable'. All equipment is checked, and before it can be used must be deemed serviceable. Back in the day an MoD Form 731 was attached to all components; it was two-sided: one green and the other red. Until equipment was checked it was deemed U/S and the red side of the label was completed and displayed on the item. These days it is all electronic and they don't use colour coding. Don't confuse U/S with the US – they don't like it!

Uckers – A game based loosely on ludo. Two or more players compete (fiercely) to move all their pieces around the board to reach home. During the game there will be snots, running snots, blobs, mixed blobs, and all manner of shouting and tactics deployed. Pieces are traditionally made from some form of explosive cartridge (spent of course because using live ones would be stupid), painted for easy identification. The board is lovingly crafted from any material available, hand painted, and lavished with care and respect. The Uckers board is often the focal point of the tea bar or crew room, and matches are announced by phrases such as 'Uckers, you f***ers?'

UOR – Urgent operational requirement. When the brown stuff hits the rotary device, people are galvanised into action; red tape disappears and normally obstructive, sorry, efficient people melt into the background. All of a sudden the impossible becomes easy, and also rather exciting. A UOR was a chance for people to get creative and try things like fitting Sidewinder missiles to a Nimrod, or using a bicycle pump to deploy chaff though the signal pistol mount on a Herc. UORs are often accompanied by the phrase, 'What could possibly go wrong?', which is clearly rhetorical because you don't want the answer.

UXB – Unexploded bomb. That is a bomb that has been deployed but that hasn't gone off. Generally a dangerous situation.

Warrant officer – The highest non-commissioned rank in the RAF. The holder of the rank is the recipient of the King's Warrant to carry out their duties. See 'Wobbly orange'.

Webbing – A convenient way for soldiers to carry all the required accoutrements for a darn good fight. Ammunition pouches, respirator haversack, bayonet frog, water bottle, kidney pouches, small pack and large pack are all strung together with strong webbing straps which hang off the soldier and means everything is to hand. The reality is a cats-cradle of stuff that is a mind-bending exercise to assemble and rubs shoulders and other contact patches when worn. Webbing has been worn by soldiers for centuries. The early stuff was probably just as useless as the stuff issued in the 50s. The modern incarnation is much better with quick release buckles and multi-adjustable fit to cater for any body shape.

Simply donning webbing turns one into a Hollywood star ready to fill the leading role of the latest blockbuster, or a security guard at a shopping centre.

Wheelbarrow – A vital item of EOD equipment designed to save the Man 1 from having to don the bomb suit and make the long walk to an IED. The Wheelbarrow is a platform with an extending arm fitted with two pigsticks (you can never have too many pigsticks) and a camera at the end. The platform is mounted on tracks (like a tiny tank) and can traverse a variety of terrain. It is remote controlled which means the operator is safe as they investigate and render safe IEDs without interrupting their tea and biscuits.

Wheels – Transport to get you where you need to be. Wheels can refer to any transport that must, at all costs, be caught on time. 'Wheels' stems from 'wheels up', the time at which an aircraft takes off.

Wobbly – Warsteiner is a strong German beer. So called because after a couple of beers one can become a bit wobbly.

HOW TO TALK LIKE AN ARMOURER

Wobbly orange – Warrant officer (WO), someone holding the King's Warrant. Typically, a rank hard won over a considerable period of service. Specialist skills associated with the rank are (but not limited to) sleeping, dribbling while asleep, wandering aimlessly, and unintentional moments of incoherence followed by intentional moments of incoherence.

WOW – Weight on wheels. This refers to a safety device fitted to aircraft. It is a switch that, when the undercarriage is lowered, cuts power to the armament systems, thereby preventing anything nasty happening. Can also be referred to as 'Wheels on ground'.

Ying-yang – A delightful way of describing lots of something. For example, 'We have bombs up the ying-yang' means we have lots of bombs.

Index

ACMI, *see* Air Combat Manoeuvring Instrumentation
Aden gun, 30mm, xii, 40–1, 91, 145, 151
Adie, Kate, 236
AEOD, *see* Airfield explosive ordnance disposal
AEOD Reference Guide, 116, 118–19
AF (after flight) checks, 38, 81, 88–9, 91, 94, 164, 168, 176
Afghanistan, 6, 150, 216–17
Agila, operation, 158
AGSE, *see* Armament ground support equipment
AGSE bay, 145
Air Cadets, 16, 18, 20
Air Combat Manoeuvring Instrumentation (ACMI), 169
Air Officer Commanding (AOC), 36–7, 236
Air publication (AP), 37, 44, 55, 135
Air Sea Rescue helicopter, 87
Aircraft bay, 147, 149
Airfield explosive ordnance disposal (AEOD), xi, 110–11
Ajax Bay, Falkland Islands, 262, 278
Akrotiri, RAF station, Cyprus, 188–9, 212–13, 235
AK-47 gun, 158, 308
Aldergrove, RAF station, 219
Ali Al Salem airbase, Kuwait, 214, 237
Allen, Dermot, 5
Amsterdam, 233-4
Ancona, Italy, 207–208, 210, 212, 221, 236
Angel, operation, 210–212

Anti-submarine bombs, 6
AOC, *see* Air Officer Commanding
AOC's parade, 36
AP, *see* Air publication
APC, *see* Armament practice camp
Armament ground support equipment (AGSE), xi, 134, 144, 147
Armament practice camp (APC), 92, 161
Armourer family, 254–5
Armourers' artwork, 96, 156
Armoury, *see* Station armoury
Ascension Island, 190, 258, 274–5
Atomic weapons, 197
Attesting, 22, 30
Avro aircraft:
    Lancaster bomber, xiii, 9–10, 83, 85, 89
    Lincoln bomber, 82–3
    Shackleton bomber, xiii, 82–3, 87, 89, 92
    Vulcan bomber, 89–92, 187, 190, 273

Babies' heads, 264
BAC Jet Provost aircraft, 42–3, 88–90, 92
Badges, 96-7
BAE Systems, 198, 251
BAE Systems Hawk aircraft, xiii, 89–90, 138
Bahrain, 237
Balkans War, 149, 207
Ballykinler, army base, 219
Barostatic Time Release Unit (BTRU), 138
Basic Engineering course, 35, 38, 41

INDEX

Basra, Iraq, 214–16
Battle of Britain, 7–9, 82
Bays:
    AGSE, 145
    Aircraft, 147, 149
    Carrier, 138, 143, 148
    Gun, xii, 144
    Launcher, 138
    Pylon, 138
    Release unit, 138
    Role, 138, 192
    Seat, xi, 135, 138, 213
    Servicing, 141, 156
BCU, *see* Bird Control Unit
Beatrice oil field, 244
Belize, 14, 161, 178–84
Benson, RAF station, 89
Berlin, 197
Berlin Airlift, 210
BF (before flight) checks, 38, 76, 78, 94, 164
Biological weapons, 115, 119–20, 206
Bird Control Unit (BCU), 88
Bird strikes, 88
Black and tan cable, 144
Black Buck, operations, 190, 258
Blackburn Buccaneer aircraft, 63, 88–9, 91–2
Blacklists, 196
Blitz, the, 9
Bloodhound missile, 89, 91
Bluff Cove, Falkland Islands, 271
BL755 cluster bomblet, 258
Boeing P-8 Poseidon aircraft, 87
Bofors gun, 257
Bomb disposal, *see* Explosive ordnance disposal (EOD)
Bomb dump, xii, 10, 50–67, 85–6, 121, 130, 134, 141, 165, 178, 188, 191–6, 206, 215, 228, 242
Bomb suit, 116
Bombs:
    anti-submarine, 6
    Cooper, 3
    General Purpose (GP), 6, 9
    High Capacity (HC), 9
    incendiary, 4, 6, 9–10, 98, 115
    loading, 10, 85, 98–9, 101, 115, 145, 147, 213, 231–2
    Medium Capacity (MC), 9–10
    Paveway, 55, 142
    phosphorous, 3, 9
    prepping, 53, 65, 83
    sweeper, 3
    1000-pounders, 92
Borneo, 187–8
Boscombe Down, RAF station, 18
Bosnia, 14, 150
Breathing apparatus (BA set), 59
Bristol Beaufighter aircraft, 9
Brize Norton, RAF station, 158, 190, 214, 252, 258, 275
Browning guns:
    machine gun, 6, 8, 82
    9mm SLP, 41, 154
Brüggen, RAF station, Germany, 58, 120, 157, 241–2
Brunei revolt, 187
BTRU, *see* Barostatic Time Release Unit
Buccaneer, *see* Blackburn Buccaneer
Buckets of sunshine, 14, 147, 242

Canberra bomber, *see* English Electric Canberra bomber
Card games, 153, 156, 164, 200
Cardington, RAF station, 24
Careers Information Office (CIO), 16–18
Carmichael, George, 3
Carrier bay, 138, 143, 148
Carrier bomb light stores (CBLS), 90, 139
Carriers, xii–xiii, 75, 134, 138–9, 141, 143–4, 147
Catania, Italy, 166, 237
CBLS, *see* Carrier bomb light stores
CBU, *see* Cluster bomb unit
Chaff and flare, 38, 149, 168, 208–209, 238
Changi airbase, Singapore, 227
Charlton, Flight Lieutenant, 109
Chastise, operation, 13

313

Chemical weapons, 28, 110, 114–15, 119–20, 199, 206
Cherry Point military base, North Carolina, 165, 172
Cheshire, operation, 207–210, 236, 238
Chilmark, RAF ammunition store, 64
Chinook helicopters, 87, 89–91, 268, 271
Chivenor, RAF station, 126, 131
Churchill, Sir Winston, 7
CIO, *see* Careers Information Office
Cluster bomb unit (CBU), 195–6, 270
Cold War, 14–15, 48, 62, 64, 71, 82, 86–87, 112, 119, 157, 161, 186, 190, 197–207, 257
Coltishall, RAF station, 18, 43
Composite servicing model, 202
Composite teams, 48
Conflicts, 186–217
    Balkans, 149, 207
    Borneo, 187–8
    Falkland Islands, 14, 20, 90, 149, 189–96, 256–83
    Gulf, 149, 198–206, 212–216, 235, 249, 252
Conran, Eric, 3
Cooper bombs, 3
Cosford, RAF station, 32, 42–5, 49, 88, 123, 143
Cottesmore, RAF station, 43
Courses, *see* Training
Criminal record when applying to join RAF, 21
Cromwell, Oliver, 60
Cross service postings, 92, 108
Cross training, 48
Crutching, xii, 141
CS gas, 28, 95, 215
Cyprus, 161, 188–9, 200, 212–15, 235, 250
    military coup, 189

DACT, *see* Dissimilar Air Combat Training
Dakar, 190, 258
Darwin, Falkland Islands, 270
Dassault Mirage aircraft, 259–60, 268
DE, *see* Direct Entrant

De Havilland aircraft:
    Mosquito, 10
    Sea Vixen, 89, 92
De la Billière, Sir Peter, 206
De Wilde cartridges, 8
Decimomannu Air Base, Sardinia, 169–71
Decker, Sally, 210
Defence Explosive Ordnance Disposal School (DEODS), 110
Depleted uranium, 252
Desert Shield, operation, 198
Detachments, 161–185
    Belize, 178–84
    Decimomannu, 169–71
    Purple Star, 154, 172–3
    Red Flag, 162–4, 168
    Rum Punch, 163
    Sigonella, 166
Detonation cord, 114
Detonators, xii, 53, 91, 114, 121, 130, 271
Dhahran airbase, Saudi Arabia, 205–206
Di staff, *see* Direction staff
Dickson, Bertram, 2
Direct Entrant, 20, 32
Direction staff (Di staff), 23, 233
Dissimilar Air Combat Training (DACT), 169
Douglas A-4 Skyhawk aircraft, 265
Dowding, Hugh, 7
Drogue, 83, 135, 138
Duty Armourer, 87, 149, 151–2, 167

Earthing, 53
East German corridor, 197–8
East Germany, 82, 198
East Kirby, RAF station, 10
Ejection seats, xi, xiii, 2, 14, 40, 60, 72–3, 78, 80, 91, 111, 134–5, 137, 197, 231, 268, 274
Ejector Release Unit (ERU), xii–xiii, 141
El Salvador, 183
Electrically operated fire extinguisher cartridge (EOFE cart), 147, 149
Empty box store, 56–7

INDEX

Engineering Record Card (ERC), 135
English Electric aircraft:
    Canberra bomber, 86, 89–91, 187, 265
    Lightning, xiii, 47, 89, 91–2, 249
EOD, *see* Explosive ordnance disposal
EOFE cart, *see* Electrically operated fire extinguisher cartridge
ERU, *see* Ejector Release Unit
ESA, *see* Bomb dump
Eurofighter Typhoon aircraft, xiii, 81, 91–92, 135, 141
Exercises, xii, 27, 94–6, 112, 119, 221, 231–2, 243–4
    See also Detachments
Exmoor, 127
Explosive ordnance disposal (EOD), 49, 107–134, 168, 183, 194, 256, 258, 261, 263, 268
    teams, 49, 107, 109–12, 115, 123–5, 130, 133, 147, 256
Explosive Storage Area (ESA), *see* Bomb dump

Fairies, 48, 76, 90, 92, 94, 150, 202
Falkland Islands, 14, 20, 90, 149, 189–96, 256–83
Falklands Diary, 256–283
FB5, *see* Vickers FB5
Field Hospital, Falkland Islands, 264, 272
Final Test Job (FTJ), 39–40, 143, 186
Finningley, RAF station, 43
Fire bottles, 147–9, 167
Firefighting, 23
Fire training, 58
Firestreak missiles, 17
Firework displays, 224–6
First Line Armament Servicing (FLAS), 77
First World War, 2–6, 17, 108, 186
Fitters course, 32, 35, 42, 46, 125, 143, 147–8, 196, 219
Fleet Air Arm, 20, 245
Florida, 163–4
FN rifle, 269–70
FOD, *see* Foreign object damage

Fokker aircraft, 4
Forces Resettlement Bulletin, 247
Foreign object damage (FOD), 72–4, 270
FTB, *see* Final Test Job
Fulton Block, RAF Cosford, 32
Fuzes, removing, xiii, 85, 114–118

Galtieri's Revenge, 263
Gaydon, RAF station, 24, 85, 87, 223, 227, 246
Gemini RIB, 258
General Purpose bombs, 6, 9
General purpose machine gun (GPMG), 41, 191, 260, 271
Geneva Convention, 96
Giraffe platform, 86
Gizzits, 156
Gloster aircraft:
    Javelin, 17, 89–90, 187–8
    Meteor, 84
Goose Bay, Canada, 163–4
Goose Green, Falkland Islands, 266, 268–70, 278
GPMG, *see* General purpose machine gun
GPU, *see* Ground power unit
Graveley, RAF station, 10
Green Label ammunition, 4
Greyhound, *see* Grumman C-2 Greyhound
Ground power unit (GPU), 68–9
Grumman aircraft:
    C-2 Greyhound, 212
    F-14 Tomcat, 213
Guard duty, 71, 220
Guardroom, 53, 152, 190
Gulf conflicts, 149, 198–206, 212–216, 235, 249, 252
Gulf of Oman, 201
Gun bay, xii, 144
Gun room, 153, 155–6, 159
Guns:
    Aden, 30mm, xii, 39–41, 91, 145, 151
    AK47, 158, 308
    Bofors, 257
    Browning machine gun, 6, 8, 82, 140

Browning 9mm Self-Loading Pistol (SLP), 41, 154
FN rifle, 269–70
General purpose machine gun (GPMG), 41, 191, 260, 271
Lewis, 6
L85 A1 (SA80), 41
PPSH 40 submachine gun, 158
Rarden cannon, 30mm, 115
Shotgun, 41
Signal pistol, 41, 82, 204
Synchronised, 4
Vickers, 4, 6
.303 Short Magazine Lee Enfield (SMLE), 41
7.62 Self-Loading Rifle (SLR), 41
Gütersloh, RAF station, Germany, 64, 233

Hacking and bashing, *see* Basic Engineering course
Halifax, *see* Handley Page Halifax
Halton, RAF station, 19, 22, 27, 32, 36, 46, 251
Handley Page aircraft:
　Halifax bomber, 9
　Victor bomber, 86, 89–90, 92
Hardened aircraft shelter (HAS), xiii, 47, 50, 64, 95, 231–3
Harpoon missiles, 144, 199, 304
Harrier, *see* Hawker Siddeley Harrier
Harris, Arthur "Bomber", 9
HAS, *see* Hardened aircraft shelter
Hatch system, 91, 153–4
Hawk, *see* BAE Systems Hawk
Hawker aircraft:
　Hunter, xiii, 62–3, 89–92, 145, 187–8
　Hurricane, xiii, 8–9
Hawker Siddeley aircraft:
　Harrier, xiii, 78, 89–92, 157, 178, 182, 184, 191–2, 257, 259, 270
　Nimrod, xiii, 67, 71, 75–7, 81, 87–92, 94, 96, 141, 164, 166, 168, 176, 199–204
Health issues when applying to join RAF, 21

Hercules, *see* Lockheed C-130 Hercules
High Capacity (HC) bombs, 9
Hiroshima, 197
HMS *Antelope*, 261
HMS *Ark Royal*, 187
HMS *Ardent*, 259
HMS *Fearless*, 260
HMS *Sir Galahad*, 260
Homestead Air Force Base, USA, 163
Honington, RAF station, 63, 228
Hornet, *see* McDonnell Douglas Hornet
Houchin GPU, 88, 162
Hunter, *see* Hawker Hunter
Hunter gun packs, 62–3
Hurricane, *see* Hawker Hurricane
Hussein, Saddam, 201, 215

IBM, 247–8
ID card, 50, 72, 153, 217–18, 246, 248, 250
IED, *see* Improvised explosive device
IEED, *see* Improvised electrical explosive device
Incendiary bomb, 4, 6, 9–10, 98, 115
Indonesia, 187–8
Improvised electrical explosive device (IEED), 114, 123
Improvised explosive device (IED), xi, 111–12, 114, 123, 272
Initial training, *see* Training, basic
Innsworth, RAF station, 190
Inskip, Sir Thomas, 7
IRA, 126, 150, 218–20
Iraq, 6, 73, 150, 155, 198–9, 201, 206, 213
Irish Republican Army, *see* IRA

Jacks, xi, 75, 86, 147, 239
Javelin, *see* Gloster Javelin
Jet Provost, *see* BAC Jet Provost
Jettison capability, 139
Jolly Green Giants, 213
JP233 airfield denial weapon, 125, 231

Kabul, Afghanistan, 216
Kalamazoo, 60–1

INDEX

KCS, *see* King's Colour Squadron
KD, *see* Khaki drill uniform
Kenley, RAF station, 8
Kenya Mau Mau crisis, 85
Kevlar helmet, 201
Khaki drill (KD) uniform, 173, 199
King Charles II, 60
King George V, 2
King's Colour Squadron (KCS), 157
King's Regiment, 214
Kinloss, RAF station, 44–6, 51, 59, 65, 67, 70–1, 74, 76, 82, 93–4, 96, 138, 143–4, 147–8, 163, 165, 168, 196, 198, 200, 203, 224–5, 240–1, 272
Kipper fleet, 163
Kuwait, 102, 198, 201, 214, 237

Laarbruch, RAF station, Germany, 157, 232
Labis, Malaysia, 188
Labuan airbase, Borneo, 187
Lancaster bomber, *see* Avro Lancaster
Lancaster House agreement, 158
Larkhill, RAF station, 222
Las Vegas, 163
LAU-7/A missile launcher, 139, 192
Launcher bay, 138
Launchers, 67, 91, 134, 138–9, 204
Leconfield, RAF station, 82–3
Leeming, RAF station, 138, 213, 215, 243
Leuchars, RAF station, 43–4, 190, 206, 240–1, 249
Lewis gun, 6
Licensing, bomb dumps, 52–3
Lightning, *see* English Electric Lightning
Limassol, Cyprus, 189, 235
Lincoln bomber, *see* Avro Lincoln
Line work, 87
Lineys, 37, 67, 80, 143, 164, 173, 177
Linking tool, xiii, 65
Loaders, 54, 141, 145, 147, 206
  R-type, 145
  VAP-60, 145, 147
  Wendy, xi, 145, 147
  Y-type, 105, 145

Loading bombs, 10, 85, 98–9, 101, 115, 145, 147, 213, 231–2
Lock wiring, 41–2, 138
Lockheed C-130 Hercules aircraft, 38, 89–92, 149–50, 167–8, 172, 174, 188–90, 199–200, 203, 209–11, 216, 221, 236–240, 273–4,
  Toilet facilities, 175–8
  XV193, 221
London, 9, 241, 243, 275
Long walk, 110, 116, 122, 124
Loraine, Captain Eustace B., 222
Loss of life, 206, 221–2
Lossiemouth, RAF station, 44–6, 62, 243
Luftwaffe, 7, 9, 109
Lyneham, RAF station, 87, 147–51, 167–8, 199–200, 203, 207–208, 221, 225
Lynx helicopter, 89, 91, 269

Machrihanish, RAF station, 162, 168
Major, John, 206, 236
Malaysia, 187–8
Manby, RAF station, 108
Marchwood military docks, 257
Marconi, 164
Marham, RAF station, 46, 64, 86, 251
Marker flares, 67, 76, 204
Marshalling, 42–3, 68, 216
Martin-Baker Aircraft Company, 135
MASS, *see* Master Armament Safety Switch
Master armament safety switch (MASS), 78–9
Mauser cannon, 27mm, xii, 39, 145
McDonnell Douglas aircraft:
  F-4 Phantom, xiii, 89–92, 194
  Hornet, 89, 213
MDC, *see* Miniature detonating cord
Mechs course, 38, 42–4, 46, 143
Medium Capacity (MC) bombs, 9–10
Messerschmitt aircraft, 8
Mexeflote, 259, 262
MiG aircraft, 82, 119, 198
Military range, 127
Mine detector, 112

Miniature detonating cord (MDC), 111
Mirage, see Dassault Mirage
Mk4 Metal Detector, 113–14
Morland, Oliver, 61
Morland, Sir Samuel, 60
Mortuary, 252
Mostar, Bosnia and Herzegovina, 210
Mount Longdon, Falkland Islands, 194
Mount Pleasant airfield, Falkland Islands, 196
Mosquito, see De Havilland Mosquito
Mutually Assured Destruction (MAD), 197
MV *Elk*, 272
MV *Norland ferry*, 192

NAAFI bar, 35, 50, 188, 251
Nagasaki, 197
Napalm, 269–71, 275
National Service, xi, 17, 24, 85, 245, 249
NATO, 14, 162, 169, 171, 197, 252
NBC gear, 28, 114–15, 119–20, 199, 206, 231
Negligent discharge (ND), 154
Nellis Air Force Base, USA, 163, 168
Net explosive quantity (NEQ), 52
Nevada, 163
Nicholson, Sir William, 2
Nieuport monoplane, 222
Nimrod, see Hawker Siddeley Nimrod
Nimrod Line Squadron (NLS), 76
North Luffenham, RAF station, 28, 110
Northern Ireland, 19–21, 219
Norway, 71, 184
Nuclear weapons, 14, 119-20, 197, 231-2

OC Arm, 53, 94–5, 151
Oman, 92, 200–202, 204–206, 249
Operations (ops), 48, 67, 70, 76, 119, 155, 163, 190, 208, 222, 255
　Agila, 158
　Angel, 210–212
　Black Buck, 190, 258
　Chastise, 13
　Cheshire, 207–210, 236, 238
　Desert Shield, 198

Options, first, 42–43
OTR (operational turn round) checks, 38, 91
Otterburn ranges, 127, 256

Padgate, RAF station, 22
Panavia Tornado aircraft, xiii, 58, 64, 78–9, 89–93, 104, 106, 138, 198, 232, 251
Passing out parade, 31
Pathfinder units, 10
Patriot missiles, 206
Paveway bomb, 55–6, 105, 142
PE, see Plastic explosive
Pendine Sands, 130, 168
Persian Gulf, 201
Phantom, see McDonnell Douglas F-4 Phantom
Phosphorous bombs, 3, 9
Pigstick, 107, 114–15, 124
Piper Alpha oil rig, 67, 244
Plastic explosive (PE), xii, 53, 114, 121–3, 125–6, 131, 225–6
Port Stanley, 191–2, 194, 196
Poseidon, see Boeing P-8 Poseidon
Post traumatic stress disorder (PTSD), 252–4
Postings, vi, 42–43, 45–49, 51, 64, 68, 108, 112, 149, 168, 196, 214, 240
Pountain, Ronald, 8
PPSH 40 submachine gun, 158
Prepping bombs, 53, 65, 83, 94, 186
Prestwick, RAF station, 167
Princess Diana, 195
Propwash sailing, 238
PSI, see Public Service Institute
PTSD, see Post traumatic stress disorder
Public Service Institute (PSI), 195
Pucara aircraft, 268–9, 273, 283
Puma helicopter, 89, 178, 184
Purple Star detachment, 154, 172–3
Pylon bay, 138
Pylons, xii, 40, 81, 138–9, 141, 184

QAS inspector, 196
QCS, see Queen's Colour Squadron

INDEX

QRA, *see* Quick Reaction Alert
Queen Elizabeth II, 248
Queen's Colour Squadron (QCS), 157
Queen's Commendation for Brave Conduct medal, 276
Queen's Flight, 243
Quenault, Louis, 3
Quick Reaction Alert (QRA), 86, 197

R loader, 145
RA, *see* Royal Artillery
Radar, 14, 92, 202–203
RAF Armament School, 108
RAF Association (RAFA) Armourers Branch 1366, vi, 254–5
RAF Bomber Command, 9
RAF Fighter Command, 7, 9
RAF forms:
  F6485, 57
  F700, 76
  F705, 76
  F7192, 293
RAF Hospital, Ely, 228
RAF police, 121, 152, 207, 275
RAF Regiment, xii, 34, 157, 199, 214–15
RAF stations:
  Akrotiri, 188–9, 212–13, 235
  Aldergrove, 219
  Benson, 89
  Boscombe Down, 18
  Brize Norton, 158, 190, 214, 252, 258, 275
  Brüggen, 58, 120, 157, 241–2
  Cardington, 24
  Chivenor, 126, 131
  Coltishall, 18, 43
  Cosford, 32, 42–5, 49, 88, 123, 143
  Cottesmore, 43
  East Kirby, 10
  Finningley, 43
  Gaydon, 24, 85, 87, 223, 227, 246
  Graveley, 10
  Gütersloh, 64, 233
  Halton, 19, 22, 27, 32, 36, 46, 251
  Honington, 63, 228
  Innsworth, 190

Kenley, 8
Kinloss, 44–6, 51, 59, 65, 67, 70–1, 74, 76, 82, 93–4, 96, 138, 143–4, 147–8, 163, 165, 168, 196, 198, 200, 203, 224–5, 240–1, 272
Laarbruch, 157, 232
Larkhill, 222
Leconfield, 82–3
Leeming, 138, 213, 215, 243
Leuchars, 43–4, 190, 206, 240–1, 249
Lossiemouth, 44–6, 62, 243
Lyneham, 87, 147–51, 167–8, 199–200, 203, 207–208, 221, 225
Machrihanish, 162, 168
Manby, 108
Marham, 46, 64, 86, 251
North Luffenham, 28, 110
Padgate, 22
Prestwick, 167
Spilsby, 10
St Athan, 24, 34–5, 91–2
St Mawgan, 91, 242
Stafford, 19, 64
Swinderby, 18–19, 21–3, 26, 28, 36
Tengah, 187
Upavon, 131, 148, 151, 230
Waterbeach, 10
West Kirby, 24
Wildenrath, 157, 218
Wittering, 49, 110, 132, 249, 256, 258, 267, 275
RAF 1250 ID card, 152
Raigmore Hospital, Inverness, 244
Rangatira ferry, 191, 194
Rapier missile, 157, 259, 268
Rarden cannon, 30mm, 115
RE, *see* Royal Engineers
Ready use armament storage (RUAS), 50
Rectifications (recs) controller, 70
Red and Green Life Machine, 262, 279
Red cards, 196
Red Flag detachment, 162–4, 168
Red flags, xii, 80, 127
Red Label ammunition, 4
Release to Service (RTS) document, 139
Release unit bay, 138

Release units, 60, 138, 141, 143, 147, 149
RFA *Sir Bedivere*, 257–8
RFA *Sir Galahad*, 260, 272
RFA *Sir Geraint*, 274
RFA *Sir Lancelot*, 263
RFC, *see* Royal Flying Corps
Rhodes Moorhouse, Will, 3
Rhodesia, 158, 249
Riggers, 18, 48, 76, 94, 139, 141, 150, 166, 243
Rock apes, *see* RAF Regiment
Rocket Wrench, 114–15, 121
Roermond Earthquake, 241–2
Role bay, 138, 192
Rotary launcher, 67, 204
Royal Army Ordnance Corps, 107
Royal Artillery (RA), 131
Royal Australian Air Force, 246
Royal British Legion, 246
Royal Canadian Air Force, 163, 246
Royal Engineers (RE), 133, 191, 194, 261, 273
Royal Flying Corps (RFC), 2–6, 17, 78, 108, 134, 222
Royal Logistics Corps, 133
Royal Naval Air Service, 6
Royal Navy, 17, 108, 133, 244
RUAS, *see* Ready use armament storage
Rum Punch detachment, 163
Russia, 71, 82, 150, 158, 198

S-type trolley, 54, 63, 145–7
SAC, *see* Security Advice Centre
Saint Barbara, 1
Salisbury Plain, 127, 131
San Carlos Water, Falkland Islands, 259, 272, 278
SAR, *see* Search and rescue
Sarajevo, 149, 207–10, 221–2, 236, 238, 240
SAS, 159, 289
Satellites, 62
Saudi Arabia, 73, 201, 205, 249
Scimitar armoured vehicle, xi, 110, 115, 147

Scud missile attack, Saudi Arabia, 205–206
Sea King helicopter, 89, 91, 244, 265, 270–1
Sea Vixen, *see* De Havilland Sea Vixen
Search and rescue (SAR), 67, 76, 87, 168, 199, 203, 244
Seat bay, xi, 135, 138, 213
Second World War, vi–vii, 7–14, 17–18, 20, 82, 108–109, 112–15, 118, 135, 157–8, 172, 186, 197
Security Advice Centre (SAC), 219
See-off crew, 68–9, 80
Seeb, Oman, 200, 202–204
Sennybridge Training Area, 162, 168
Servicing, 37–38
  First Line Armament Servicing (FLAS), 77
  Flight, 38, 174
  Maintenance, xi, 37, 56, 134, 138, 142, 145, 194
Servicing bay, 141, 156
Shackleton bomber, *see* Avro Shackleton
Shaibah, Iraq, 215
Short Sunderland aircraft, 20, 89
Shrike electrical power unit, 114, 122
Sidewinder missiles, 65, 139, 190, 192, 199
Sigonella, Italy, 166, 234, 237
Singapore, 14, 187–8, 227
Skyflash missiles, 192, 194
Skyhawk, *see* Douglas A-4 Skyhawk
Small arms, 40, 49, 57, 60–2, 112, 126, 147–9, 151–60, 186, 197, 209, 259
Sonobuoys, 75, 203–204
Sooties, 18, 48, 76, 94, 150, 166
Soviet Union, 14–15
Spartan armoured vehicle, xi, 110, 147
Special Forces (SF), 207–208
Spilsby, RAF station, 10
Spitfire, *see* Supermarine Spitfire
Split, Croatia, 208
Squadrons:
  RAF Regiment, 157, 214
  XIV, 106
  1 (F), 257
  5, 5

INDEX

9, 73
15, 232–3, 249
20, 187–8
26, 214–15
27, 46
45, 108, 187
47 SF, 208, 213, 236
55, 86
57, 86
60, 187
63, 215
64, 8
100, 86
202, 244
617, 13, 105
5131, 46–7, 49, 109–10, 112, 123–4, 133, 278
Square bashing, 24, 31
SS *Atlantic Conveyor*, 267–8
SS *Canberra*, 259
St Athan, RAF station, 24, 34–5, 91–2
St Mawgan, RAF station, 91, 242
Stack cards, 53, 60, 62
Stafford, RAF station, 19, 64
Standard bearer, 254–5
State board, 70–1
Static water tank (SWT), 57–8
Station armoury, xi, 86–87, 126, 131, 144, 147–56, 158–9, 168, 186, 215
Steamers, 112
Stethoscope, 115–16
Stingray torpedoes, 204
Strange, Louis, 3
Suez Crisis, 85
Sukarno, President, 187
Suncorite, 143
Supermarine Spitfire aircraft, xiii, 8–9, 246
Sweeper bombs, 3
Swinderby, RAF station, 18–19, 21–3, 26, 28, 36
SWT, *see* Static water tank
Synchronised guns, 4

Taceval, *see* Tactical evaluation
Tactical evaluation, 112, 233, 308
Tail unit, xiii, 54–5, 105, 242
TATs, *see* Trade Ability Tests
Tea bar, xii, 42, 51, 96, 144, 161, 196
Teeny weeny airways (Army Air Corps), 263, 272
Tengah, RAF Station, Singapore, 187
Terrorism, 217–21
Three greens, 80
Tool shadow board, 73
Tomcat, *see* Grumman F-14 Tomcat
Tornado, *see* Panavia Tornado
Torpedoes, xiii, 59–60, 76, 108, 161, 163–5, 199, 204
TR (turn round) checks, 38, 81, 88, 164
Trade Ability Tests (TATs), 47
Training:
   Aircraft Assisted Escape Systems, 40
   Airfield phase, 42
   Basic, 22, 31, 46, 120, 157
   Basic Engineering, 35, 38, 41
   Bomb disposal, 34
      8B1, 110
      8B3, 110
      8B4, 110
   Bombs, Components and Pyrotechnics, 40
   Final Test Job (FTJ), 39–40, 143, 186
   Fire, 58
   Fitters, 32, 35, 42, 46, 125, 143, 147–8, 196, 219
   Guns, 154
   HGV, 34
   Mechs, 38, 42–4, 46, 143
   NBC, 28, 120
   Small arms, 40, 49
   Tracked vehicle driving, 110
   Trade, 31, 33, 36–7, 44, 48–9, 246
Training cell, 47–8, 94, 144
Trenchard, Lord, 1, 15
Trenchard Museum, 251
Trepanning, 112, 118
Trichloroethylene, 143
Tucson, 55, 146
Turret Armourer, 82–3
Twin Towers attack, 212

Two Boats village, Ascension Island, 258
Typhoon, *see* Eurofighter Typhoon

Uckers, 67, 143, 156
UK Mobile Air Movements (UKMAMs), 207–208
Unexploded bombs (UXB), xi, 108–119, 122, 131, 193, 195, 263, 265–6, 274–5
Uniform, 31–4, 95, 156, 162, 173, 211, 217–18, 221
United Nations (UN), 207–208
Upavon, RAF station, 131, 148, 151, 230
UXB, *see* Unexploded bombs

V bombers, 24, 85
Valiant bomber, *see* Vickers Valiant
VAP-60 loader, 145, 147
Vehicle access to RAF stations, 51, 219
Very pistol, 148
Vickers aircraft:
    FB.5, 4
    Valiant bomber, 85
Vickers gun, 4, 6
Victor bomber, *see* Handley Page Victor
Victor OCU, 86
Vulcan bomber, *see* Avro Vulcan

Warsaw Pact, 110, 112, 119, 197
Waterbeach, RAF station, 10
Weapons practice, 127
Wendy loader, xi, 145, 147
Wessex helicopter, 190, 275
West Freugh range, 258

West Germany, 14, 197
West Kirby, RAF station, 24
Westlands, 249
Wheelbarrow, 112–13, 124–5
Wildenrath, RAF station, Germany, 157, 218
Wittering, RAF station, 49, 110, 132, 249, 256, 258, 267, 275
Women's Royal Air Force (WRAF), 14, 26–7, 41, 220
WRAF, *see* Women's Royal Air Force
Wrecks work, 71
WW1, *see* First World War
WW2, *see* Second World War

X stations, 109

Y loader, 105, 145

Zagreb, Croatia, 149, 207–208
Zimbabwe, 158

9/11 incident, 212
16 Field Hospital Paras, 272
45 Commando battalion, 262
114 tail units, 55, 242
957 card, 53
1366 RAFA branch, vi, 254–5
    Chairman, 254–5
    Honorary Welfare Officer (HWO), 254–5
1563 Flight Pumas, 96
4021 Locator, 112–13